Contents

Foreword One

Ismael Fernández Mejía
ISOCARP President (2009-2012)

This ISOCARP Review is about living conditions in the world's cities. Industrialisation, the accompanying rural to urban migration, and the consequent rapid growth of urban centres, has often come at a heavy price. It has consigned millions to the most basic housing conditions and to being cheap labour if they have a job at all, while exposing them to the effects of acute air and water pollution, debilitating disease and heightened mortality. This is both a phenomenon of the past, but also of the present, as can be seen in the huge informal settlements in and around many fast developing cities.

How then to ensure that our urbanising areas are planned and managed so that they are truly liveable cities, wherein the well being of their communities gains practical reality? Here we come back to the notion of sustainable development and to its three pillars, the economic, the social and the environmental; thus, rewarding livelihoods where the needs of employees are properly catered for, access to good quality housing, education and other services, and a healthy environment that caters for our physical, psychological and cultural needs and, globally, for the well being of our planet.

With this Year's Review, we continue with a sequence of sustainability themes. So, its predecessor Reviews have addressed city sprawl (2008), low carbon cities (2009) and sustainability in the context of the developing world (2010). In that last case we focussed, in particular, on the needs of the poorer developing countries, for example, many of those in Africa. In *Liveable Cities*, our emphasis is upon those fast urbanising countries that are des-

tined to become the economic superpowers of tomorrow. Thus, the book starts with contributions from India and Brazil and concludes with a section on China.

However, *Liveable Cities* also includes case studies and strategies drawn from many other parts of the world. For example, it highlights the entirely new approaches displayed in the preparation of the latest plan for Amsterdam, and in the legacy planning for the 2012 Olympic Games, important work on urban climatology and its link to planning and design, and Singapore's impressive recreation/biodiversity initiative, its park connector network.

Finally, I should like to thank the many authors involved in this collection of 16 papers, the editorial team which was drawn from both Europe and China, and everyone else who has had a part to play. I wish to congratulate them for their hard work which has led to this fascinating book on liveable cities.

Foreword Two

Qiu Baoxing
President of Urban Planning Society of China and Chairman of the Local Organising Committee

This year's ISOCARP Review focuses on the theme of the 47th ISOCARP World Congress: Liveable Cities - Urbanising World, Meeting the Challenge. This was held in Wuhan, China in October 2011.

Located at the economic and geographical center of the country, Wuhan has been a vital industrial base in China. Founded 3,500 years ago, Wuhan had become one of the top four cities in the late Ming Dynasty, and has preserved a host of historical and cultural relics to date. The city is endowed with abundant natural resources, in particular the Yangtze River and Han River that flow through it and its substantial area of lakes. Supported by 78 institutions of higher learning, Wuhan boasts rich human resources and outstanding competitiveness in education and technology. The East Lake Area of Wuhan has become the second largest agglomeration of technological talent in China.

Wuhan is undergoing a rapid urbanisation process. The total population now exceeds 9.78 million and the urbanisation level is over 70 %. The central urban area of Wuhan had a population of 5.4 million in 2009. It faces challenges comparable to those of other big cities in their urbanizing process, such as rapid population growth, rural-urban migration, urban sprawl, pollution, environment degradation, housing supply, employment etc. The discussion of this topic at the Congress and in this Review will be significantly helpful to Wuhan towards building a liveable city.

This ISOCARP Review has three main parts: (i) Countries and City Regions; (ii) Studies and Strategies; and (iii) China Reports. The topics of the five Chinese papers seek to provide a panoramic view of the urbanising process in this country through their coverage of the ecological spatial planning of a megacity, i.e. Wuhan, appropriate forms of local governance for low carbon cities, emergency planning for disaster situations, affordable housing and suitable target groups and industrial heritage as a form of cultural infrastructure. These papers represent the latest research and practice achievements of Chinese planning professionals.

I would like to express my gratitude to the authors, editors and all other people involved in the preparation of this publication. Thank you!

Liveable Cities: Urbanising World An Introduction to the Review

Chris Gossop

Shi Nan

The Topic

This ISOCARP Review is about the task of shaping our cities and city regions in ways whereby they can be made more sustainable and more liveable. The challenge for planning and city management is to accomplish this in the face of a scale and pace of urbanisation that almost overwhelms the imagination. A few years ago we reached the stage where over half of the world's population lived in urban areas, and current projections suggest that this will have risen to 70% by 2050. For the most part, this continued urbanisation will happen in the world's developing regions, where, according to UN HABITAT, the annual urban population increase amounts to some 50 million a year[i]. The predicted outcome is many new cities of over 10 million population ('megacities') amid very many smaller, but still substantial, settlements.

As the previous two Reviews have highlighted, one of the greatest challenges faced by our planet is that of anthropogenic climate change[ii, iii]. The cities are a major source of the greenhouse gases that are contributing to that change, and they will have to be a major part of any solution. Despite the failure of the world's leaders, so far, to agree to a global deal on climate change action, it is encouraging to see that many cities are responding to the issue with important new initiatives. A key task for ISOCARP and other planning organisations is to gather and spread this knowledge so that the lessons learned can inform practice around the world. We believe that ISOCARP's Review series makes a useful contribution on this front.

Progress towards mitigation will be heavily dependent upon the way we plan and design our cities, including our approach to the renewal of outworn areas. We will need more, and better, planning as one ingredient on the vital pathway towards more sustainable, lower carbon cities, where there is a diminished use of finite resources, especially oil. Moreover, many cities will be directly threatened by the effects of climate change. Particularly at risk will be those in coastal areas – including several of the world's megacities – where a combination of sea level rise, coastal erosion, saltwater contamination and heightened storms will put the environment, and living conditions under increased stress.

Climate change will often impact worst on the urban poor, generally those least able to cope with its effects. The inexorable move in developing countries from rural areas to the cities has meant, in many places, the rapid growth of slums and squatter settlements having minimal infrastructure and often in places that are most vulnerable to floods and landslides. Another characteristic of this urbanisation is the often extreme spatial polarisation – between the wealthier and poorer housing areas, the up market suburban areas, on the one hand, and the tenements and slums on the other. Often that polarisation, and the consequent fear of crime amongst the wealthier people, manifests itself in the segregation of upper income households as gated communities.

On the economic front, globalisation and economic restructuring have had complex effects upon the world's cities and their labour markets. Big disparities have emerged in terms of income while the economic downturn that

began in 2008 has led to further restructuring and a widespread increase in unemployment. An accompanying feature has been the rapid growth of the informal economy. While this has been perhaps a 'saving grace' for some economies, it has trapped many millions in low profit, very insecure activities offering few prospects for the future.

The factors summarised above are among the many matters discussed in the 16 case studies that follow. While these are drawn from around the world, there is an emphasis on the world's fast developing countries, the economic superpowers of the near future. Fittingly, five of the papers stem from China, in recognition of the fact that this book is published in parallel with the holding of ISO-CARP's 47th World Congress in Wuhan, central China. Those papers form the third of three sections; the other two address 'Countries and City Regions' and 'Studies and Strategies'

The Case Studies – A Guide

01 Countries and City Regions

Our case studies begin with an overview of the state and prospects of Indian cities, in a vast developing country that is on the cusp of becoming an economic superpower. In her paper *Making Indian Cities Liveable: the Challenges of India's Urban Transformation,* Shipra Narang Suri paints a picture of a country where, on the one hand, the problems of the cities overwhelm the ability of weak public authorities to respond to them and, on the other; there are some striking examples of local solutions that are working well. In numerical terms, there is no doubt that India's problems are massive with some 80 million urban dwellers living below the poverty line, almost a quarter of the total urban population. In the words of the author *'Informal settlements, informal livelihoods, homelessness, insecurity, various types of pollution and declining green areas are the bane of most Indian cities. Combined with emerging concerns about climate change and the regular occurrence of natural disasters, Indian towns and cities seem to be sitting on a ticking time bomb'.*

The paper explores the challenges for India's urban transformation based upon three aspects of liveability, namely **inclusion** - implying social integration and cohesion, **resilience** - adaptability, flexibility and balance and **authenticity** - maintaining the local character of the city, while accommodating social, economic and technological changes. It provides some impressive examples of schemes that are making cities more liveable in these ways and it concludes with some ideas for the future. Those point to the clear need for new planning and urban management mechanisms that tackle effectively the realities of India's cities today and the physical and social conditions of its informal settlements.

We turn next to a second emerging economic giant, namely Brazil where rapid urbanisation since the 1930s has manifested itself in a range of ways not unlike those of India. In *The Urban Reform Agenda and the Struggle for Liveable Cities in Brazil,* Edesio Fernandes describes its effects as a nationwide urban crisis *'characterised by a combination of sociospatial segregation, negative environmental impact, and escalating informal development'.* These problems, together with a growing housing deficit and poor housing conditions generally have accumulated over the years, assisted by government neglect. Moreover, turning things round means having to *'change the wheels with the car moving'.*

But as the author describes, urban reform has been advanced substantially since the

late 1980s with the aim of generating more liveable, sustainable, efficient, safer and fairer cities. A new legal-urban order has emerged and this has been consolidated by the enactment of the 2001 City Statute, and the setting up of a Ministry for Cities and the National Council of Cities. Under the new agenda, over 1400 municipalities have implemented their master plans and there has been much more citizen participation than before.

However, while significant steps have been taken at both the federal and the municipal level, the effectiveness of planning and urban management has been limited as a result of rising land values (a consequence of Brazil's recent economic growth) and, related to that, to the lack of ambition of many master plans which have failed to impose obligations on land and property owners. The closing message is that still further legal reform is needed, although the effectiveness of that will depend upon the extent to which it can be translated into a new sociospatial pact that can be politically appropriated by the stakeholders.

The other two case studies in this section are drawn from the Netherlands, a medium sized European country which has long been a laboratory for planning and the advancement of new ideas and practice on the concept of the liveable city. The first study, *The Netherlands in Transition: The Planning of Low Carbon, Sustainable and Liveable Cities in the Utrecht Region,* by Martin Dubbeling, complements an essay published in the ISOCARP Review Low Carbon Cities. This latest study focuses on the way that, in the context of a new Dutch administration, national and local climate and energy targets are being translated into spatial policy, strategy and physical planning in Utrecht, a central province of the Netherlands.

Utrecht's drive on these fronts is firmly anchored within a vision of a region determined to maintain its leading position in terms of its knowledge based industries and centres, its culture, and the quality of its cities and the surrounding landscape. The paper gives many examples of specific developments, which significantly advance practice in terms of environmental performance and liveability; these include transit oriented development. For their part, the large municipalities of Utrecht and Amersfoort have set stringent goals in terms of CO_2 reduction and energy transformation and these are linked to creating new opportunities for economy.

In terms of the overall structure of the region, Dubbeling highlights the planning of the A12 zone which connects the City of Utrecht with other municipalities in the region; that involves, amongst other things, higher densities and mixed uses in locations that are accessible by a variety of means of transport, and intensified 'green/blue' planning, providing a fine environment for the citizens of today and tomorrow. It remains to be seen how the longer term aspirations of Dutch planners on climate change will be realised in practice, but the pathfinder developments already in place give reasonable grounds for optimism.

For the student of international planning, the miscellany of strategies for the long term growth and development of the world's capital cities has been a source of endless fascination. Thus ISOCARP is particularly pleased to have been able to publish an essay on the latest vision for Amsterdam and its regional hinterland (Amsterdam 2040). This contribution by Zef Hemel, *WikicitY: Open Planning for a Liveable Amsterdam 2004-2011*, is partly about the plan itself, but more particularly about the process, the extraordinary story telling that has created the new vision. This tenth major plan for the Dutch capital started from the premise that plan making had got itself into a rut, that the system had become ossified, and that something fundamentally new was required to reinvent planning as an essen-

tial force for the future. There was also the pragmatic point that planning needed to be simplified and made more efficient.

While it was later to become a plan from the bottom up involving every segment of the community, the process started from a new way of communication put together by the city's planners – a story about a possible future for the city. Each time the story was told in public platforms, it was developed, becoming like a Wikipedia entry put together by thousands of people. The impenetrability of standard approaches to communication by planners had been replaced by a new way of engaging people, and it is claimed that this has been far more effective. Practising planners and politicians have long sought to involve the public in the planning choices that need to be made, but the results have been very mixed. While no one approach is likely to be right for every situation, could it be that Amsterdam has provided a new template for participation that may be of much wider use?

02 Studies and Strategies

We begin the second section of this Review with an alternative vision for the rapidly expanding urban regions of the world, an approach which would be based upon neither the continuing expansion of existing cities nor acceptance that the alternative must be formless sprawl. In his essay *Beyond Cities: Is an Urban Planet even Possible?*, Jeremy Dawkins outlines a radically different development future for parts of East Asia and other rapidly growing world regions.

That alternative future is based upon the findings of an ISOCARP Urban Planning Advisory Team (UPAT) for the Philips Center of Health and Well-being, Singapore, an exercise which Dawkins led. The UPAT concluded that the management of a rapidly urbanising region would require, amongst other things, an adaptive strategic land use planning approach ('mosaics'), an adaptive strategic network planning approach ('fishnets'), and a radical governance approach termed 'regional commission'. And beyond that, its success would depend on strong global measures to (amongst other things) price carbon and value natural capital.

This complex package charts an entirely new planning approach which spans layers of scale from the equivalent of 1000 sq.km (the region) down to 1 sq.km (urban living areas) and imagines ten 'practical solutions' that would be possible steps towards these outcomes as well as capable of being implemented immediately, everywhere. They include the mapping of energy resources in advance of development, measures to exploit opportunities for food production and a strategy of advance landscaping. In place of prescriptive planning we have smarter planning, taking the necessary bold decisions at the outset, for example on essential infrastructure, but keeping decisions on other matters open, thus allowing the plan to respond to the changing circumstances of future decades.

While the actual and potential impacts of global climate change resulting from greenhouse gas emissions and deforestation have become a major preoccupation for many national governments and city decision makers, and were a driving factor behind the conclusions of the Singapore UPAT, we should not forget that other, older example of anthropogenic climate change, the urban heat island. In their article *Towards a Liveable Urban Climate: Lessons from Stuttgart*, Michael Hebbert and Brian Webb of the University of Manchester describe how the physical design and material form of a city directly modifies its climate and how climatic variables – temperature, wind patterns, humidity, precipitation and air quality have a vital impact upon liveability.

The paper looks in some detail at the inspirational example set by the German City of Stuttgart which has a long tradition of applying urban climatic analysis in city planning. Stuttgart's *Klimaatlas* provides a written description of its local climate supported by analysis maps at a scale that corresponds to that of the city's land use maps. These maps identify eleven 'climatopes' which provide guidance for planning decisions at strategic and neighbourhood level, for example through highlighting those green spaces that deserve particular protection because of their influence on the local micro-climate, and those parts of the terrain that should remain undeveloped because of their role as channels for urban ventilation.

However, the paradox is that, while the science of urban climatology is now well established, and while we have clear examples of good practice such as Stuttgart, city planning generally has become less climate aware. As the authors conclude, planners need to put micro-climatic observation and mapping back on their agendas, both to inform decisions that directly affect liveability and as a powerful contribution towards urban strategies for carbon mitigation and climate change adaptation.

The ways that we travel and transport goods both within and between our cities have a powerful influence on city form and liveability. The next two essays address two very different scales of transport related planning, the international represented by a key European transport corridor and that of the individual city worldwide. In his paper *Strategies for Integrated Spatial Development along the European North-South Railway Link,* Professor Bernd Scholl examines a vital 1200km transport corridor which provides one of the most important railway connections in Europe. This project has great significance at many levels: thus, it is a project of European significance, it contributes to mobility in and between regions and, with its trans alpine tunnels, it plays a vital role in terms of the environment, through the fostering of rail travel as opposed to road.

However, there is as yet no proper overall strategy that connects railway and settlement development along this corridor and the author's case studies point to the need for much closer coordination and cooperation between the various stakeholders, especially in the cross border areas. This is already a highly populated area and, for effective planning, much of its future growth will need to occur through redevelopment associated with the upgrading of the rail system; that, in turn, will mean reaching a balance between the needs of the different categories of rail transport, i.e, goods, regional passenger rail and high speed traffic, and local, regional and international journeys. Looking ahead, much reliance is being placed on the work of the strategically designated EU Interreg Project CODE 24 which, by 2013, is to have completed an overview of all the central difficulties and conflicts and recommended solutions to be taken up by the participating countries and the EU. The eventual decisions will have considerable implications for the living conditions of many communities along this major transport route.

In the second transport paper, *The Contribution of Mobility to Liveable Cities,* Pierre Laconte first charts the rise of the car and the huge impact of its success upon the form of our settlements. Especially at the extreme, as seen in the endless suburban expansion in parts of the USA, but also more generally, the dominance of the car and the freedom that it offers the individual has been achieved at the expense of human health and the quality of life. The paper proceeds to discuss 'sustainable mobility' which, in essence, requires an integrated transport policy combining urban planning, parking controls and a significant role for public transport so this becomes once again the mode of transport for all and not just the elderly and the poor.

Aspects of that mix are in place in many progressive cities and the author provides useful examples. Copenhagen ticks several boxes. Thus, it is a relatively compact city with an advanced public transport system that includes an expanding driverless metro network. It is also a healthy city with extensive pedestrian areas and a well developed cycle network that encourages 36% of commuters to use bikes. Another city characterised by its integrated, sustainable transport system is Singapore which applies congestion pricing, auctions new licence plates as a way of restraining car ownership and, again, has excellent public transport. An obvious message from this paper and its various exemplar cities is that tried and tested planning and other mechanisms are there to secure healthier, more liveable cities on a much wider basis. The question that then arises is whether local politicians will have the courage to advance comparable solutions in places where their voters have become so wedded to the car.

Singapore features again, but in a very different guise, in the next essay by Lena Chan, Cheng Hai Sim, Meng Tong Yeo and Kartini Omar-Hor *Linking People, Linking Nature: the Park Connector Network of Singapore.* Through careful planning and management this island city state has reconciled its crowded space (with its population density of over 7,000 persons per sq.km) and its continuing development need with the maintenance of a rich biodiversity. In its quest for positive solutions, a unique biodiversity conservation model has been created which champions environmental sustainability as an essential part of the necessary balance.

This paper is about Singapore's park connector network (PCN), the rationale for which is to foster the enjoyment and well-being of people living in highly urbanised areas. By linking Singapore's National Parks, Nature Reserves, Nature Areas, major parks, streetscape, and other open green and blue spaces through the

PCN, recreational areas are made more accessible to the public. As an attractive nature resource, the PCN also offers a visual and psychological respite for people living in an island state where there is no large hinterland or rural areas to escape to during the weekends. The network, which will be 300km long when completed, caters for cyclists as well as walkers and has a commuter function as well as a recreational one. This fine initiative deserves to be much better known internationally and it is hoped that the publication of this paper will contribute to that end.

In their paper *Skolkovo: City of the Future as a Russian Hi Tech Hub*, Fedor Kudryavtsev and Victoria Bannykh describe the vision for a new 'scientific city' close to Moscow that is intended to offer attractive working and living conditions for leading researchers, engineers, designers, software programmers, managers and financial specialists, with the aim of advancing new technologies and other products able to compete on the global market. Backed strongly by President Medvedev, the Skolkovo Innovation Centre is to be planned, managed and developed in a very different way to normal practice in modern-day Russia.

Thus, new laws define the Skolkovo Innovation Centre as a 'geographically separate facility' which is to have its own modes of taxation, city regulations and building standards, for example. It is to be governed by a single minded management company responsible for all issues relating to the development and functioning of the Centre, including housing. The underlying purpose is to foster an R&D environment conducive to technological innovation and its commercialization, coupled with lasting value for Russia through a new generation of scholars.

The master plan for Skolkovo has emerged following an international competition, a mechanism that is quite unusual in Russia.

It has a distinctive structure of development clusters, connected, mixed use developments set in a natural landscape. As the paper details, this is to be an energy efficient city with low carbon emissions and high environmental standards generally. As with all projects there is no guarantee that the results will live up to the vision. The ingredients for success would appear to be there, but time will tell.

The final paper in this section is about one of the most complicated development challenges in Europe. In their paper *The London 2012 Olympic Park: Planning for a Sustainable Legacy*, Dan Epstein, Jo Carris and Emily Moore describe the way that the long term needs of one of the most economically and socially disadvantaged parts of London, the Lower Lea Valley are being addressed in conjunction with the planning of the 2012 Olympic Games. That transition from Games mode to legacy is to be delivered through a sequence of three masterplans: a Games time plan, a transformation plan (by means of which the removal of the many temporary facilities makes way for serviced development plots for permanent developments) and a legacy plan (showing a conceptual model of the site fully developed over a period of 20-30 years, depending on market conditions). This process is hugely ambitious and appears not to have been attempted before in conjunction with a major sporting event, certainly at this scale. As the authors say, it will be many years before its full success can be evaluated.

The paper is also about sustainability in its various guises, all of which are intimately linked to this book's theme of liveable cities. The Olympics scheme will be seen to be a success in liveability terms if it can lift the fortunes of this poor area of London through the creation of new businesses and jobs, boost household incomes and improve the well being of its people. On the last of those fronts, the vastly improved environment that will be a major part of the Games legacy should help greatly. And the techniques that are being employed to make the 2012 Games 'the greenest ever' should be capable of much wider application as part of a sustainable, low carbon future.

03 China Reports

The five papers from China begin, appropriately, with one by Liu Qizhi, Hei Mei and Wang Yun which addresses the planning of Wuhan, the host city for ISOCARP's 47th World Congress. In their paper, *Planning the Ecological Spatial System of the Megacity of Wuhan*, the authors first set the scene by describing the historical development of three towns at the confluence of the Yangtze and Han Rivers, settlements that became today's Wuhan with its population of nearly 10 million living within a built area approaching 500 km². Faced with continuing massive urbanisation which is extending that area by 30 km² annually, Wuhan's planners face the immense challenge of how this scale of growth can best be directed.

The paper addresses, in particular, the question of ecological and landscape protection and how valuable resources can best be safeguarded so that demands for private development and gain do not override the public good, for example public access to lakesides. Wuhan is seeking to achieve this balance through a planning structure that defines boundaries for its ecological resources based upon 'two axes, two rings, six wedges and multiple corridors' and, alongside this, to identify those areas where construction is generally prohibited or restricted. In general, development is to be concentrated within the central city area and around the new town clusters of the peripheral areas.

As the authors conclude, the success of this planning approach in the face of the current development pressures requires a precise definition of those ecological areas and a

boundary for Wuhan's urban development that is firmly enshrined in local law and regulation.

The need for effective environmental protection is assuming growing importance in China as the effects of rapid urbanization become increasingly clear. That is manifest in the concerns expressed by China's leaders about land consumption, which over the longer term threatens to hinder the country's ability to feed itself, and about the effects of industry and transportation in respect of air and water pollution and soil contamination. There is also a growing awareness of the link between greenhouse gases and climate change which has led to decisions at the level of the Chinese Government to reduce the carbon intensity of its development (carbon dioxide levels per unit of GDP), to develop alternatives to fossil fuel energy and to increase the extent of its forested areas. Significantly, China is also developing a substantial renewable energy industry.

In concert with other governments across the world, China understands that much of the necessary action to tackle climate change will need to take place at the level of the cities. That has led to the concept of low carbon cities and it has caused planners and other decision makers to explore the sorts of action that might be on the agenda. However, as Stanley Yip argues in his paper *Local Governance of Low Carbon Cities: Is our Local Planning system Ready Yet?,* there has been less said about how this might be done. Yip's thesis is that a prerequisite for action is the need to localize the climate change issue and to develop co-benefits so that local political and community support can be gained. At present there is a question mark over the readiness of current governance modes, the statutory planning process, the knowledge base and the decision making framework. Yip's paper provides some useful ideas as to how the governance issue might best be tackled.

We turn next to the potential for the reuse of older industrial buildings forming part of China's heritage. In his paper *Industrial Heritage as a Cultural Infrastructure,* Professor Dong Wei describes the rich industrial history of many cities and towns in China. Besides the things that we normally consider as infrastructure, for example transportation, electricity, communications and drainage, there exists another kind of infrastructure, which includes culture, the urban pattern and the environment. These ingredients make one city different from any others, and make the world rich and diverse in cultures and life styles. As one of the elements of culture, China's industrial heritage reflects the origins of urban modernization, and needs to be viewed in the context of social development.

Following an interesting discussion about the tension between the theory and practice of heritage conservation, and between the concept of 'authenticity' and maintaining 'the spirit of place', the author acknowledges that on industrial heritage questions an academic balance has been struck between the purposes of conservation and urban redevelopment, and between theory and practice. This is largely because the industrial heritage is mostly of high value in terms of reuse and restoration, given its scale, its comparative modernity, its structure and the space available. This means that the results of conservation usually blend well with the purposes of urban redevelopment. Indeed, industrial heritage is now the newest cultural resource for cities and the principle of its conservation and reuse is consistent with the dominant Chinese ideology of historical continuity and the handing down of tradition.

The world has been afflicted by a seemingly large number of natural disasters over the last few years and these have resulted in many deaths and huge disruption within the countries involved. And many countries, even the largest ones, find themselves stretched to their limits. China has certainly had its share of such disasters, a recent example being that of the Wenchuan earthquake of 2008. In their comprehensive paper *Devising an Adaptable Urban Shelter and Evacuation System in Disaster Situations* Su Jing-Yu, Liu Chao-Feng and Wang Wei discuss the long term planning requirements for future disaster situations of varying scales, up to the level of an extreme disaster.

The paper points to some of the shortcomings of the previous approach. For example fixed shelters may be inappropriate for concurrent natural disasters, such as parallel or sequential incidences of earthquakes, tsunamis, and typhoons. Also they may not readily adapt to the different stages of natural disasters. There is a need too for the shelter system to be closely connected to other urban systems for disaster prevention and rescue, such as firefighting, public security, medical treatment, supply of goods and materials, emergency command, maintenance and management systems. In a time of growing worries about man-made climate change and its effects, with the likelihood that the number and scale of emergencies will grow, this experience from China could, sadly, be of considerable relevance to governments around the world.

The final case study by Zhang Jie and Jiao Yang, *A Study of Target Groups for Affordable Housing* stems from China's switch towards a market economy. While the steady growth in commercial housing development over the last ten years has resulted in improved housing conditions for urban residents, there is an emerging problem of affordability for some sectors of the population. As has long been realized in certain developed countries, for example the United Kingdom, such market housing may be out of reach for many households, justifying a continuation of some forms of public housing programme. However, in between the options of purchasing a dwelling or relying on social housing, intermediate solutions have been found to extend the availability of market housing to those on relatively modest incomes.

That is what the mechanism described in this paper seeks to do. Thus, the target groups for affordable housing comprise a stratum of lower-middle to middle-income households, which account for about 40% of the total urban population. To ensure viability it is necessary for the government to provide the land required, together with the supporting infrastructure, tax breaks, low-interest loans, effective and transparent entry and exit mechanisms and the legal and regulatory framework. However, the housing involved would not be accessible, or affordable, to those on the lowest incomes for whom other types of housing, such as low rent housing, would continue to be required.

We hope that you will enjoy reading this latest issue of our popular publication on international planning.

References

i   UN HABITAT (2009) *Planning Sustainable Cities*, Earthscan
ii ISOCARP (2009) *Low Carbon Cities* (Review 05) ISOCARP, The Hague
iii ISOCARP (2010) *Sustainable City: Developing World* (Review 06), Routledge

01

COUNTRIES AND CITY REGIONS

Making Indian Cities Liveable: the Challenges of India's Urban Transformation

Shipra Narang Suri

Figure 1: Typical Indian urban scene, with mixed uses and mixed modes of transport – Lal Chowk in Srinagar. Photograph © Harish Narang

Shipra Narang Suri

Setting the Context: India's Urban Transformation

India's urbanisation is a paradox of sorts. The country's urban population is undoubtedly vast at 377 million (2011 Census). In international terms, however, India's urban growth can hardly be described as rapid. Despite the fact that the fastest urbanization rates are being witnessed in the developing world, India's urban population increased from 17.3 per cent in 1971 to just 23.3 per cent in 1981, and 27.78 per cent in 2001. The 2011 Census figures reveal that just over 31 per cent of the country's population is presently living in urban areas, lower than, for example, China, Indonesia, Mexico or Brazil (HPEC 2011). But there are over 80 million people living below the poverty line in India's urban centres; a quarter of the total urban population lives in slums. Informal settlements, informal livelihoods, homelessness, insecurity, various types of pollution and declining green areas are the bane of most Indian cities. Combined with emerging concerns about climate change and the regular occurrence of natural disasters, Indian towns and cities seem to sitting on a ticking time bomb.

The other characteristic of India's urbanisation is that it is 'top-heavy', which means that the larger cities (metropolises, which have over a million residents, and Class I cities, which have 100,000+ residents) have witnessed much more rapid growth than smaller towns. In 2001, nearly 70 per cent of the country's urban population resided in the 393 Class I cities. The unequal spatial distribution of urban populations across the country has been a cause for concern for the policymakers at the highest level in successive five-year plans (Kundu 2011). At the same time, urbanisation strategies currently being implemented or proposed seem to advance the same trend.

For example, the proposals put forth by a recently constituted High-Powered Expert Committee for Estimating the Investment Requirements for Urban Infrastructure Services (HPEC) are likely to create 87 cities with population of 1 million and above by 2030 (HPEC 2011).

These outcomes of India's urban transformation pose enormous challenges for the country's planners and policymakers. The formal planning system has seen little change since independence, and most towns and cities rely on inflexible master plans which are more often than not outdated by the time they are completed. Rigid development control norms which are flouted at every step, and a weak governance system which can neither guide nor enforce, completes the sorry picture. Recent policy innovations such as the National Urban Renewal Mission launched in 2005 have triggered some changes, but have sidestepped the existing planning processes, which seem too complicated to change. Other recent events, including increasingly frequent violent protests on issues such as rural land acquisition for urbanisation and industrialisation, and the widespread political posturing on the issue, seem once again to pitch urban centres versus rural areas, or "India" versus "Bharat", as the country is commonly known in Hindi. Many thinkers and policymakers understand that this is a false dichotomy, but the latter in particular are unable to take any stand which apparently 'favours' urban areas, urban residents, or even the urban poor, over their rural counterparts.

Given this scenario, many of India's cities have taken it upon themselves to introduce innovative measures in urban planning, management and governance, demonstrating vision, creativity, and a departure from business as usual. Improvements in public transport are becoming increasingly common and characterised by innovative planning and the use of modern technology – Delhi, for instance, has pioneered the use of Compressed Natural Gas, a low-polluting fuel, for all modes of public transport, while Ahmedabad has launched an extremely successful Bus Rapid Transit system. Disaster risk management plans are being developed, institutionalised and implemented, as has been done by Mumbai, to protect cities and their residents from natural and man-made disasters. Renewal and revitalisation of older areas within cities is also being promoted, by cities such as Ahmedabad, Jaipur, Pondicherry and Varanasi. Urban infrastructure, water and sanitation systems are being revamped – in fact this is the overarching focus of recent policy reforms; safety and security in public spaces is being enhanced through improved infrastructure and more responsive policing; and communities are being empowered through skill development, participation and partnerships in a number of cities across the country.

This article attempts to build a broad picture of India's urban transformation and the major challenges of liveability faced in Indian cities, based on a conception of liveability that includes notions of **inclusion** (implying not only social integration and cohesion, but also enabling the widest range of stakeholders to make the best of the opportunities a city offers, as well as participate actively in decision-making), **resilience** (referring to adaptability, flexibility and balance; the ability of a city to "invent" or "re-invent" itself in response to shocks and stresses, to harmoniously accommodate old and new values, and to adapt the functions and requirements of the city), and **authenticity** (which involves maintaining the local character of the city, the local heritage, culture and environment, while evolving and accommodating social, economic and technological changes).[1] As Indian towns and cities have expanded, they have become less inclusive for the poor, for women, and for other socially disadvantaged groups. In addition, the imperatives of development and 'modernisation' are taking a toll on the historic character

of many cities. They are also struggling to become more resilient in coping with natural and man-made disasters, crime and insecurity, and conflict among various societal groups.

Using a wide range of illustrations and examples, this paper argues that to build liveable cities in India, a fundamental shift in the approach to urban planning and development is required, and concludes with some ideas that might contribute towards such a change.

The Changing (?) Mechanics of Planning

Urban planning and local governance in Indian cities

Urban planning in India has traditionally taken the form of master plans, usually developed and implemented by specially constituted development authorities which are outside the purview of the local administration and hence not directly accountable to the local population (unlike local governments which have an elected council that is accountable to the citizens). The lack of coordination between urban planning and local governance was sought to be corrected through the adoption of the 74th Constitutional Amendment Act (CAA) in 1992, which proposed that Urban Local Bodies (ULBs) be established and strengthened in order to improve the quality of the urban environment, provide services in a more responsive and effective manner, and enhance participation of local stakeholders in decision-making processes. The amendment has been described as

> "...the first serious attempt to ensure stabilization of democratic municipal government through constitutional provisions." (Savage and Dasgupta 2006: 43)

While the Act directly addressed the issue of planning (the first of the functions assigned to ULBs under the Twelfth Schedule which is part of the Amendment Act), this aspect has remained marginal to the development of India's towns, cities, districts and regions. According to a report prepared by the National Institute of Urban Affairs (NIUA) in 2005 assessing the implementation of the 74th CAA in 27 states and one Union Territory, District Planning Committees (DPCs) and Metropolitan Planning Committees (MPCs), which according to the Act should be established by each Municipal Authority, are yet to be established in most states.[2]

The ineffectiveness of planning has become endemic across Indian cities. Ansari (2004) points out some key drawbacks of the Master Plan, including the limited attention paid to social and economic development aspects, financial resource mobilisation for the implementation of the plan, as well as the long time needed for plan preparation and the limited stakeholder involvement. Economic planning or local economic development strategies are rarely incorporated into the spatial planning exercise, with the result that the plans are unrealistic and impossible to implement (Sridharan 2008).

> "What emerges [...] is largely a bundle of half-baked ideas incorporated into a proposed land use plan that planners insist should be implemented in its entirety, at all costs." (Ansari 2004: 15)

Furthermore, the implementation of urban plans in Indian cities is hampered by the fact that water and sewerage systems, power and telecommunication services, roads and public transport, housing and slums, are controlled by other parastatal bodies or line departments of central and state governments. Local governments are responsible only for solid waste management, maintenance of public spaces, and some basic repair and maintenance of

other services such as roads, street lighting and drainage systems.

The launch of the Jawaharlal Nehru National Urban Renewal Mission (JNNURM) towards the end of 2005 has significantly influenced both the local governance and urban planning systems in India's large cities. Covering 63 cities across the country, the JNNURM's overarching goal is to encourage reforms and fast track planned development of the identified cities, with a focus on improving efficiency in the delivery of urban infrastructure and services. Community participation and building accountability of local authorities towards citizens are the other objectives of the Mission (Government of India 2005b).[3]

One of the prerequisites for any city to access funds under the JNNURM is the preparation of a City Development Plan (CDP). To support cities in this process, the JNNURM secretariat has produced a Toolkit containing guidelines for CDP preparation. The Toolkit suggests that a multi-stage process be adopted for the preparation of a CDP, including an assessment of the current situation, development of a vision for the future in consultation with stakeholders, strategy formulation and the development of a City Investment Plan (Government of India 2005a).

While this is indeed a welcome step forward, and has encouraged the cities included to formulate CDPs, one is unable to decipher how different these plans are, or will be, from old-fashioned master plans (other than including an Investment Plan). It is also unclear whether CDPs will replace master plans as the key statutory document for planning, or are to be developed in addition to master plans. It is too soon, of course, to comment on the extent to which each CDP has been implemented, and its long-term impact on the city concerned. The JNNURM demands that over the duration of the Mission urban planning become a designated function of elected local bodies. However, without significant institutional reforms to streamline and reorganise the responsibilities of local bodies and various parastatal (unelected/ technical) organisations, the development and implementation of the CDPs prepared for cities in the next phase of JNNURM (see below) could well remain as fragmented as it has been in the past.

A revised version of the JNNURM is now in the pipeline. Titled unimaginatively as the "New Improved JNNURM" (NIJNNURM), the new scheme will target all cities and towns, small or big, and will focus on capacity creation within the local governments. Funding will be linked to a city-specific reform agenda, rather than imposing one-size-fits-all solutions on large, medium and smaller urban centres. Regarding the governance of planning, it is proposed to strengthen Metropolitan and District Planning Committees, with Urban Development Authorities and Unified Metropolitan Transport Authorities as their technical arms. City planning would be made a function of elected local governments rather than Urban Development Authorities (HPEC 2011). It remains to be seen if this version of the Urban Renewal Mission would be any more effective as compared to the previous one, especially vis-à-vis planning.

Addressing the complex and contentious issue of urban land

Of course, urban planning reforms cannot be complete without addressing the issue of land. Urban land has always been, and continues to be, a contentious subject in most Indian cities. Like urban development and local governance, land is also a state subject under the Indian federal system. The central government provides policy advice and guidance in this area, but it is up to the state governments to adopt any central policies or directives (Banerjee 2002). One of the major legal instruments which has significantly impacted (in fact, hin-

dered) the development of urban land in the country has been the Urban Land Ceiling and Regulation Act (ULCRA) of 1976, which was applied in cities with populations of 200,000 or more in the year 1971. The key objectives of this Act were to

"...curb the activities of private land developers, to check undesirable speculation, to operate a land bank to keep land prices within reasonable limits and to ensure plan development with special reference to the needs of the poorer segment of the population." (Sivam 2002: 529)

Although these goals were undoubtedly noble, the Act led to the freezing of large tracts of land in the big cities, ostensibly for planned development. The slow pace of such development, in turn, led to a scarcity of developed land and skyrocketing prices. Land acquisition also became more and more expensive for development authorities, as well as being a cumbersome process fraught with litigation, which in turn fed the cycle of low supply and high demand (Gnaneshwar 1995; Sivam 2002). Thus, in effect, the Act shut out the urban poor from the housing market in most large cities, Delhi being a prime example. In 1998, the central Act was finally repealed. Most states have also repealed the corresponding state acts. Some states have also made other attempts to reduce barriers to private supply of land, such as reforming Rent Control Acts.

In recent years, two other initiatives have been tried to overcome the existing constraints. These are: (i) township development and (ii) land pooling and readjustment. The Integrated Township Policy, adopted by certain states, is an attempt to mobilize the private sector for the supply of land for urban housing, infrastructure, and other public purposes. Under this mechanism, a developer assembles land by paying private landowners the prevailing market price, without the deployment of Land Acquisition Act (LAA) provisions to acquire land. This is unusual in India, where land is historically seen as a public good, and its acquisition a state function. The role of the public sector in this process is restricted to that of a facilitator and a regulator of town planning, environmental, and social welfare norms (Joshi 2009).

Another effective approach being deployed for the delivery of serviced land for urban expansion in the periphery of cities, mainly in the western Indian state of Gujarat, is known as the 'Development Plan–Town Planning Scheme' mechanism. Under the Gujarat Town Planning and Urban Development Act (GT-PUDA) of 1976, a two-stage process is outlined for urban development. The first step is the preparation of a statutory Development Plan (DP) for the town or city as a whole, which also demarcates the area of the rural hinterland where the city is expected to expand. In the second stage, the expansion area is divided into a number of smaller areas, usually

between 1 and 2 sq km each, and for each of these, a Town Planning Scheme (TPS) is prepared. This is a combined land reconstitution, infrastructure development, and financing proposal (see Figure 2). Although this is a tedious process, it has been, and continues to be an effective instrument for development planning, infrastructure development, financing and implementation (Ballaney and Patel 2009).

While these measures are innovative and are being usefully deployed in a number of cities, in the long term, the supply of urban land can only be freed by removing constraints such as rent control, high stamp duty and development charges, restriction on sale or conversion of agricultural land, and the weak land title/record and protection system (IDFC 2009).

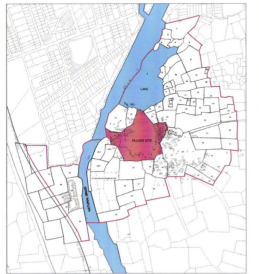
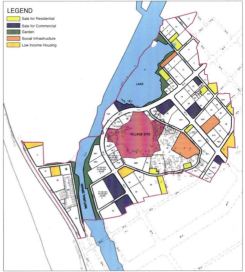

Figure 2: Before and after maps of Vinzol-2 Town Planning Scheme in the south of Ahmedabad, western India.
Courtesy EPC Development Planning and Management (EPCDPM), Ahmedabad

Responding to the Challenges of Liveability

This paper does not attempt to provide a comprehensive overview of every single challenge or concern faced by Indian cities today. Rather, it aims to focus on some critical areas which have a close connection with the concepts of inclusion, resilience and authenticity, including some which have consistently been of concern to policymakers and citizens alike (e.g. urban housing, services and transport), as well as issues which have recently emerged

(or, re-emerged) and captured the imagination of urban stakeholders (e.g. revitalisation of historic districts within cities, security and social inclusion). For each of these, the major challenges are enunciated first, followed by a few examples of innovative interventions which aim to address these.

Urban housing, infrastructure and service delivery

The challenges of urban housing, especially for low-income populations, infrastructure provision, and the delivery of a variety of urban services including (among others) water, sanitation, education and health, are long-stand-

Figure 3: Pavement-dwellers in the city of Delhi. Photograph © Maud Hainry, courtesy UNESCO New Delhi

ing concerns for Indian policymakers. According to the latest National Sample Survey reports, there are over 80 million poor people living in the cities and towns of India. While this figure is contentious and debated, at the same time it is widely accepted that 'shelter poverty' is much larger than income poverty in urban areas. This is mainly a result of heavily distorted land markets and an exclusionary regulatory system that fails to accommodate the needs of the poor, or adequately address the challenges of slums, informal settlements and pavement dwellings. An adequate, affordable formal housing supply for the urban poor doesn't seem to be a priority area for policy-makers, even though land values are escalating sharply and the 'market' is clearly

excluding the poor. A resettlement policy is urgently required which lays down guidelines to minimize displacements and ensure the rehabilitation of people affected by projects, based on human rights to adequate shelter. As slums are a state subject according to the Indian constitution, state slum laws also need to be reviewed across the country (Risbud 2009).

In terms of services, too, Indian cities lag behind on almost all counts. It is estimated that water supply is available for an average of 2.9 hours per day, across all Indian cities and towns; less than 20 per cent of waste water is treated; and solid waste management is grossly inadequate. National benchmarks have recently been developed for the four key

Figure 4: Typical scene in the older part of an Indian city, with overcrowding, dilapidated buildings and crumbling infrastructure. Photograph © Marina Faetanini, courtesy UNESCO New Delhi

service sectors, viz., water supply, sewerage, storm water drainage and solid waste management (Vaidya 2009).

Urban transport, however, is one area which is witnessing quite some innovation. Mobility is a serious challenge in most Indian cities and towns, mainly due to inadequate transport infrastructure, an unbalanced modal split heavily favouring private transport, and little integration between land use and transport planning. However, public transport is increasingly coming into focus, with a range of options being tried, from improved and environment-friendly bus services, introduction of bus rapid transit, and the development of metro rail systems. Integration of transport and land use planning is a key suggestion of the National Urban Transport Policy adopted in 2006, and Transit-Oriented Development is slowly becoming a strategic focus in several key cities, such as Delhi. The capital has seen the development of the most extensive metro-rail network in the country over the past decade, which now ferries upto 1.7 million commuters every day on seven lines. In addition, all public service vehicles in the National Capital Territory run on Compressed Natural Gas (CNG), a much cleaner fuel than diesel. This policy, when introduced in 2001-02 under directives of the Supreme Court of India, was extremely unpopular, and riddled with several glitches, the most important one being limited availability of CNG and the long queues that snaked for several kilometers outside the handful of stations which supplied the fuel. These, however, have now been addressed effectively, and the capital is relatively free of diesel smoke. Between 2000 and 2008 carbon emissions had plummeted by 72% while SO2 emissions decreased by 57%, thanks to 3,500 CNG buses, 12,000 taxis, 65,000 auto rickshaws and 5,000 mini buses running on CNG (Hohne, Burck et al. 2009).

The experience of the Bus Rapid Transit (BRT) corridor, on the other hand, was not as positive in Delhi, and the corridor was never extended beyond roads covered in the first phase. Delhi, and other Indian cities, would do well to learn from Ahmedabad in this respect (see Box 1, Figure 6).

Figure 5: Buses and auto-rickshaws plying on CNG in Delhi. Photograph © Harish Narang

Figure 6: Aerial view of the Janmarg BRTS corridor, Ahmedabad. Photograph © CEPT University, Ahmedabad

Box 1: The Ahmedabad Bus Rapid Transit System – demonstrating innovation in policy, technology and implementation

The Janmarg BRTS, as the BRTS system in Ahmedabad is known, is a much-lauded initiative for many reasons. Developed under the broader vision of "Accessible Ahmedabad", which aimed to redesign the city structure and transport systems towards greater accessibility, efficient mobility and a lower carbon future, the Janmarg BRTS was inaugurated in 2009. The project itself aimed to provide high quality, reliable public transport services comparable to a much-more expensive metro system, which would attract users from all classes of society. Extensive technological applications such as Automatic Vehicle Tracking and passenger information systems, the use of smart cards, surveillance and security systems, and Area Traffic Control Systems at junctions ensured superior service and helped build a brand identity for the Janmarg system. Dedicated right-of-way for the buses and median bus stations with barrier-free access and at-level boarding enhance accessibility and save time. Innovative public-private partnership arrangements have been used to provide footbridges, landscaping and maintenance of the corridor, as well as operation and maintenance of a pay and park system. The Janmarg BRTS today carries an average of 125,000 passengers per day using 70 buses. Financed initially through a combination of JNNURM (central government) funds (35%), Gujarat state contribution (15%) and local government contribution (50%), Ahmedabad Janmarg Limited, the company incorporated to manage the system, today generates a daily revenue of about Rs. 0.75 million and meets all its operating costs, including bus cost.

Source: www.ahmedabadbrts.com, CEPT University documentation

Urban renewal and revitalisation of historic areas

Urbanisation, along with the pressure it creates on urban land and services, also has a significant bearing on the older/historic areas within cities, often leading to deterioration and decay, as well as the loss of harmony and a sense of place. Unfortunately, this dimension of liveability is frequently neglected by policy-makers. This is, of course, not unusual as traditionally, across the developing world, rehabilitation and conservation of historic and inner-city districts receives little attention in urban development policy, with the focus mainly on monuments, or remains of monuments, or at the most, sites or complexes containing a number of monuments or other historic structures (Steinberg 1996). The emphasis on modernisation – including modern housing, transport and infrastructure – means that older city areas (which present a range of complex problems and cannot be 'modernised' easily) are ignored, therefore continue to decline, and are eventually torn down. In India, too, the urbanization of poverty and poor planning on the one hand, and the desire to 'modernise' and 'develop', on the other, have combined to play a rather destructive role vis-à-vis urban heritage (Menon 2005).

According to a recent UNESCO publication, historic areas in India are faced with multiple challenges, including those relating to poverty, migration and exclusion; inadequate housing, poor infrastructure and a deteriorat-

Figure 7: Inner-city housing above the spice market in Shahjahanabad, Delhi
Photograph © Marina Faetanini, courtesy UNESCO New Delhi

Figure 8: Evening prayer ("Aarti") on the banks of the Ganges river in the holy city of Varanasi. A popular religio-cultural ritual witnessed by thousands of residents and visitors. Photograph © Harish Narang

ing living environment; land tenure, ownership and tenancy; weak governance and conflicting interests; and finally, lack of political will to address these complex issues (UNESCO 2010). As historic areas provide economic and residential opportunities to a large number and wide range of residents and migrants, they also become melting pots for very diverse groups of people. At the same time, they can become ghettoes for the urban poor and those working in the informal sector. With deteriorating urban services, overcrowded housing conditions and lack of interest on the part of many owners in maintaining their properties, historic districts in Indian cities increasingly resemble urban slums. Conflicting interests of the poor and the middle-classes, who prefer a sanitised, restrictive approach to urban conservation, and the lack of political will to resolve these, mean that historic districts continue to suffer from neglect and decay. The

fragmented governance framework vis-à-vis cities has also played a part in the neglect of urban heritage. While the Archaeological Survey of India focused its attention predominantly on individual or groups of monuments, the Town Planning Acts and the work of development authorities only emphasised new development (and to a lesser degree, some urban renewal). Historic districts or areas within cities, thus, fell between the institutional cracks. According to Ravindran (2005)

"[There are] no regulations to guide their [old cities'] development, no base maps to propose improvements, and no intellectual space devoted to planning them."
(Ravindran 2005: 11)

Clearly, the development and renewal of historic districts in cities, with their complex and layered built form, wide-ranging economic activities and multiple uses, need to be addressed as a whole, rather than as a sum of many parts. An important step was taken in 2004 in the form of the INTACH Charter, which proposed a concept of "Heritage Zones", described as 'sensitive development areas, which are a part of larger urban agglomeration possessing significant evidence of heritage' (Menon 2005). The Heritage Zone concept emphasises that the conservation of architectural heritage and sites must be undertaken in a holistic manner, and should go hand in hand with the imperatives of routine development process. An example of the application of the heritage zone concept can be found in the newly prepared City Development Plan for the city of Ujjain, which divides the city into 18 'kshetras' (areas or zones), each of which is unique and

treated differently in the overall plan. Detailed master plans are being developed for each of these kshetras (UNESCO 2010).

Some of these issues of liveability faced by historic areas in Indian cities are being addressed within the broader City Development Plans (CDPs) prepared under the aegis of JNNURM. Guidelines issued by the Mission emphasise that heritage conservation must be integrated with the overall plan for the city - an important step forward from the older approach of focusing on the conservation of monuments and structures, often virtually in isolation from their surrounding environment (Government of India 2006). However, while these guidelines are undoubtedly progressive, they still don't go far enough in terms of being

Figure 9: A view of the restored French quarter in Pondicherry, southern India.
Photograph © INTACH Pondicherry Chapter

'people-centric'. The emphasis is far more on what heritage can do for the city in terms of revenue raising and increasing tourism inflows, rather than what it does to promote social cohesion and inclusion, sustain livelihoods, and serve as an important integrative symbol of the city (among others). There is little space devoted to the concept of 'urban revitalisation', and even less to principles of sustainable development or social inclusion, which must form the basis of any revitalization effort.

At the same time, innovative urban renewal and revitalization initiatives are by no means entirely at the mercy of national legislation or policy. Ahmedabad, in the western Indian state of Gujarat, and Pondicherry, a centrally governed territory in the south, are cases in point (See Box 2).

Box 2: Revitalisation of the historic urban core in Ahmedabad

The municipal corporation of Ahmedabad in western India has recently been awarded the top prize for being the best-managed urban local body among the 63 local governments participating in the JNNURM programme. In the news lately for its well-designed and popular Bus Rapid Transit system described earlier, the city has also been leading the way in the conservation of the walled city area and the traditional neighbourhoods therein (pols) since 1996. Undertaken in a participatory and holistic manner, this exercise has focused on creating awareness among different sections of society, and adopting a fresh approach, towards urban conservation and revitalisation. The interventions are not just about the physical conservation of heritage monuments, but also aim to protect intangible heritage as well as improve living conditions in the pols. Further, it aims to revive local governance in the walled city through extensive and continuous public participation, particularly recognizing the panch, key community leaders involved in information dissemination, as formal representatives of the community. Cultural revival is also a key focus area. One of the most successful elements of the project, which has also been replicated in other cities subsequently, is the Heritage Walk. The Heritage Walk passes through a number of well-preserved old neighbourhoods and raises awareness about their architectural, cultural and socio-economic significance. It not only targets tourists but also inhabitants of the city, aiming to build a sense of urban identity and belonging.
The urban revitalisation efforts are currently led by the Ahmedabad Heritage Centre, established in 2001 by the Ahmedabad Municipal Corporation (AMC) in collaboration with the French Government. The Centre was preceded by a Heritage Conservation Cell set up within the AMC in July 1996, to oversee and coordinate all heritage conservation efforts, in partnership with a number of civil society organisations. The Cell introduced a bye-law in the General Development Control Regulations which prohibited any heritage property from being pulled down without its prior permission. Other measures adopted include the reduction in property tax on traditional buildings, and the reduction of the Floor Space Index (FSI) from 3 to 1.8. In addition, the municipal budget sanctions approximately Rs 5 million (US$ 100,000) every year to sustain conservation activities in the area. Since waste management is integral to the process of revitalisation of the walled city, the Heritage Centre has also initiated a garbage collection and disposal programme for the same.

Source: AHC 2008; Nayak and Iyer 2008

Urban security and inclusion

Despite all its positive impact, urbanisation often brings in its wake many kinds of security challenges. In India, like many other countries, the most obvious one is the increasing vulnerability of urban areas to natural and man-made disasters – both climate- and non-climate related. Flash floods (e.g. seen in Mumbai in the year 2005), earthquakes (most recently in Kashmir (2005), Andaman Islands (2004) and Gujarat (2001), countless urban fires and other such disasters regularly affect poorly planned settlements and buildings which usually disregard the most basic building bye-laws and safety standards. The result is loss of life as well as livelihoods, mainly for the poor who live on precarious sites (e.g. along railway tracks, close to land-fill sites, or on low-lying land), in overcrowded conditions, and without many basic services such as water, sanitation and health care. Large parts of the city of Delhi lie in the floodplain of the River Yamuna, and are especially vulnerable. Mumbai is susceptible to rising sea levels, as large sections of the city are built on land reclaimed from the sea, and to heavy monsoon rains, which can cause serious havoc as the natural storm water drainage systems of the city have been haphazardly built over. Kolkata has witnessed frequent and increasingly severe cyclonic storms over the past few years, and is also facing a freshwater crisis, while Chennai is increasingly at risk of being struck by tidal waves (Banerjee 2011).

National policymakers have attempted to respond to these issues by creating a National Disaster Management Authority (NDMA), which was established under the aegis of the Disaster Management Act of 2005 and is headed by the Prime Minister. Since its inception, the NDMA has adopted numerous guidelines on preventing and responding to natural and man-made disasters. At the city level, too, many innovative initiatives are seen. Mumbai's disaster management approach, adopted by the city authorities after the flash floods of 2005, is a key example (See Box 3).

Yet another form of urban insecurity is rising crime. Urbanisation also leads to an increasing gap between the rich and the poor, between the formal and the informal. One of the results of these imbalances is exclusionary development, which is manifested in the separation of poorer settlements from the enclaves of the middle-classes and the rich, the abandonment of certain neighbourhoods, the development of an "architecture of fear", and the stigmatisation of districts or communities (UN-HABITAT 2000). At the same time, crime also limits the access of vulnerable populations such as women, youth and the elderly to urban spaces, which has serious implications for liveability in cities.

Rising crime afflicts not only the rich, but also the poor. Contrary to the widely-held belief that poverty, and the poor, are the most important cause of crime, the latter are in fact the most vulnerable as they don't have the means to defend themselves. Urban violence erodes their social capital and prevents social mobility and progress, especially that of the youth, who in turn get increasingly disenchanted (UN-HABITAT 2000). Furthermore, poorer women and girls are the most affected by crime and violence, both in their unprotected dwellings and on the streets, as they have no protection, and often no recourse. In India, past efforts have focused mainly on domestic violence and sexual harassment at the workplace, sexual assault and rape, but some recent initiatives have also attempted to reduce violence against women in public spaces, and increase safety and inclusion.

The National Capital Territory of Delhi, for example, while being in the vanguard with respect to many urban innovations, has not been able to successfully tackle the problem of gender-based violence, especially in its streets, squares, parks and public transport

Box 3: Upgrading Mumbai's disaster management capabilities

The city of Mumbai as it exists today is formed by the merger of 7 islands in the city area with 4 islands and hilly areas in the suburbs. Much of the area is reclaimed from the sea. The city has a gravity-based drainage system. During high tide, flood-gates have to be closed to stop the ingress of sea water, as a result of which there is no drainage of storm water. Water logging and floods occur when heavy rains combine with high tide conditions. The drainage network is over 150 years old and not designed for current rainfall levels. The population of greater Mumbai is over 20 million today, and it is the financial and entertainment capital of the country. The greatest challenge, however, lies in the density of its population. As compared to the national density of 382 people per square kilometre (sq. km.), the density of population in suburban Mumbai is 20,925 per sq. km., while that in the island city is 20,038 per sq. km. In these circumstances, when disaster strikes, it has the potential to affect a very large section of the population. The flash floods of July 2005 were one such event. Starting at 0830 hours on the 26th July, 2005, 994 mm of rainfall was recorded over a period of 24 hours, which resulted in water logging in several suburbs, overflow of the Mithi River, and flooding of the Western Express Highway. Nearly 500 people lost their lives in the flash floods and landslides, and about 200 died due to various deluge-related illnesses. 2,000 dwellings were completely destroyed while over 50,000 were par-tially damaged. 40,000 commercial establishments were also affected. Railway tracks were submerged and services on all railway lines were suspended as a consequence. The airport was also flooded and temporarily closed. Power supply was disconnected in most parts of Mumbai's western suburbs on the night of the 26th July due to the danger of electrocution.
Following the devastating floods, the Municipal Corporation of Greater Mumbai (MCGM) has significantly upgraded its disaster management system and capacities. The Disaster Management Unit (DMU) of the Corporation now serves as a strong and effective command and control centre, coordinating preparedness as well as response activities between the administration, field units and various stakeholders. The DMU is equipped with an ar-ray of communications systems (land lines, hot lines, cellular phones, wireless, Very High Frequency (VHF) etc.), and is linked with 14 key agencies on hotlines. Each agency provides regular updates about the situation in the city. To issue warnings and enable evacuation, MCGM has installed 35 rain gauges at 28 locations across the city. The data from these sta-tions is transmitted to the DMU at 15-minute intervals. The gauges are calibrated to raise an alarm if rainfall intensity exceeds 10 mm in 15 minutes.
Real-time information is provided to citizens on the website www.mumbaimonsoon.in. This portal also contains information on traffic and public transport diversions during floods. The DMU also engages with the population by organizing frequent training programmes on disaster preparedness for communities, school and college students and corporate houses. The Unit is currently preparing a multi-hazard disaster plan for the city.

*Source: http://siteresources.worldbank.org/PHILIPPINESEXTN/Resources/05_Mumbai_
Presentation_20080513.pdf, www.mumbaimonsoon.in*

systems. This lack of safety for women, both experienced and perceived, significantly undermines their right to the city – the right to move around freely; to use and access public spaces and services; to make choices about their place of residence, work, or leisure; and more broadly, to make the most of the opportunities the city has to offer (Narang Suri 2010).

To address these challenges, the Department of Women and Child Development, Government of Delhi, in collaboration with UNIFEM, UN-HABITAT and Jagori (a women-focused NGO), has developed a Strategic Framework on Women's Safety. This Framework is the first attempt in the country to address the issues of women's safety systematically and comprehensively (see Box 4).

Box 4: Towards a Strategic Framework for women's safety in Delhi

The Draft Strategic Framework for Women's Safety in Delhi is a groundbreaking document which has been developed through an extensive process of stakeholder consultations. The Framework draws on the findings of a large-scale safety survey of over 5,000 respondents conducted across the city, as well as several Safety Audits and focus group discussions organised over the past few years by Jagori, a leading non-governmental organisation working on women's issues in Delhi and other Indian cities. The survey and other instruments revealed that sexual harassment is seen as a major threat to women's safety in public spaces in Delhi, with the roadside seen as the most unsafe place, followed closely by public transport, as well as waiting areas for public transport. Trust in the police is extremely low, and bystanders too refuse to get involved in incidents of harassment. Some groups such as poor women who live and work on the streets, the physically challenged, as well as students and other migrants from the north-eastern parts of the country, are particularly vulnerable.

The Framework identifies seven major areas of intervention in order to address the issue of women's safety in public spaces, which would clearly also have a positive impact on the safety and security of the general population. These are: urban planning and design of public spaces; provision and management of public infrastructure and services; public transport; policing; legislation, justice and support to victims; education; and, civic awareness and participation.

For each of these seven themes, the Framework proposes a mix of physical, institutional and policy interventions, which can be carried out in the short-, medium- and longer-term. These would require the involvement of various arms of the government as well as civil society, and in some cases, the private sector. Many of these have already been acted upon, for example, the installation of GPS in auto-rickshaw and taxi services; training of public transport staff; and introduction of women-only coaches in the Delhi Metro. The biggest challenge, however, lies in transforming attitudes towards women and women's safety in public spaces, including those of key policy makers, political leaders and high-level officials, as well as ordinary citizens.

(Source: Narang Suri 2010)

Building Liveable Cities: The China Model, or is there Another Way?

Unlike China, where urbanisation is a heavily directed and planned effort, urban growth in India can be described as largely organic and chaotic, with the planning and provision of housing, infrastructure and basic services constantly playing catch-up (often unsuccessfully) with such growth. The result is seen in the way larger Indian towns and cities are being regularly retrofitted to keep up with the demands of the burgeoning population. However, the HPEC report cited earlier notes that:

"To achieve both inclusion and economic growth will [...] require shifting the focus of policy from creating physical infrastructure to delivering services." (HPEC 2011: XXIII)

Indeed, to make Indian cities liveable from the perspective of inclusion, resilience and authenticity, which are intricately interconnected, and cannot be achieved independently of one another, there needs to be a fundamental shift in the way planners and policy-makers approach urban development. Learning from the success stories as well as many failed initiatives, a few factors emerge as central to making Indian cities liveable.

• Planning legislation needs to be overhauled, in conjunction with the legal framework relating to urban land. Conventional master plans have proved to be unwieldy and impossible to implement, while new-age Comprehensive Development Plans have yet to be brought into the mainstream of the legislative framework. Land management needs to be made more efficient and transparent, with a role for both the state as well as private developers.
• Creation of extensive infrastructure, often at massive cost, not unlike China, is often seen

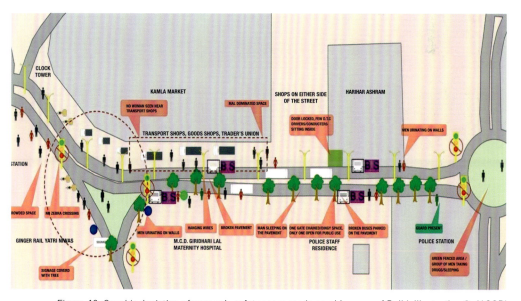

Figure 10: Graphic depiction of women's safety concerns in an older area of Delhi. Illustration © JAGORI

by political and business leaders as the key to resolving the urban problems. More importantly, however, Indian cities need more equitable as well as efficient systems of planning, stakeholder engagement and provision and management of services. Addressing urban poverty, lack of decent shelter and urban services, and the challenges of slums and homelessness need to be accorded the highest priority.

- Safety and security in cities cannot be viewed as an optional extra, but is a central concern of liveability. Security against natural and man-made disasters, as well as crime, can be enhanced significantly through better planning practices, implementation and enforcement of appropriate zoning and building regulations, and the provision of basic amenities such as water, sanitation, and electricity/lighting. This will in turn contribute significantly to making cities resilient as well as inclusive.
- The approach towards historic city centres needs to shift from heritage conservation to sustainable urban revitalisation. This is critical in order to make it people-centric in general, and pro-poor, in particular. Historic districts not only provide a sense of place and authenticity to cities, but are also important economic and social hubs whose development needs to be integrated with the rest of the city.
- Finally, better and more reliable spatial as well as socio-economic data is needed in order to make policy decisions that are suitable to different stakeholders in Indian towns and cities. This requires not only technological solutions but also a change in mindset, and also needs to be built into planning education systems and curricula.

As India stands on the verge of being an economic superpower, urbanisation is a phenomenon that can no longer be ignored or relegated to the backburner. Many Indian cities, their citizens and administrators, researchers and thinkers are taking innovative steps to address the challenges of liveability, but bringing about change across 4,000+ urban centres which are home to nearly 380 million people needs more than one-off initiatives. Laws and policies need to be changed, institutions need to be transformed, capacities need to be upgraded, and most importantly, citizens need to be empowered, if India's cities are to fulfil their enormous potential and become liveable for generations to come.

Endnotes

1. These ideas are currently under development as part of the work of a think-tank on Liveable Cities set up by the Philips Centre for Health and Well-being, of which the author is a member.

2. Since local government is a state matter according to the Constitution of India, the 74th CAA had to be adopted individually by each state legislature before it could be applied to the local authorities under its jurisdiction.

3. A similar initiative focusing on small and medium towns is the Urban Infrastructure Development Scheme for Small and Medium Towns (UIDSSMT). Planned and integrated development of urban areas is one of the stated objectives of this programme.

References

AHC (2008). Walled City Revitalisation Project Ahmedabad, Ahmedabad Heritage Centre.

Ansari, J. H. (2004). "Time for a new approach in India." Habitat Debate 10 (4): 15.

Ballaney, S. and B. Patel (2009). Using the 'Development Plan—Town Planning Scheme' Mechanism to Appropriate Land and Build Urban Infrastructure. India Infrastructure Report 2009. Land - A Critical Resource for Infrastructure. New Delhi, Oxford University Press for IDFC. 190-204.

Banerjee, B. (2002). Security of Tenure in Indian Cities. Holding Their Ground: Secure land tenure for the urban poor in developing countries. A. Durand-Lasserve and L. Royston. London, Sterling (VA), Earthscan. 37-58.

Banerjee, I. R. (2011). How safe are our cities? The Times of India. New Delhi. March 27, 2011.

Gnaneshwar, V. (1995). "Urban Policies in India - Paradoxes and Predicaments." Habitat International 19(3): 293-316.

Government of India (2005a). Formulation of a City Development Plan. New Delhi, Ministry of Urban Development, Ministry of Housing and Urban Poverty Alleviation.

Government of India (2005b). Jawaharlal Nehru National Urban Renewal Mission (JNNURM): Overview. New Delhi, Ministry of Urban Development, Ministry of Housing and Urban Poverty Alleviation.

Government of India (2006). A supplement to Toolkit on formulation of City Development Plan: Focus on Heritage. New Delhi, Ministry of Urban Development, Ministry of Housing and Poverty Alleviation.

Hohne, N., J. Burck, et al. (2009). Scorecards on best and worst policies for green new deal, WWF and E3G.

HPEC (2011). Report on Indian Urban Infrastructure and Services. New Delhi, National Institute of Urban Affairs.

IDFC (2009). India Infrastructure Report 2009. Land - A Critical Resource for Infrastructure. New Delhi, Oxford University Press for IDFC.

Joshi, R. (2009). Integrated Townships as a Policy Response to Changing Supply and Demand Dynamics of Urban Growth. India Infrastructure Report 2009. Land - A Critical Resource for Infrastructure. New Delhi, Oxford University Press for IDFC. 167-175.

Kundu, A. (2011). "Politics and Economics of Urban Growth." Economic & Political Weekly XLVL (20): 10-12.

Menon, A. G. K. (2005). Heritage Conservation and Urban Development: Beyond the Monument. Heritage Conservation and Urban Development. Hyderabad, India, INTACH.

Narang Suri, S. (2010). Safe City Free of Violence Against Women and Girls Initiative: A Draft Strategic Framework for Women's Safety in Delhi. New Delhi, Jagori.

Nayak, D. and A. Iyer (2008). "The case of Ahmedabad: Heritage Regulations and Participatory Conservation." Context V(1): 175-182.

Ravindran, K. T. (2005). Cities within Cities: Plurality and Community Participation in Indian Cities. Heritage Conservation and Urban Development, Hyderabad, India, INTACH.

Risbud, N. (2009). The Poor and Morphology of Cities. India Urban Poverty Report 2009. New Delhi, Oxford University Press. 177-198.

Savage, D. and S. Dasgupta (2006). Governance Framework for Delivery of Urban Services. India Infrastructure Report 2006 - Urban Infrastructure. 3i-Network. New Delhi, Oxford University Press. 42-58.

Sivam, A. (2002). "Constraints affecting the efficiency of the urban residential land market in developing countries: a case study of India." Habitat International 26(4): 523-537.

Sridharan, N. (2008). "Globalisation of Urban India." Economic and Political Weekly (March 8, 2008): 26-31.

Steinberg, F. (1996). "Conservation and Rehabilitation of Urban Heritage in Developing Countries." Habitat International 20(3): 463-475.

UN-HABITAT (2000). Prevention of Urban Crime: Safer Cities Concept Note. Nairobi, Safer Cities Programme, UN-HABITAT.

UNESCO (2010). Historic Districts for All - India. A Social and Human Approach for Sustainable Revitalisation. New Delhi, UNESCO.

Vaidya, C. (2009). Urban Issues, Reforms and Way Forward in India. New Delhi, Department of Economic Affairs, Ministry of Finance, Government of India.

The Urban Reform Agenda and the Struggle for Liveable Cities in Brazil

Edesio Fernandes

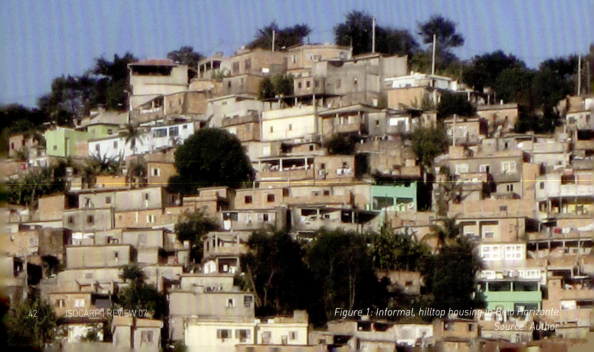

Figure 1: Informal, hilltop housing in Belo Horizonte
Source: Author

Edesio Fernandes

Introduction

Brazil has experienced one of the most drastic processes of socioeconomic and territorial re-organisation in the developing world as a result of rapid urbanisation since the 1930s.[1] According to the latest national census, over 83% of the total population of 190 million people lives in urban areas, and there is an enormous concentration of population and economic activities in a very small part of the national territory. All the relevant figures and available data clearly indicate the staggering scale and complex nature of this process, which has been widely discussed in an extensive literature. Put briefly, rapid urbanisation in Brazil has generated a nationwide urban crisis characterised by the combination of sociospatial segregation, negative environmental impact, and escalating informal development. The escalating housing deficit has been estimated as 7 million units, while some 15 million other families live in inadequate conditions. At the same time, there are about 5.5 million under-utilised properties in the country and an enormous stock of serviced, but vacant, plots of land.[2] Living and housing conditions in urban areas have long been precarious for a large proportion of the population.

The exclusionary nature of the growing process of urban development globally has renewed the calls for the promotion of urban reform in Brazil and many other countries. Like Brazil, many low- and middle-income countries are currently in the uncomfortable position of having to "change the wheels with the car moving", given the grave social, urban, and environmental problems that have accumulated over years, and even decades, of rapid urbanisation and governmental neglect. This task has been complicated further by the effects of the changes in the nature and dynamics of the traditional urbanisation process within the context of the ever-changing global economy. More than ever, stakeholders in several countries understand that the importance of getting the regulatory and institutional frameworks right cannot be underestimated. The promotion of urban reform takes times and it requires continuity and systematic responses at all governmental levels in order to address the scale of the existing problems. It also requires other fundamental factors such as capacity building, approval of articulated policies according to a clearly defined public agenda, and the allocation of the necessary resources.

It is in this context that the Brazilian experience deserves to be better known. An important process of urban reform has been slowly, but consistently, promoted in Brazil since the late 1980s, aiming to generate more liveable, sustainable, efficient, safer, and fairer cities. Significant legal and institutional changes have been introduced at the national level, creating a whole new legal-urban order that was consolidated with the enactment of the 2001 City Statute and the installation, in 2003, of both the Ministry of Cities and the National Council of Cities. More recently, record-breaking investments by the federal government in housing, sanitation, infrastructure, especially through the Plan to Accelerate Growth – PAC, the "My House, My Life" Housing Programme, and other social programmes have raised a new set of questions to be addressed by policymakers in the country.

This national legal order has been complemented by the impressive enactment of a whole generation of Municipal Master Plans: some 1,400 such plans have already been formulated all over the country since 2001, and it is the nature of their contents, as well as their effective enforcement, that will deliver the new urban-legal order consolidated by the City Statute – thus determining that the overall living and housing conditions are effectively been improved.

Above all, the Brazilian experience clearly shows that urban reform requires a precise, and often elusive, combination of renewed social mobilisation, legal reform, and institutional change. This is a long, open-ended process, the political quality of which resides ultimately in the Brazilian society's capacity to effectively assert its legal right to be present and actively participate in the decision-making process. The rules of the game of urban development and management have already been significantly altered; what remains to be seen is whether or not the newly created legal and political spaces will be used at all govern-

mental levels in such a way as to advance the urban reform agenda in the country. There is still a long way to go in Brazil, and there are many serious obstacles to overcome.

This article describes the main aspects of the process of urban reform in Brazil. Following a brief account of the historical context, the article will discuss the new legal-urban order that has been created in Brazil since the promulgation of the 1988 Federal Constitution; special emphasis will be placed on the provisions of the internationally acclaimed 2001 City Statute. The article will then describe the new institutional apparatus that resulted from the creation of the Ministry of Cities and the National Council of Cities in 2003, as well as discussing some of the main problems affecting these new institutions since their creation.

As a conclusion, it will be argued that, while significant progress has already been made towards the realization of the urban reform agenda in Brazil, the socioeconomic, political, institutional and legal disputes over the control of the land development processes have increased. The renewal of social mobilisation at all governmental levels is crucial for the consolidation, and expansion, of this new inclusive and participatory legal-urban order.

The Origins of the Urban Reform Movement

Despite a longstanding tradition of political, legal, and financial centralisation during most of the urbanisation process, until recently the federal government had failed to formulate and implement comprehensive national land and urban policies, or even to put together a basic institutional infrastructure to deal with the many concerns affecting cities and the growing urban population. In fact, prior to the creation of the Ministry of Cities in 2003, both the lack of a proper governmental response at the federal level and the elitist and exclusionary nature of the actual governmental intervention through the few existing programmes were some of the main factors determining the exclusionary nature of land and urban development in Brazil. This was aggravated further by the conditions of political exclusion resulting from the centralised and authoritarian legal system in force until the promulgation of the 1988 Federal Constitution, which undermined not only the legal-political powers of municipal government, but also the quality of the representative democracy system at all governmental levels.

Another fundamental factor in the creation and reproduction of this process was the prohibitive, obsolete legal order still affirming the anachronistic paradigm of the 1916 Civil Code, thus reinforcing the historical tradition of unqualified private property rights.[3] As a result, until recently the scope for significant state intervention in the domain of property rights through land policy and urban planning was minimal, especially at the municipal level.[4] While most municipalities still have only a set of basic laws – determining the urban perimeters and traditional constructions codes – only from the mid-1960s did a new generation of more ambitious planning laws start to be enacted in some of the main cities, although initially they were regularly legally contested.

From the mid-1970s and especially early 1980s on, important cracks appeared in the longstanding military regime, as a result of a powerful combination of factors: the growing social mobilisation through trade unions, civic organisations, social movements, residents' associations, groups linked to the progressive branch of the Catholic Church, and other collective channels; the re-organisation of traditional political parties and creation of

new ones expressing renewed political claims for politico-institutional change, particularly through democratic elections and the strengthening of local government; and also, to a lesser extent, to the rearrangements within land and property capital. The first significant attempts at the democratisation of urban management at the municipal level could be identified in the mid-1970s.[5]

As a result of the growing process of social mobilisation and political change, an important federal law was approved in 1979. This aimed to regulate urban land subdivision nationally, as well as providing basic elements for the regularisation of consolidated informal settlements in cities. Soon afterwards, some progressive environmental laws were also enacted, including a groundbreaking legal recognition in 1985 of a civil public action to defend diffuse interests in environmental matters, *locus standi* being extended to the emerging NGOs.[6] At the municipal level, the first land regularisation programmes were formulated in 1983 in Belo Horizonte and Recife.[7]

A national Urban Reform Movement then emerged and started to gain momentum, within the broader political opening process aiming to promote the redemocratisation of the country.[8] With the increasing strengthening of a new sociopolitical pact, there was a wide recognition of the need for deeper legal and political changes in the country, thus leading to the remarkable, though, in many respects, flawed 1986–88 constitution-making process.

The New Legal-Political Order for the Cities Approved by the 1988 Federal Constitution

The urbanisation process in Brazil started in the 1930s and had its peak in the 1970s - during which period several federal constitutions were promulgated in 1934, 1937, 1946, 1967 and the 1969 general amendment. Until the 1988 Federal Constitution came into force there were no specific constitutional provisions to guide the processes of land development and urban management. It was the original chapter on urban policy introduced by the 1988 Constitution that set the legal-political basis for the promotion of urban reform in Brazil.

Since the constitution-making process was itself the subject of an unprecedented level of popular participation, much of this constitutional chapter was developed on the basis of the "Popular Amendment on Urban Policy". This had been formulated, discussed, disseminated and signed by more than a hundred thousand social organisations and individuals involved in the Urban Reform Movement. This "Popular Amendment" recognized the following general principles: autonomy of municipal government; democratic management of cities; the social right to housing; the right to the regularisation of consolidated informal settlements; the social function of urban property; and the need to combat land and property speculation in urban areas. Another important "Popular Amendment" proposed the approval of a series of constitutional provisions recognising the collective right to a balanced environment.

Following a process of intense disputes in the Constituent Congress, a progressive chapter on environmental preservation was eventually approved, together with a groundbreaking, though limited, chapter on urban policy.[9]

Most of these popular claims were recognised to some extent. The right to the regularisation of consolidated informal settlements was promoted through the approval of new legal instruments aiming to render such programmes viable, both concerning settlements formed on private land (*usucapiao* rights, that is, a special form of adverse possession rights in five years, to be declared by a judicial decision as a result of which land occupiers become full legal owners) and on public land ("concession of the real right to use", a form of leasehold). The need to combat land and property speculation in cities was explicitly addressed, and new legal instruments were created for this purpose, namely, subdivision, utilisation and construction compulsory orders; progressive property taxation; and a punitive form of expropriation. The principle of the democratic management of cities was fully endorsed, as the 1988 Constitution provided a series of legal-political instruments aiming to widen the conditions of direct participation in the overall decision-making process.

The autonomy of municipal government was also recognised in legal, political and financial terms, to such an extent that Brazilian federalism is considered to be one of the most decentralised in the world. There are three governmental levels in Brazil – federal state and municipal. However, the urbanisation process in the country has essentially been a process of metropolitanisation, there currently being several metropolitan areas, which are not recognised by the legal-institutional system. This makes it impossible to formulate public policies to deal properly with quintessentially metropolitan matters such as sanitation, transport, housing, etc. However, the 1988 Constitution did not take a proper stand on the matter of metropolitan administration, transferring to the federated-states the power to do so.[10]

At that juncture, there was no political consensus on the recognition of the social right to housing. Regarding the recognition of the principle of the social function of urban property, there were heated debates between antagonistic groups, and as a result the following formula was approved: private property is recognised as a fundamental right provided that it accomplishes social functions, which are those determined by municipal master plans and other urban and environmental laws. By making the principle of the social function of urban property conditional on the approval of municipal planning laws, the intention of conservative groups seemed to be to make this principle merely rhetorical. The limited Brazilian experience with city and master planning so far had been largely ineffective in terms of its power to reverse the exclusionary conditions of urban development. On the contrary, informal land development had largely resulted from the elitist and technocratic nature of city planning. Faced with the impossibility of approving another, more progressive constitutional formula, the Urban Reform Movement then decided to make the most of the situation and subvert the approved provision, by consciously investing in the formulation of municipal master plans throughout the country that would be both inclusive and participatory.

Local Experiences in the 1990s and the Expansion of the New Legal-Urban Order

The promulgation of the 1988 Constitution inaugurated a whole new legal-urban order,

and its possibilities began to be realized throughout the 1990s by means of a series of progressive local experiences. Many municipalities approved new urban and environmental laws, including some master plans; in fact, Brazil became an interesting urban planning and management laboratory, with new strategies and processes establishing new relations between the public, the community, the private, and the voluntary sectors where urban land development was concerned. New land regularisation programmes were formulated and began to be implemented by several municipalities.[11]

Special emphasis was placed on the political quality of all such processes, with popular participation being encouraged in various areas, from the definition of urban policies in "City Conferences" to the introduction of an innovative participatory budgeting process.[12] Since then, municipalities such as Porto Alegre, Santo Andre, Diadema, Recife and Belo Horizonte have gained international recognition.

However, the lack of regulation of the urban policy chapter in the 1988 Constitution through federal legislation, as is the tradition in Brazil, led to a series of legal-political difficulties, which were fomented by groups opposed to the advance of the new legal-urban order. This undermined the extent and the scope of the promising local experiences. As a result, the organisations involved in the Urban Reform Movement decided to consolidate and expand the urban reform movement itself, initially by creating the National Forum of Urban Reform (NFUR) in the early 1990s.

Comprising a wide range of national and local organisations and movements, the NFUR was instrumental in promoting the urban reform banner and agenda nationally. Three of its main targets in the 1990s were the incorporation of the social right to housing in the 1988 Constitution; the approval of a federal law regulating the constitutional chapter; and the approval of a bill of law, originating from a popular initiative using the new possibilities created by the 1988 Constitution, which proposed the creation of a National Fund for Social Housing. At the same time, the NFUR also called for the creation by the federal government of an institutional apparatus at the national level to promote urban planning and policy in Brazil.

A long process of social mobilisation and a fierce political struggle lasted throughout the 1990s and into the new century, within and outside the National Congress. In 1999, a new federal law regulated the action of "civil society organisations of public interest" so as to allow them to receive public money. The social right to housing was eventually approved by a constitutional amendment in 2000, and the federal law creating the National Fund for Social Housing was finally enacted in 2005. Of special importance was the enactment, in 2001, of the internationally acclaimed "City Statute", the federal law on urban policy.

The Pioneering Legal Framework Approved by the 2001 City Statute

The above-mentioned constitutional provisions were regulated and expanded on by the groundbreaking 2001 City Statute, which explicitly recognised the "right to the city" in Brazil.[13] Resulting from an intense negotiation process which lasted for more than ten years, within and beyond the National Congress, the City Statute confirmed and widened the fundamental legal-political role of municipalities in the formulation of directives for urban planning, as well as in conducting the process of urban development and management.

The City Statute broke with the longstanding tradition of civil law and set the basis of a new legal-political paradigm for urban land use and development control. It did this especially by reinforcing the constitutional provision recognising the power and the obligation of municipal governments to control of the process of urban development through the formulation of territorial and land use policies, in which the individual interests of landowners necessarily co-exist with other social, cultural and environmental interests of other groups and the city as a whole.

The City Statute elaborated on the principle of the "social functions of property and of the city", thus replacing the individualistic paradigm of the 1916 Civil Code. In addition, the Statute provided a range of legal, urban planning and fiscal instruments to be used by the municipal administrations, especially within the context of their master plans, to regulate, induce and/or change the current course of urban land and property markets according to criteria of social inclusion and environmental sustainability. All such instruments can, and should, be used in a combined manner aiming not only to regulate the process of land use development, but especially to induce it, according to a "concept of city", to be expressed through the municipal master plans. Municipalities were given more scope for interfering with, and possibly reverting to some extent, the pattern and dynamics of formal and informal urban land markets, especially those of a speculative nature, which have long brought about social exclusion and spatial segregation in Brazil. In fact, the combination of traditional planning mechanisms – zoning, subdivision, building rules, etc. – with the new instruments – compulsory subdivision, construction and utilisation orders, extrafiscal use of local property tax progressively over time, expropriation-sanction with payment in public bonds , surface rights; preference rights for the municipality, onerous transfer of building rights, etc. – opened a new range of possibilities for the construction by the municipalities of a new urban order which can be economically more efficient, politically fairer, and more sensitive to the gamut of existing social and environmental questions.

Moreover, the City Statute indicated several processes for municipalities to integrate urban planning, legislation and management so as to democratise the local decision-making process and thus legitimise a new, socially orientated urban-legal order. Several mechanisms were recognised to ensure the effective participation of citizens and associations in urban planning and management: audiences, consultations, creation of councils, reports of environmental and neighbourhood impact, popular initiative for the proposal of urban laws, public litigation, and above all the practices of the participatory budgeting process. Moreover, the new law also emphasised the importance of establishing new relations between the state, the private and the community sectors, especially through partnerships and linkage "urban operations" to be promoted within a clearly defined legal-political and fiscal framework.

The 2001 legislation also improved on the legal order regarding the regularisation of consolidated informal settlements in private and public urban areas, enabling municipalities to promote land tenure regularisation programmes and thus democratise the conditions of access to land and housing. As well as regulating the abovementioned constitutional instruments of *usucapiao* and concession of the real right to use, the new law went one step further and admitted the collective utilisation of such instruments. Subsequently, still in 2001, given the active mobilisation of the NFUR Provisional Measure no. 2.220 was signed by the President, recognising the subjective right (and not only the prerogative of the public authorities) of those occupying public land until that date to be granted, under certain circumstances, the "concession

of special use for housing purposes", another form of leasehold rights.

All municipalities with more than 20,000 inhabitants, among other special categories, were given a deadline of five years to create and approve their master plans.

The City Statute has been complemented by important new federal laws enacted subsequently, namely those regulating public-private partnerships (2004) and intermunicipal consortia (2005). More recently, several federal laws were enacted in 2008, 2009 and 2010, aiming to facilitate the regularisation of informal settlements, particularly those occupying federal land. There has also been a nationwide discussion on the proposed, thorough revision of the 1979 Federal Law, which governs the subdivision of urban land.

This gradual, fundamental process of legal reform has also been supported by a significant process of institutional change, in which the creation of the Ministry of Cities in 2003 deserves special mention.

Institutional Reform at the Federal Level

Throughout the urbanisation process, there was no adequate institutional treatment of the urban questions at the federal level. Given President Fernando Henrique Cardoso's celebrated academic and political background, the lack of a national urban policy and a corresponding institutional apparatus during his government (1995-2002) was particularly frustrating. There were some isolated, sectoral programmes scattered through several ministries dealing with aspects of the broader urban question, but there was no national urban policy to articulate them, especially because the then existing urban policy secretariat had insignificant powers and few resources.

Only with the election of President Lula in 2003 was an original decision made to create the Ministry of Cities. It is important to stress that the new Ministry was not created merely as an executive decision by the new President, but as his response to the social claim long defended by the NFUR and other stakeholders, which fact confers a special form of legitimacy on the Ministry of Cities.

The Ministry consists of an Executive Secretariat presiding over four National Secretariats, namely, housing, environmental sanitation, public transportation and mobility, and land and urban programmes. Among other tasks, the Executive Secretariat has focused on building the capacity of municipalities to act, initially through a national campaign for the elaboration of multipurpose municipal cadastres. As well as formulating national programmes on their respective subjects, the four Secretariats have been involved in several negotiations with the National Congress to promote further changes in the regulatory framework in force, with a relative degree of success so far.

An important initiative has been the National Campaign for Participatory Municipal Master Plans, which has been instrumental in boosting the discussion and mobilisation nationally around the issue. The above mentioned approval of municipal master plans is a legal requirement affecting about 1,700 Brazilian municipalities, and it is the political and technical quality of this process that will eventually determine the extent to which the possibilities of the new legal-urban order proposed by the City Statute will be realized.

For this gigantic task to be properly fulfilled there was an enormous need for municipalities to be provided not only with capacity building and financial resources, but also with adequate technical information and conceptual formulations. Educational "kits" have been widely distributed, grants have been given to municipalities and registered consultants committed to the urban reform agenda; a "bank of experiences" has been created, organising materials from more than 700 ongoing experiences; a virtual network disseminates experiences and information; and seminars and all sorts of meetings have been promoted throughout the national territory, always in partnership with local institutions.

Problems and constraints

Significant progress has already been made in the implementation of the urban reform agenda nationally, and the Ministry of Cities has gained increasing institutional credibility, social legitimacy, and political influence. However, the Ministry of Cities still faces many serious problems, the most immediate being its precarious institutional organisation, small team, and limited budgetary resources.

There is still a serious problem of fragmentation to be overcome in the way interrelated urban policies are formulated within the Ministry and in its relationship with other ministries. Only in 2007 was a new national sanitation policy approved by federal law. With due respect to the importance of the recently approved National Fund for Social Housing, as well as to the improvements already made to previously existing federal programmes through *Caixa Economica Federal*, the fact is that a new, comprehensive and articulated national housing policy has not yet been formulated. Federal investment in both areas, housing and sanitation, has significantly increased since 2003, indeed breaking historical records, but, given the longstanding governmental neglect of those matters and the extent of the accumulated social debt, the total budget is still limited. The ambitious "My House, My Life" national housing programme swiftly launched in 2009 in response to pressure from developers and promoters affected by the national effects of the global economic crisis bypassed the process of discussion of the national housing policy conducted by the Ministry of Cities; as mentioned below, some of its impacts have been questionable.

The creation of the Ministry of Cities has certainly given more visibility to the long neglected urban concerns, but with this recognition new disputes have also emerged – including disputes over the control of the Ministry of Cities itself. With the growing recognition of the political dimensions of the urban questions, fierce political disputes have resulted from the constant realignment of the questionable political coalition supporting President Lula. As a result, while all the four National Secretaries were kept in office, in 2005 the first Minister and Executive Secretary, from a left-of- centre political party, were replaced by people nominated by a conservative, populist political party less in tune with the principles of the urban reform agenda. At the same time, the Urban Development Commission of the National Congress, which for a long time had only played an insignificant role, has been gaining more political visibility and influence, and not all of its members fully embrace the reform agenda. More recently, the fact that the Ministry of Cities controls the enormous financial resources earmarked for PAC and the housing programmes has increased the interest of conservative, centre-right political parties that support the governmental coalition. It has also attracted the attention of the newly elected President Dilma Rousseff, who has recently nominated a conservative politician not clearly committed to the urban reform agenda as the new Minister.

Given all these constraints, the Ministry of Cities has been systematically investing in the establishment of partnerships of all sorts – within the federal government, through intergovernmental relations, with the National Congress and the Judiciary, with the private sector, and with the organised social movements, NGOs, and academia.

A fundamental part of this process has been the intimate link between the Ministry of Cities and the National Council of Cities.

The National Council of Cities

Perhaps the most remarkable aspect of the new political-institutional apparatus that is currently being created in Brazil has been the installation of the National Council of Cities.

In April 2003, President Lula called for a national mobilisation to discuss a list of land, urban and housing policy goals, through a series of municipal "City Conferences" in which delegates would be elected to participate in State Conferences, and eventually in the National Conference planned to take place in October 2003. It was expected that some 300 or so municipalities, out of the 5,571 existing, would have the time and the conditions to organise local conferences. As it happened, over 3,000 municipalities did so, as did all 27 federated-states. At the National Conference, over 2,500 delegates discussed the initial national policy directives on urban development, as well as the range of specific proposals on sectoral housing, planning, sanitation, and transportation national policies. They all voted on the definition of the final list of principles that should guide the formulation of national policies by the Ministry of Cities.

Moreover, one of the most important deliberations of the 1st National Conference of Cities was the creation of the National Council of Cities, with representatives from all sectors of stakeholders being elected. The National Council consists of 86 members, 49 representing segments of civil society (popular movements, workers' unions, NGOs, academic institutions, and the business sector) and 37 representing federal, federated-state and municipal administrations. All the members are elected for a two-year term. Citizen participation in the Council's deliberations is

Figure 2: Informal development (favela) on the hilltops of Rio de Janeiro
Source: Author

thus widely ensured, and the Ministry of Cities is legally required to follow and respect such deliberations.

The 2nd National Conference of Cities took place in December 2005, again as the culmination of a nationwide mobilisation process. Some 2,500 delegates and 410 observers from all federated-states and different social segments discussed a more articulated National Urban Development Policy, aiming to generate "fairer, democratic and sustainable" cities. The 3rd Conference took place in November 2007, again involving the participation of over 2,500 delegates; it aimed to take stock of previously approved pans and programs, as well as discussing the National Housing Plan. Perhaps involving a lesser degree of popular participation, the 4th National Conference took place in June 2010, discussing "Advances, difficulties and challenges in the implementation of the urban development policy".

The National Council of Cities has met on several occasions so far, issuing several important resolutions, and it has gradually been recognised as a most important sociopolitical forum. This recognition is unequivocal among the stakeholders more directly involved with the urban concerns discussed by the National Council. However, it still needs to be fully acknowledged by the federal government as a whole, particularly when it comes to fully accepting the National Council's deliberations as well as translating them into proper budgetary provisions. It is also crucial that the National Council is empowered to control the Ministry of Cities, so that the urban reform agenda that justified its creation is not replaced by a series of narrow, client driven relations.

In any case, the promotion of the National Conferences and the action of the National Council have already made a difference to the course of urban policy in Brazil, and have conferred a unique degree of sociopolitical legitimacy on the decision-making process.

For this reason, both initiatives were given the 2006 UN-Habitat Scroll of Honour Award.

Current Challenges for the City Statute and the Ministry of Cities in Brazil

It is undeniable that the approval of the City Statute consolidated the constitutional order in Brazil as to the control of the process of urban development, aiming to re-orient the action of the state, the land and property markets, and society as a whole, according to new legal, economic, social, and environmental criteria. Its effective materialisation in policies and programmes will depend on the reform of the local legal-urban orders, that is, the overall regulatory and institutional framework put together at the local level to govern land use development by the municipalities, particularly through the approval of adequate master plans. The role of municipalities is crucial so that the exclusionary pattern of urban development can be reversed in the country.

Over 1,400 municipalities have already implemented their master plans to some extent, and, 10 years after the enactment of the City Statute, several studies have recently begun to assess their efficacy from the viewpoint of how they have promoted both inclusiveness and participation. It is still early to make any definitive assessments, but there are strong elements suggesting that – even fully acknowledging the diversity of situations and the several problems and constraints affecting popular participation - while the new tradition of master planning is indeed more participatory than ever before, the socioeconomic, political and institutional disputes over the control of land development processes have worsened. This very much reflects Brazil's

recent economic growth and the growing, record-breaking values generated by dynamic, and often speculative, land and property transactions in the country.

It seems that many, if not most, municipal master plans have not been totally successful in the promotion of sociospatial integration, especially in that, by keeping the tradition of regulatory planning, they have failed to directly intervene in the land structure. Many new master plans have failed to territorialise their proposals and are not backed up by adequate spatial plans; many have limited themselves to the approval of conventional regulatory plans, especially zoning and land use regulations, but have failed to adopt the new urban tools so as to intervene more directly in the urban structure by determining obligations to land and property owners.

Also, most of those few others that have made use of such new urban planning tools – especially the sale of building rights – have done so without having clearly determined a redistributive context for the application of the newly found financial resources, thus reinforcing traditional land and property speculation and sociospatial segregation processes. Technically complex and even somewhat obscure, many plans have not taken into account the limited capacity local administrations have to act so as to implement them. Indeed, the effective implementation of the approved laws is the main challenge faced by the social movements, urban managers, legal professionals and politicians committed to the promotion of urban reform in Brazil.

While it is undeniable that the process of urban reform in Brazil has been given an enormous boost with the recent legal and institutional reforms, there are many problems to be overcome and serious challenges to be confronted at the federal level, and the new laws and institutions should not be taken for granted.

At this juncture, it should be briefly mentioned the great impact the Plan to Accelerate Growth (PAC, launched by President Lula in 2007), may have to advance urban reform and the consolidation of the federal institutional apparatus in Brazil. The record amount of financial resources – initially announced as US$300 billion – in infrastructure, sanitation, land regularization and other fields – initially over three years, but extended by President Dilma Rousseff - has raised a new set of questions to be addressed by policymakers, namely:

- Are there adequate projects in place for the application of the new financial resources?
- Do the public administrations, especially at the municipal level, have the necessary conditions to manage such projects and resources in a proper and efficient manner?
- Are there adequate channels and processes in place to enable social, fiscal and judicial control of the expenditure, so as to prevent client driven use of the resources, not to speak of corruption?

It is still premature to make a consistent and fair assessment of the impact of PAC, but there are already strong elements suggesting that a significant part of the new resources is being wasted given the lack of administrative capacity and institutional efficiency, when it is not being politically manipulated or, even worse, appropriated in corruption schemes.

The same applies to the federal housing program "My House, My Life" launched by President Lula in 2009 and extended by President Dilma in 2011, promising to build and deliver over 1,000,000 houses over three years, which also involves record-breaking investments by the federal government. Again, it is still premature to make a consistent and fair assessment of the impact of the programme. However, there are already elements suggesting that, apart from the above mentioned problems with administrative capacity and

institutional efficiency, by failing to engage with the land structure – and thus make use of vacant and under-utilised private and public land and property - the programme has encouraged a significant increase in land prices as well as the construction of thousands of housing estates in precarious peripheral areas. This has reinforced the traditional pattern of sociospatial segregation.

The City Statute itself has already been the subject of several proposed changes at the National Congress, many of which, if approved, might undermine its potential. So far, the discussion of such legal bills has been stalled in the Urban Development Commission. Moreover, the continuity and the quality of the action of the Ministry of Cities will depend on how the existing political disputes and contradictory interests will be accommodated. The very existence of the Ministry has been questioned, especially by some people who would like to see it merged with other ministries within the context of a streamlined federal government.

On a broader level, the full realization of the urban reform agenda by the Ministry of Cities will depend on how the federal government as a whole understands the centrality of urban questions. Critical to this understanding will be the promotion of more interministerial integration and intergovernmental articulation. The Ministry of Cities will also need to be provided with a more consistent institutional infrastructure and capacity to act, and the necessary resources for the promotion of the whole new set of social policies and programmes. The control of urban development cannot be left only to market forces; but nor can it be left to municipal government alone.

Figure 3: High rise blocks in Belo Horizonte with informal housing on the mountain slopes beyond Source: Author

There is a crucial role for the federal government, as well as the federated-state governments.

At a more internal level, the Ministry of Cities needs to promote better integration between its Secretariats and respective programmes. The approval of a comprehensive housing policy aimed at the urban poor is of utmost importance, in part to slow the process of informal development. For this purpose, the clear definition of a national policy on the utilisation of federal land and property is particularly necessary. The definition of an articulated territorial organisation policy and system of cities is also crucial, including an adequate treatment of the pressing matter of metropolitan administration. More emphasis should be placed on the attempts to reconcile the "green" and the "brown" agendas in the country. Existing partnerships need to be reinforced, and new ones should be formed.

Conclusion: Possible Lessons from the Brazilian Experience

All in all, the Brazilian experience has clearly shown that, if urban reform aiming to generate more liveable cities requires combined institutional change and legal reform, it also fundamentally depends on nationwide social mobilisation. This is indeed a highly political process, and the constant renewal of social mobilisation in Brazil, through the NFUR and other collective channels, within and outside the state apparatus, is the *sine qua non* for the advance of the urban reform movement in the country.

The urban reform process is naturally an expression of the country's specific historical conditions and political processes, but impor-

tant universal lessons can be learned by other countries and cities interested in promoting social inclusion in cities.

Besides the above-mentioned sociopolitical, institutional and administrative requirements, the Brazilian case has stressed the importance of redefining the legal system to create the bases of an inclusive land and property governance framework, in which new legal concepts and principles (especially the recognition of collective rights), institutional mechanisms and sociopolitical processes are properly articulated. The perspective of urban reform also requires broader access to judicial courts to help push the legal boundaries from inside the legal system, as well as to guarantee the effectiveness of the legislation in force.

This is a process of renewed fierce disputes though, and, difficult as it is, changing the rules of the game is no guarantee that the game will be played accordingly. In fact, the enactment of progressive laws may perversely contribute to the creation of a legal discourse and practice that demobilises civil society, thus keeping unchallenged, if not legitimising, the main foundations of the exclusionary *status quo*. There is a growing literature discussing the possibilities, limits and intrinsic contradictions of participatory processes, especially participatory budgeting and municipal master planning processes.[14]

Also in this respect, the materialisation of the possibilities of any redefined legal system and its translation into a new sociospatial pact will depend on how it is legally and politically appropriated by the stakeholders. As Jean-Jacques Rousseau clearly understood, houses make a town, but citizens make a city.

Endnotes

This article draws from, updates and expands upon, articles published by the author in 2007 and 2010; see Fernandes (2007a; 2007b; and 2010).

1. Data on the urbanisation process in Brazil can be found in several sources, the main one being the site of the Brazilian Institute of Geography and Statistics – IBGE (www.ibge.gov.br); for some recent analytical studies, see Fernandes and Valenca (2001).

2. I have discussed the legal basis of the historical process of urban development in Brazil elsewhere; see Fernandes (2002a).

3. Although it is less popular in Brazil than it is internationally, the impressive case of Curitiba demonstrates that many problems with the legal order may be successfully overcome if there is a solid political-institutional pact in place; in any case, Curitiba is indeed the exception that proves the rule, because of the conservative and even exclusionary nature of the city planning strategies adopted in that city until recently. For a general reference, see Schwartz (2004); see also Fernandes (1995c).

4. See Kowarick (1994) for analyses on the social mobilisation processes in Sao Paulo.

5. For a detailed analysis of the civil public action, see Fernandes (1995b; 1994).

6. For a critical analysis of the first stage of the regularisation programme in Belo Horizonte, see Fernandes (1993).

7. For a broader analysis of the urban reform movement, see M. L. de Souza (2001).

8. For an analysis of the constitutional chapter on urban policy, see Fernandes (1995a) and Fernandes and Rolnik (1998); for a discussion of the environmental chapter, see Fernandes (1996a; 1992a).

9. For an analysis of the Brazilian experience of metropolitan administration between 1973 and 1988, see Fernandes (1992b).

10. I have discussed the ongoing experiences of land regularisation in Brazil in some detail elsewhere; see Fernandes (2002b, 2000).

11. For a critical analysis of the participatory budgeting process, see C. Souza (2001); see also Fernandes (1996b).

12. For a broad discussion of the new urban-legal order and the City Statute, see Fernandes (2007b).

13. For a detailed analysis of the National Programme, see Fernandes (2006).

14. For a critical analysis of the experiences of participatory budgeting, see Fernandes (2010).

References

Fernandes, Eedesio

(2010). Participatory Budgeting Processes in Brazil – 15 Years Later. In Kihato, C., Masoumi, M., Ruble, B. A., Subiros, P. & Garland, A. M. (Eds.) *Urban Diversity – Space, Culture and Inclusive Pluralism in Cities Worldwide* (pp. 283-300). Baltimore: The John Hopkins University Press and Washington, DC: Woodrow Wilson Center Press.

(2007a). Implementing the urban reform agenda in Brazil. *Environment & Urbanization,* 19 (1), 77-189.

(2007b). Constructing the Right to the City in Brazil. *Social and Legal Studies,* 16 (2), 201-219.

(2006). Principles, bases and challenges of the National Programme to Support Sustainable Urban Land Regularisation in Brazil. In Huchzermeyer, M. & Karam, A. (Eds.) *Informal settlements – A perpetual challenge?* (pp. 62-83). Cape Town: University of Cape Town Press.

(2002a). Providing security of tenure for the urban poor: the Brazilian experience. In Durand-Lasserve, A. & Royston, L. (Eds.) *Holding their Ground – Secure land tenure for the urban poor in developing countries* (pp. 101-126). London: Earthscan.

(2002b). Combining tenure policies, urban planning and city management in Brazil. In Payne, G. (Ed.) *Land, Rights and Innovation – Improving Tenure Security for the Urban Poor* (pp. 209-232). London: ITDG.

(2000). The legal regularisation of favelas in Brazil: problems and prospects. *Third World Planning Review,* 22 (2), 167-187.

(1996a). Constitutional Environmental Rights in Brazil. In Anderson, M.R & Boyle, A.E. (Eds.) *Human Rights Approaches to Environmental Protection* (pp. 265-284). Oxford: Oxford University Press.

(1996b). Participatory Budget: a new experience of democratic administration in Belo Horizonte, Brazil. *Report* 11 (December), 23-25.

(1995a). *Law and Urban Change in Brazil.* Aldershot: Avebury.

(1995b). Collective Interests in Brazilian Environmental Law. In Robinson, D. & Dunkley, J. (Eds.) *Public Interest Perspectives in Environmental Law* (pp. 117-134). Chichester: Wiley Chancery Law.

(1995c). Curitiba, Brazil: Successfully Integrating Land Use and Transport Policies. *Report* 5 (June), 6-9.

(1994). Defending Collective Interests in Brazilian Environmental Law: An Assessment of the Civil Public Action. *RECIEL - Review of European Community & International Environmental Law* 3 (4), 253-258

(1993). The legal regularisation of "favelas" in Brazil - The case of Belo Horizonte. *Social & Legal Studies* 2 (2), 211-236.

(1992a). Law, politics and environmental protection in Brazil. *Journal of Environmental Law* 4 (1), 41-56.

(1992b). Juridical-institutional aspects of metropolitan administration in Brazil. *Third World Planning Review* 14 (3), 227-243.

Fernandes, E. & Rolnik, R. (1998). Law and Urban Change in Brazil. In Fernandes, E. & Varley, A. (Eds.) Illegal Cities - Law and Urban Change in Developing Countries (pp. 140-156). London: Zed Books.

Fernandes, E. & Valenca, M. (2001). (Eds.) Urban Brazil: past and future. Geoforum Special Issue, 32. London: Elsevier.

Kowarick, L. (1994). (Ed) Social Struggles and the City. The Case of São Paulo. New York: Monthly Review Press.

Schwartz, H. (2004). *Urban Renewal, Municipal Revitalization – The case of Curitiba, Brazil*. Alexandria, VA: Hugh Schwartz.

Souza, M. L. de (2001). The Brazilian Way of Conquering the "Right to the City": Successes and Obstacles in the Long Stride Towards an 'Urban Reform'. *DISP* 147 25-31.

Souza, C. (2001). Participatory budgeting in Brazilian cities: limits and possibilities in building democratic institutions. *Environment and Urbanization* 13 (1), 159-184

The Netherlands in Transition

The Planning of Low Carbon, Sustainable and Liveable Cities in the Utrecht Region

Martin Dubbeling

Figure 1: The Netherlands has centuries of experience in harvesting wind energy. The traditional wind mill from 1897, now a national monument, originally drained the Eemspolder and is the most northern situated windmill on the mainland of the Netherlands. Its name, 'The Goliath', suggests that, in its time, this windmill was a huge building. Nowadays this windmill is dwarfed by contemporary windmills. Photo: Sake Elzinga

Introduction

The Netherlands is world renowned for the way in which urban planning, infrastructure, ecology and the environment form an integral part of the practice of spatial planning and urban design. The country has a vigorous and open economy, an entrepreneurial society with its metropolis situated on a compact delta which is vulnerable to climate change. The Netherlands has four layers of public administration, the State (central government), the provinces and the municipalities which, together with the regional water boards, are responsible for spatial planning and the future development and structure of the Netherlands' cities, infrastructure and national landscape. At the start of 2011 and following a change of government the responsibilities of each of the three tiers of government and how they can work together was re-evaluated and set out in the 'Administrative Agreement 2011-2015'[1]. Central government, the provinces and the municipalities are almost constantly working on strategies, policies and plans for the development and redevelopment of low carbon, sustainable and liveable city regions and cities for the coming decades.

All three tiers of government are charged with the task of making Dutch cities ready to face the future: less dependent on fossil fuels, with reduced emissions of greenhouse gases, and able to cope with the expected rise in sea level and climate change. Policy and targets in the area of reducing CO_2 emissions and energy transition are more likely to succeed when they become an essential part of spatial policy and planning. The Province of Utrecht and the larger cities in this region, in particular, are taking major steps in this area. This article describes how the newly elected central government, the Province of Utrecht and the six larger towns in Utrecht are turning their climate and energy targets into spatial policy, strategy and physical planning. This stands in sharp contrast with the situation as reported in the ISOCARP Review 05 Low Carbons Cities[2], especially in the way the responsibilities between the state, provinces and municipalities are redefined and redivided.

The Administrative Agreement

The Netherlands faces a major challenge: cutting government spending while at the same time strengthening the economy. The Administrative Agreement between the State, provinces, municipalities and regional water boards is supposed to help to create a government apparatus which is lean and efficient with a clear division of tasks between the four levels of administrative authority. The underlying principle of the Dutch Government apparatus of the last decade 'decentralize whatever can be, centralize whatever has to be' is put into practice. This means that, wherever possible, the implementation of tasks is devolved to the municipalities or provinces. Central government is responsible only for national concerns such as national defence and foreign policy, but is also involved, alongside other

levels of administration, in the spatial economic structure, public health, flood defences, the nation's unique landscape features and cultural heritage, plus the national and international transport networks. Central government set out this vision in the draft National Policy Strategy for Infrastructure and Spatial Planning[3].

The core tasks of the provinces will lie in spatial development and the physical surroundings. The provinces will act as regional coordinators for the development of integrated development strategies, the interplay of interests as well as promoting and safeguarding complementarity between the cities and city regions within the province. The municipalities will be responsible for creating a safe and pleasant environment in which to live and work, and their tasks will lie in the social, economic and spatial domains. In the spatial domain this will be spatial planning in the widest sense, in which it will be important to find the right balance between the environment, nature, water, the economy and housing, etc. This policy will be laid down in policy strategies and zoning plans. The task of the regional water boards is to manage water quality and quantity in the regional water systems. As part of this task the water boards are responsible for the flood defences and for ensuring that there is sufficient clean water.

The Administrative Agreement states that the public authorities will work together to ensure coherent spatial policy and task allocation across the administrative layers and levels of scale in the areas of housing, water, mobility, economic activity, the climate, energy, the environment and cultural heritage. This spatial policy must ensure that the Netherlands:

• Can develop further economically, so that investing in the Netherlands continues to be attractive to national and international businesses;

- Continues to be accessible by land, water and air;
- Puts its energy supply in order and ensures that energy is available for the future;
- Is protected against flooding and surplus water, and continues to be safe even under climate change;
- Is a pleasant, healthy and attractive place to live and work, where people can enjoy nature, culture, and recreation, with a good balance between all these functions[4].

Energy Report 2011

The Administrative Agreement refers to the goals set out for economic innovation and making the energy supply more sustainable as formulated in the Energy Report 2011 published by the Netherlands Ministry of Economic Affairs, Agriculture and Innovation. Central government continues to work towards achieving the EU climate target, reducing 80 - 95% of CO_2 emissions in 2050 by comparison with 1990. The provincial authorities, municipalities and water boards too are dedicated to creating more sustainable energy and achieving climate targets. Based on their own goals and resources, they are continuing to work towards energy conservation and increasing the share of sustainable power generation. The provinces and municipalities are adjusting the spatial criteria for this, while fostering economic innovation and change. The underlying principle of the Energy Report is a form of energy management which is more sustainable and less dependent on increasingly scarce fossil fuels. The state wants to benefit from the strength of the Dutch energy sector. This will bring growth, jobs and revenue. The energy policy has three main concerns: transition to a cleaner energy supply, the economic outlook for the energy sector and the need for a reliable energy supply[5].

The Energy Report sets out the aspiration of achieving a low carbon economy by 2050. It indicates that the best way of doing this will be through an international climate agreement and it will be necessary to make the transition to a more sustainable form of energy management. This transition should be good for the Dutch economy. Under the motto of "not 'green' or growth, but 'green' and growth" the Energy Report advocates capitalising on the strength of the energy sector and encouraging cooperation with research institutes and industry in the development of new energy technologies. This is the only way that the Netherlands will be able to further develop renewable energy and maintain its international position as an energy producing country. This will bring growth, jobs and revenue. The Energy Report further assumes a balanced mix of national and international green energy and grey (i.e. fossil) energy. It describes the present reality which, for the time being, means that Europe will continue to be dependent on fossil fuels and that the Netherlands' position as a gas producer and world leader in the technological field of capturing and storing CO_2 will be important for the Dutch economy. It further assumes that, in the near future, the Netherlands will also need nuclear energy because this will help to further diversify energy sources and does not lead to CO_2 emissions. The Energy Report sets out five main pointers for the future:

- A modern industrial policy based on innovation, the development and commercial viability of renewable energy technologies, the positioning of the Netherlands as a knowledge-based economy and as a gas exchange for North-West Europe. This will not only create jobs and economic activity, but also help to safeguard supply;
- Increasing the share of renewable energy, provided that the energy supply becomes more sustainable, in a way which is economically viable and that renewable energy

becomes a standard part of the internal European energy market;

- Keeping all energy options open as we move towards a low carbon economy in 2050 with a balanced mix of green and grey energy in an integrated energy market together with CO_2 reductions brought about through an increased share of renewable energy, energy conservation, and nuclear energy, together with CO_2 capture and storage;
- Based on the principle of 'green growth', making a 'Green Deal' with society with the aim of taking real steps towards a sustainable society. A sustainable society will not happen by itself, it is a joint process involving both society and government. Energy conservation and renewable energy will be important elements in the Green Deal;
- Investing in a properly functioning European energy market with an adequate infrastructure which facilitates cross-border integration of national grid operators. An adequate energy infrastructure is vital for an energy supply which is clean, secure and affordable.

The Energy Report clearly shows that the built environment and transport take up a very large proportion of the total energy consumption in the Netherlands and that these constitute a major source of CO_2 emissions. There is also considerable potential for savings in both these sectors. Policy and targets in the area of reducing CO_2 emissions and energy transition are more likely to succeed when they are made an indispensable part of spatial policy and planning. However the Energy Report does not go much beyond the development of intelligent transport systems, promoting electric cars, and improving the energy labelling of new and existing buildings.[6] The Energy Report keeps all the options open when it comes to green, grey and nuclear energy, and makes no credible choice. The Energy Report therefore falls short when it comes to formulating adequate and effective policy on the necessary changes to be made in the built environment.

The aim of moving towards a low carbon economy and society in 2050 will require a revolution in the area of smart public transport and an entirely different way of organising and planning urban regions and cities.

National Policy Strategy for Infrastructure and Spatial Planning

In the spring of 2011 the Dutch Government presented its draft National Policy Strategy for Infrastructure and Spatial Planning. The subtitle 'Keeping the Netherlands competitive, accessible, liveable and safe' already indicates something of the document's nature and goals. After its adoption, this Policy Strategy will replace the Spatial Planning (2006) and Mobility (2004) Policy Documents and the Randstad 2040 Structural Vision (2008) in order to provide room for the provinces, municipalities, citizens and businesses to take the initiative and continue to develop economically. Central government has made it clear that it cannot and does not wish to continue to do and control everything. The Policy Strategy specifically notes that the spatial differences in the Netherlands are widening. The rapid population growth in previous decades is now behind us. In the next 25 years perhaps another one million or so Dutch citizens will be added to the cities, mainly in the west of the Netherlands. More than half of the country's municipalities will soon start to feel the effects of a shrinking population and an ageing one. In most areas the demand for more offices, industrial estates and residential areas will be much less than it has been in recent decades. As a result, obsolescence and vacancy levels will become an increasingly apparent problem.

In many respects, especially in the way the re-sponsibilities between the state, provinces and municipalities are redefined and redivided, the draft National Policy Strategy for Infrastruc-ture and Spatial Planning constitutes a break with the past and with the policy of the last few decades. Central government is focusing on strengthening the international position of the Netherlands and promoting the interests of the country as a whole. These interests concern the main networks for the transport of passengers and goods, energy and the environment, flood defences and environmen-tal quality (air, noise, soil, water and external security) and the protection of world heritage sites such as the Waddenzee (Wadden Sea), and the Nieuwe Hollandse Waterlinie (New Waterline defences). These three main goals have been subdivided into 13 themes of national importance and included in national commissions for seven designated so called MIRT regions under the Long-Term Programme for Infrastructure, Spatial Plan-ning and Transport, along with the North Sea coast. The seven MIRT regions are North-West Netherlands including the Amsterdam metropolis region (the northern wing of the western conurbation known as the Rands-tad), the southern wing of the Randstad, the South Western delta, Brabant-Limburg, East Netherlands, Utrecht and North Netherlands. In this way central government has indicated what it is responsible for and the results it wants to achieve. While at the same time, the state gives the provinces and municipalities room to act in response to their own regional and local situation, make their own decisions and tailor their activities accordingly.[7]

It should be noted that developing low carbon, sustainable and liveable cities and regions will mainly become the concern of the provinces and municipalities, possibly in concert with one another. The stated ambitions and themes of the Energy Report 2011, such as a low carbon economy by 2050 and entering into a

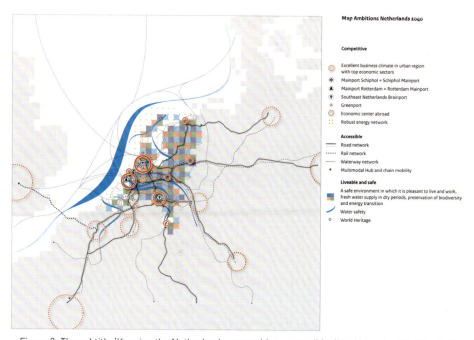

Map Ambitions Netherlands 2040

Competitive

- Excellent business climate in urban region with top economic sectors
- Mainport Schiphol = Schiphol Mainport
- Mainport Rotterdam = Rotterdam Mainport
- Southeast Netherlands Brainport
- Greenport
- Economic center abroad
- Robust energy network

Accessible

- Road network
- Rail network
- Waterway network
- Multimodal Hub and chain mobility

Liveable and safe

- A safe environment in which it is pleasant to live and work, fresh water supply in dry periods, preservation of biodiversity and energy transition
- Water safety
- World Heritage

Figure 2: The subtitle 'Keeping the Netherlands competitive, accessible, liveable and safe' of the National Policy Strategy for Infrastructure and Spatial Planning is represented in the Map Ambitions Netherlands 2040 Source: Draft National Policy Strategy for Infrastructure and Spatial Planning

"Green Deal" with society are hardly, if at all, reflected in the draft National Policy Strategy for Infrastructure and Spatial Planning. It is recognised, however, that the transition to more sustainable fuels will take up more space. To ensure that the Netherlands sets aside enough land for wind energy, central government, together with the provinces, has designated preferred areas for large scale wind farms. Alongside this, international

energy relations will be strengthened and the energy infrastructure made more suitable for decentralised electricity generation.[8]

The ex ante evaluation of the National Policy Strategy for Infrastructure and Spatial Planning by the Netherlands Environmental Assessment Agency (PBL) advocated careful steering of the energy transition. The evaluation further emphasized that the built environ-

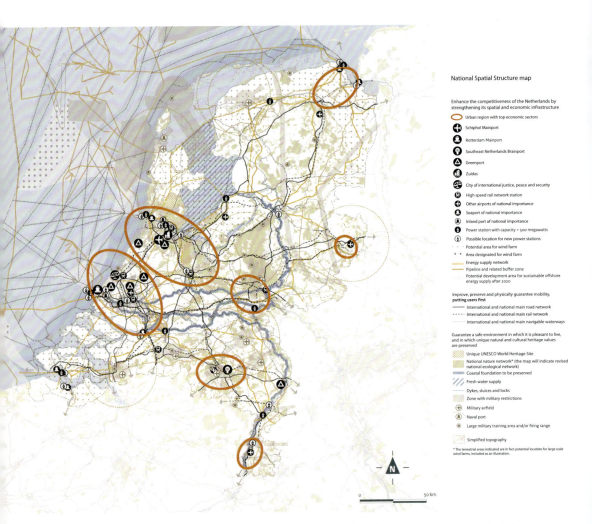

Figure 3: The National Spatial Structure Map from the (draft) National Policy Strategy for Infrastructure and Spatial Planning illustrates the way that the Netherlands is enhancing its competitiveness by strengthening its spatial and economic infrastructure. Source: Draft National Policy Strategy for Infrastructure and Spatial Planning

ment can contribute to the energy targets. The heating and cooling of buildings demands a great deal of energy and a lot can be saved by connecting the heat flows between individual buildings, and using waste heat from industry. There is also an enormous benefit to be gained through better insulation of existing homes and commercial buildings, because a large proportion of the buildings that will be standing in 2050 have already been built. This means that it is vital to look at the restructuring of the existing building stock in order to meet energy targets. In other words, it is a matter of improving the heat management in towns and cities in innovative ways, with information and clear rules, such as energy labelling for buildings, and by linking projects, for example, in heating networks.[9]

The Utrecht 2040 Mission

With 1.2 million inhabitants, the Province of Utrecht is one of the most densely populated and at the central point of the Netherlands. It forms part of the northern wing of the Randstad, one of Europe's strongest economic centres. Utrecht lies at the centre of one of the country's largest metropolitan networks which will drive economic and social developments over the next few decades. It is here that the motorways, railway connections and waterways converge which connect other parts of the Netherlands with one another. In this way it acts as a logistical hub for the major

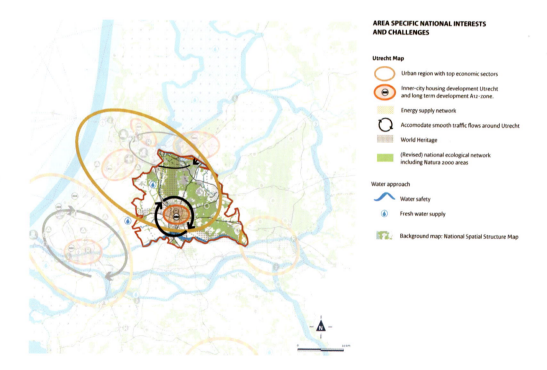

Figure 4: The Utrecht Region is part of the Amsterdam metropolis region. The (draft) National Policy Strategy for Infrastructure and Spatial Planning states that the proper functioning of the Utrecht region as the Dutch 'hub' with its complex intersection of road, rail and waterways is one of the primary tasks of national importance Source: Draft National Policy Strategy for Infrastructure and Spatial Planning

development axes along the A1, A12 and A2 motorways. With the trend from 'main ports' to 'brain ports', the Utrecht region is increasingly becoming a meeting point for know-how and creativity. Utrecht owes this opportunity to the three mainstays of the region: its leading position in terms of knowledge-based activities and culture, its central position, and the quality of the cities and surrounding landscape.

In its strategy and mission 'Utrecht 2040: sustainable and attractive', the Province of Utrecht states that it intends to be a province which does not shift the burden to other places on earth and later generations. Making choices with a view to the consequences elsewhere and later is seen as a moral duty and a strategic task. Within the overall picture of maintaining and strengthening the three mainstay qualities of the region, six goals are set; these indicate where the major societal issues and spatial tasks will lie in the coming decades. The Utrecht 2040 strategy is the prelude to the draft policy strategy for the period 2013-2025 and describes a province:

• Where there is for room for a good quality of life (housing, work and nature);
• With an innovative knowledge-based economy;
• Which is accessible by car, bike or public transport in a better environment;
• Which is climate neutral and able to cope with climate change;
• Where everyone counts and can participate at school, in their neighbourhood and in their profession;
• With more diversified nature and an attractive landscape.[10]

The economic strength of Utrecht lies as much in its central location as in its highly educated population, the knowledge-intensive sectors (such as Utrecht University, the Royal Dutch Meteorological Institute (KNMI) and the National Institute for Public Health and the Environment (RIVM) research institute) as well

as the creative sectors, business and financial services and the life sciences (Utrecht Science Park). The particular features of the surrounding landscape, including key areas of the National Ecological Infrastructure (EHS) and the presence of cultural heritage features in the form of the 'Roman Limes', representing the border line of the Roman Empire at its greatest extent in the second century AD, and the Nieuwe Hollandse Waterlinie which are candidates for the list of World Heritage Sites, also contribute to this strength. On the edge of the Randstad, Utrecht acts as a buffer zone between the metropolitan dynamism on the one side and the peace and spatial tranquility of the East Netherlands on the other. This position gives the region the relaxed urban atmosphere and quality of life which makes the area so attractive. These are its past and future critical success factors.[11]

In the 2011-2015 Coalition Agreement of the Provincial Council of Utrecht, the provincial executive designated as its core tasks economic and spatial development, nature and the landscape, accessibility, as well as cultural and historical heritage. Sustainability forms an integral part of these core tasks. The Province of Utrecht is well aware of its position and responsibilities as a hub and its central position in the Netherlands. Policy tasks include restructuring and making more intensive use of existing work sites in combination with energy conservation and reducing CO_2 emissions, together with inner city development and strengthening the quality of the rural area, as well as the flood defences, energy transition and accessibility.

The Coalition Agreement also addresses how to make sustainable energy possible in the spatial context. The accommodation of wind power is thought to be constrained by landscape quality considerations. The preliminary draft Provincial Spatial Planning Policy Strategy 2013-2025 document nevertheless includes wind energy sites. If accepted by the municipalities and if the market takes the lead, the plans for wind energy could be further developed. However, other forms of sustainable energy are preferred, such as solar energy, waste heat, thermal energy storage, geothermal energy, biomass and farm energy, which have less impact on the quality of the landscape.[12]

The draft National Policy Strategy for Infrastructure and Spatial Planning states that the proper functioning of this Dutch 'hub' with its complex intersection of road, rail and waterways is the primary task of national importance. Other tasks in the draft Policy Strategy include building and maintaining the flood defences along the Lek and Lower Rhine rivers and the freshwater supply via the main water system, implementing and protecting the (revised) National Ecological Infrastructure (EHS), including the Natura 2000 areas, making the main energy network robust and complete and accommodating the exploitation of

geothermal energy and thermal energy storage in the region. The redevelopment and urbanisation of the A12 zone in the urban landscape between the towns of Utrecht, Nieuwegein and Houten is also designated as a task of national importance. The Utrecht region experiences considerable pressure on its space because of the heavy demand for housing in combination with the limited space available for this.

The economy and the number of households in Utrecht is expected to continue to grow until 2040. Until 2040 there will be continuing demand in the Utrecht region for more than 100,000 homes, alongside the need to replace some 20,000 homes. Given the complexity and scale of the inner city task and the relationship between this task and the function of the 'Utrecht hub', central government and the region have reached agreements about this. They have furthermore agreed that, in principle, some of the demand for housing in the Utrecht region (15,000 homes) will be met in Almere.[13]

Box 1: Definitions and Ambitions

The following three ambitions are often voiced in the Netherlands: CO_2 neutral, climate neutral and energy neutral. These terms are often used interchangeably as if they mean the same thing, though this is most certainly not the case. CO_2 neutral is understood to mean: a situation where fossil energy consumption (and related CO_2 emissions) measured throughout a year is no more than zero and no energy is consumed that is not put back into the system from a renewable source. Climate neutral refers to a situation where the above definition of neutrality encompasses all greenhouse gasses. Energy neutral goes one step further because in this case the total energy requirements of a company

or a whole area must come from renewable sources and the storage of CO_2 in new forestry areas or underground is not permitted.

Figure 5: Wind energy is important in preventing climate change. Photo: Sake Elzinga

Third Industrial Revolution

For the further development of the task set out in the Utrecht 2040 strategy as well a climate-neutral and climate resilient province which is dependent only to a limited extent on fossil fuels, the Province of Utrecht in 2010 called in the US economist and energy strategist, Jeremy Rifkin. In his report Rifkin outlines a path in which economic development and the realisation of climate goals go hand in hand. Rifkin expects that, given the finite nature of fossil fuels, in the longer term a worldwide energy transition will start to take place, together with a huge demand for all kinds of products and services. Rifkin, who is also an advisor to the European Commission, makes a clear link with the economy and for his reports and recommendations draws on a large network of people in the private sector, such as Philips, Cisco and Kema. Rifkin's recommendations, with the grand title *Utrecht Roadmap to a Third Industrial Revolution*, provides building blocks for a clean economy in 2040. These involve the consistent pursuit of an energy conservation policy and the application of new, sustainable energy sources. Rifkins *Third Industrial revolution* is based on five principles:

• Energy efficiency;
• Use of renewable energy resources;
• Use of buildings as power plants;
• Development of hydrogen and other energy storage technologies;
• Shift to smart grids and electric plug-in vehicles.[14]

According to Rifkin, it will be impossible to end CO_2 emissions in Utrecht completely within 30 years. This is because a large proportion of these emissions are related to the old housing and building stock and the infrastructure. Only at extremely high cost would it be possible to become completely climate neutral within 30 years for heating and other purposes. In addition, many new technologies would have to be applied and a new generation of technicians and engineers would be necessary to manage them. This is not something which can be achieved in one generation. To become climate neutral it will therefore be necessary to find compensation elsewhere.[15]

In his report Rifkin makes an important link between the energy transition and the economic opportunities which this offers. He even calls it an 'Economic game plan'. This is precisely the approach adopted by the Province of Utrecht. It is not a separate programme in which the province will steer the energy transition, but one linked to the economic policy of the Province of Utrecht. In the economic policy plan for the province of Utrecht three essential elements are identified: life sciences, the creative industries and economic sustainability. The last theme is still in its infancy, but with such centres of knowledge as the University of Utrecht, the University of Applied Sciences Utrecht, the Utrecht Sustainability Institute (USI), KNMI, RIVM and TNO, the Province of Utrecht has a lot to offer in terms of a starting point for an economic sustainability cluster. The focus of the province in the coming period will be mainly on creating the right conditions to strengthen this cluster, for example, by combining demand and creating economic added value by encouraging innovation. This means that the province intends to take steps to reduce CO_2 emissions in the restructuring of commercial estates and make sustainability and quality of life a visible part of the inner city task. Through the Ontwikkelingsmaatschappij Utrecht (OMU – Utrecht Development Agency), the Province of Utrecht will take part in projects to break the impasse surrounding these tasks. When it comes to the energy issue, the province supports initiatives with a team of energy experts that delivers first aid for technical, financial, legal and organizational bottlenecks. Other examples in which the

Box 2: Remco van Lunteren, Provincial Executive for Mobility, Economy and Finance

"For a Provincial Executive, these are exceptional and exiting times to work on the transition towards a more sustainable society in the Netherlands. The framework in which the State, the provinces, municipalities and water boards work together on the governance and the future of the Netherlands is very fast and dramatically changing. The challenges of today and tomorrow require these administrative authorities, businesses and knowledge institutes to cooperate together in working on experimental projects, new funding models and pave the way for innovations. Governments have less to spend, that is why we need to get rid of the usual means of grants and subsidies and to become more creative. I am convinced that the future approach of becoming a more sustainable province of Utrecht needs to be quite different than before. Climate is important, but not the only issue that is at stake. We need to recognise it much more as an economic opportunity, if not economic necessity, based upon the reality that fossil fuels will be quickly run out and thus more expensive. Thanks to the "Roadmap" we know very well how difficult this task is and which opportunities can be capitalised upon. As a province we have the task to facilitate the transition towards a sustainable economy and live-

able spatial environment. In the Provincial Spatial Planning Policy Strategy we explicitly focus on working together with the municipalities in the Utrecht region in order to reserve space for sustainable energy as well as to intensify the inner cities, transform the A12 zone and improve and develop the light rail connections."

Figure 6: Remco van Lunteren, Provincial Executive for Mobility, Economy and Finance

province is involved are knowledge and innovation in the area of deep geothermal energy, facilitating biogas hubs to support transport and supply of biogas, project management group for smart grids and administration for a guarantee fund.

In his report Rifkin also makes another import link between the issue of the energy transition and its spatial impact. He has made a rough estimate of what would be required to achieve a climate neutral region by 2040: importing 120,000 freight vehicles a year carrying bio-

EPRI | ELECTRIC POWER
RESEARCH INSTITUTE

Figure 7: This diagram of a smart grid illustrates in which way local energy sources, buildings and electrical vehicles are interconnected. Source: Utrecht Roadmap To a Third Industrial Revolution

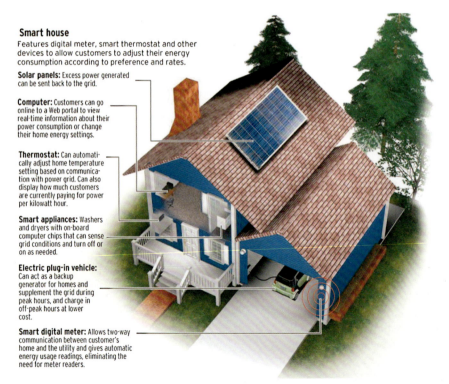

Smart house
Features digital meter, smart thermostat and other devices to allow customers to adjust their energy consumption according to preference and rates.

Solar panels: Excess power generated can be sent back to the grid.

Computer: Customers can go online to a Web portal to view real-time information about their power consumption or change their home energy settings.

Thermostat: Can automatically adjust home temperature setting based on communication with power grid. Can also display how much customers are currently paying for power per kilowatt hour.

Smart appliances: Washers and dryers with on-board computer chips that can sense grid conditions and turn off or on as needed.

Electric plug-in vehicle: Can act as a backup generator for homes and supplement the grid during peak hours, and charge in off-peak hours at lower cost.

Smart digital meter: Allows two-way communication between customer's home and the utility and gives automatic energy usage readings, eliminating the need for meter readers.

Figure 8: The common situation of a house that is connected to the power grid only to consume energy might be outdated in the near future. A smart home connected to the smart grid will be able to upload, store and download energy in a way similar to the internet. Source: Utrecht Roadmap To a Third Industrial Revolution

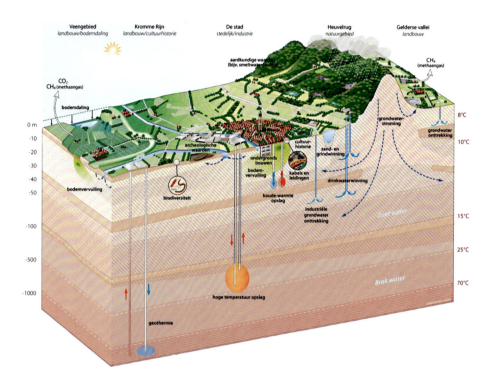

Figure 9: According to Rifkin, geo-thermal energy is one of the renewable energy resources necessary for a clean economy in the Utrecht Region 2040. Source: the Utrecht 2040 Mission

mass or 1600 large-scale wind turbines in the beautiful open landscape. Given the spatial complexity of the Province of Utrecht previously referred to (densely populated intersection of road, railway and waterway network, nature/landscape) this is not a realistic prospect. But providing the room for energy and other forms of innovation and for large scale generation of sustainable energy is probably the most important pre-requisite in relation to the province's core task in the spatial domain. The province itself cannot develop any sustainable or conventional energy projects. It will be the market players, such as project developers, power generation companies, housing associations and groups of residents who will do that. The task of the province will be to provide clarity at an early stage for these parties regarding where they can develop their initiative. This is what the Provincial Spatial Planning Policy Strategy is intended to do.

Utrecht's Spatial Planning Policy Strategy

The preliminary draft of the Provincial Spatial Planning Policy Strategy sets out spatial policy for the period 2013-2025. This document centres around the question of how to ensure that the region remains an attractive place to live and work and for recreation, while maintaining the balance between people, the environment (planet) and the market (profit). The spatial planning policy strategy sets out three main development themes: a sustainable residential environment, bustling villages and towns and an attractive rural area. These themes will contribute most to the attractiveness, liveability and spatial quality of the province.

With the development of a sustainable environment in which to live, the province is preparing for climate change. The spatial planning policy strategy restates the province's goal of being a climate-neutral province and climate-resilient by 2040. To achieve this goal the province already needs to take this into account in its spatial planning. Part of this will include increasing the share of sustainable energy sources. This is desirable not only to achieve this aim, but also from the point of view of becoming less dependent on fossil fuel sources. To cope with climate change it is important that the soil, water system and flood defences are sustainable and robust. Where water levels are too high, the excess has to be safely channelled away and the dikes are intended to further reduce the likelihood of flooding. The Province of Utrecht wants its towns and cities to continue to be attractive, healthy and safe places to live and work and recognizes that a sustainable living environment is also a factor in the decision where to locate a business, one which is expected to become even more important in the future[16]

Sustainable energy is considered to be a 'provincial concern'. This means that the province can address this concern in various ways. The goal of making the territory of the Province of Utrecht climate neutral by 2040 not only involves reducing CO_2 emissions but also achieving a situation where the province is no longer dependent on the finite supply of fossil fuels. The spatial task here is to provide space for the sustainable generation of energy and the facility to bring together those functions which supply or demand heat or energy. For this purpose the Province of Utrecht will aim for energy self-sufficiency in its regional development. The province will ask the municipalities and developers to include a section in spatial plans on how the plan takes energy conservation and the application of sustainable energy sources into account. The province also intends to stimulate the use of all forms of sustainable energy: wind energy, biomass, deep geothermal energy, thermal energy storage, solar energy, hydropower and the use of waste heat. Spatial frameworks have been drawn up for wind energy and biomass. The basic principle here is that, in view of the spatial impact of wind turbines, preference will be given to other forms of sustainable energy. Besides the Spatial Planning Policy Strategy, the province will also draw up a strategy on the theme of the subsoil which looks at the opportunities for and threats to thermal energy and geothermal energy storage.

Besides low carbon and fossil fuel independence, a territory which has been organised to be climate-neutral by 2040 has the added benefit of better air quality. It further provides opportunities to maintain and even improve the quality of the physical surroundings. Energy conservation and the generation of sustainable energy also offers opportunities in relation to Utrecht's sustainable economy. To attain climate neutrality the task is to greatly reduce energy consumption through conservation and innovation on the one hand, and to generate the energy that is needed in a way which is

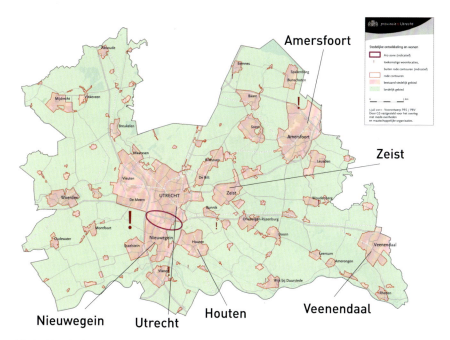

Figure 10: the Utrecht Region - Amersfoort, Veenendaal, Utrecht, Houten, Nieuwegein, Utrecht and Zeist
Source: the preliminary draft of the Provincial Spatial Planning Policy Strategy

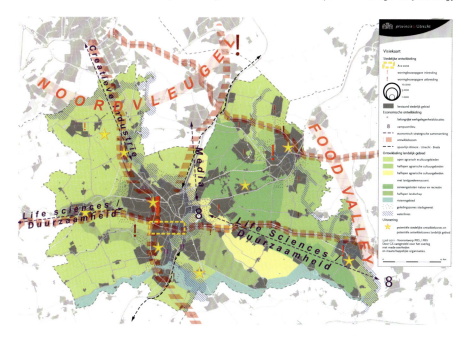

Figure 11: The preliminary draft of the Provincial Spatial Planning Policy Strategy sets out spatial policy for the
period 2013-2025. The strategy identifies three main development themes: a sustainable residential
environment, bustling villages and towns and an attractive rural area

sustainable on the other. This relates to both central power generation of large amounts of energy as well as bringing together various functions which demand heat and energy and can supply heat and energy. The province has estimated the spatial capacity for the production of sustainable energy until 2020. If all the realistic options for biomass, solar energy, geothermal energy, etc. were to be used and the province achieves the nationally agreed goal of 50 MW in wind energy, then this will provide for the sustainable generation of 10% of the Province of Utrecht's energy needs. This means that the province will not meet the goal of 20% of sustainable energy generation as intended in the Spatial Planning Framework. The transition to a sustainable energy supply is expected to progress slowly during the period of the Policy Strategy document (2013-2025). The Province of Utrecht does not expect that this will influence the objective for 2040 to be climate neutral. A characteristic of a transition is a slow start with several small scale innovations, followed by a 'take off' and acceleration phase where visible structural changes take place. In the period between 2025 - 2040 the province expects the many innovative initiatives and projects that already take place, to develop into a fully grown sustainable economy that is independent from fossil fuels.

The Province of Utrecht does not consider wind energy to be the most suitable option in this transition. The goal in itself and the related sites for wind energy are limited essentially to the agreement made with central government to provide for 50 MW of wind energy on land. When it comes to biomass the province is much more generous. Considerations such as fitting the necessary plant into the landscape and the effect of increasing traffic are, of course, also critical factors. The province wants to make the processing of biomass spatially possible based on a positive land use ratio. In the urban regions the responsibility will rest mainly with the municipalities and the

same goes for energy conservation and the application of sustainable energy. [17]

Plans and Initiatives in the Larger Towns and Cities of Utrecht

More than half the residents of the Province of Utrecht live in the six larger towns and cities of Utrecht (311,250 inhabitants), Amersfoort (146,500 inhabitants), Veenendaal (62,250 inhabitants), Nieuwegein (61,000 inhabitants), Zeist (61,000 inhabitants) and Houten (49,000 inhabitants). Utrecht and Amersfoort are the larger and older cities with a historic centre. Nieuwegein, Houten and Zeist are satellite towns of Utrecht and the town of Veenendaal is more closely linked to Ede and Wageningen in the Province of Gelderland.

The two larger municipalities in the Province of Utrecht, in particular, are highly ambitious when it comes to the areas of climate, reducing CO_2 emissions and the energy transition. The municipality of Amersfoort has laid this down in a Climate Action Plan[18] and the policy document 'Amersfoort: a city that cares about the future'[19], while the Utrecht municipality has this in its planning and implementation programme 'Utrecht's Energy'.[20] These include the goals to make the municipality of Amersfoort a CO_2 neutral municipality by 2030 and Utrecht a climate neutral municipality by 2030 (see Box 1). These goals have not been plucked from the air, but are the result of preparatory policy and research over the years. The programmes of the two councils (last elected in 2010) see CO_2 reduction and sustainability not only as a necessity but also as an opportunity for the economy and a way to improve the environment we live in. The two programmes emphasise largely the same things, specifically the building and renovation

Figure 12: The tower of the Utrecht Dom with a red shawl is the symbol of the energy efficiency of the historic centre of the City of Utrecht. Source: Municipality of Utrecht

of existing and new residential areas and commercial estates in a way which is CO_2 neutral, intensive use of space, the sustainable and local generation of power, clean air through sustainable mobility and creating a green and pleasant living environment.[21]

The planning and implementation programme 'Utrecht's Energy' is solid and full of such aims and policies. Given that 80% of CO_2 emissions come from the cities, the programme assumes that the emphasis of the drive to reduce CO_2 emissions will lie in the existing stock of housing and industrial buildings, in the private sector and in mobility in the cities. Major CO_2 reductions can be achieved by improving the relatively old stock of housing, offices and commercial premises. In mobility too, there are general opportunities for

CO_2 reduction: in a compactly built city like Utrecht, those opportunities are even greater. The distances involved are small as a result of which quieter, cleaner, safer and more sustainable mobility options (e.g. bicycle, public transport, electric transport) would appear to be the more natural choice.[22]

Thus, there is all the more reason to get to work at the urban level. This can be done, among other things, by improving and extending the district heating which started being laid as long ago as 1923, partly in the historic centre, and in 2005 provided for a quarter of the city's heating needs. The heat supplied is the waste heat from two power stations in the city, combined with auxiliary (stand-by) district heating plants. This results in a reduction of 50% of CO_2 emissions compared with traditional individual heating systems in every building. The heating network has branches not only into the post-war residential areas of Kanaleneiland and Overvecht but also extends to the neighbouring municipality of Nieu- wegein and the eastern part of the Leidsche Rijn urban development.[23] By adding biomass as source of energy in the two power stations, the district heating network becomes more sustainable.

Another key objective is to reduce energy consumption in the extensive historic inner city of Utrecht, where there are over 4.500 large and impressive historic buildings like churches, museums and university faculties. The municipality is investigating the feasibil- ity of deploying a combination of interven- tions to reduce energy consumption without

damaging the historic cityscape and the listed buildings. For the time being, the focus is on renovation and careful insulation, together with smart building services, smartly utiliz- ing the district heating network and the use of thermal storage in the ground. In this way the municipality considers not only individual buildings but also looks at connected parts of the extensive historic inner city. [24] It is working on a number of key sustainable projects, such as the Science Park on the Uithof university campus, the station area and the Rijnenburg urban development district with 7,000 homes, the master plans for which provide for them to be made more sustainable. These projects also derive to some extent out of the strategy policy for the period 2015-2030 drawn up by the municipality in 2004.[25] This strategy sets out tasks such as optimizing and intensifying

Figure 13: Artist impression of the redevelopment of Utrecht Central Station. The ambition is to become the most sustainable railway station in Europe. Source: Municipality of Utrecht.

Figure 14: Artist impression of the redevelopment of Utrecht Central Station connecting the historic city of Utrecht
Source: Municipality of Utrecht

the use of the urban space and making the urban water system more sustainable, although measures related to the areas of climate, reducing CO_2 emissions and energy transition are more recent innovations.

Amersfoort municipality has a policy strategy for 2030 in preparation in which sustainability constitutes one of the important themes. Indeed, under the course which the municipality has set for itself, sustainability will be the guiding principle in the further development of this bustling city. Moreover, it is one of the main tenets of the 2010-2014 Coalition Agreement. This concerns the interpretation of the broad term sustainability: the coherence between socio-cultural, environmental and economic measures (people, planet and profit), such that the effects elsewhere and on later generations are recognized. The positioning and strength of the city of Amersfoort is at the heart of its ambition to further develop into a vital and sustainable city as part of the northern wing of the western conurbation known as the Randstad, with a central role for the Amersfoort region. Another related task is the renewal and more intensive use of the existing urban area.[26]

The Steering Document which provides the essential starting point for the Amersfoort Spatial Policy Strategy 2030 sets out eight spatial planning goals and looks more closely at the context and dilemmas which will arise in drawing up the policy strategy. One of the eight spatial planning goals, a specific response to climate change, aimsto facilitate a CO_2 neutral city as far as is spatially possible by 2030. The municipality is fully aware of the scale of this task. To achieve this goal energy consumption will have to be reduced as far as possible. Realistically, however, the likely gains in that area will be limited. Most can be achieved in the built environment and through sustainable mobility. This is why an energy transition is needed, i.e. switching from the use of fossil fuels to the generation of sustainable energy. All promising forms of sustainable energy must be utilized in order to meet this goal. Examples include solar roof panels, energy storage in the ground, utilizing biomass and wind energy. It is important to create the right conditions to ensure that optimum use can be made of these opportunities. Some forms of sustainable energy, such as wind turbines, are at odds with other spatial planning goals, such as the aim to create an attractive green city which is a pleasant place to live in. [27]

Figure 16: One of the experimental low energy houses in Nieuwland in Amersfoort, built in the early 1990s, demonstrated all kinds of techniques and systems Source: Wissing Town Planning and Urban Design

Figure 15: The masterplan for the future residential area Rijnenburg. As the Province of Utrecht has set goals in order to reserve space for sustainable energy as well as to intensify the inner cities, transform the A12 zone and improve and develop the light rail connections, it is unlikely that this residential area will be built in the near future. Source: Municipalities of Utrecht and Juurlink and Geluk Urban Planning and Landscape Architecture

Figure 17: The sustainable residential area Nieuwland in Amersfoort consists of 4,500 houses. One thousand of them are covered with solar cells Source: Wissing Town Planning and Urban Design

In recent decades, Amersfoort has made a name for itself with its Nieuwland sustainable residential district with 4,500 homes. This residential area is one of the first of its kind in the Netherlands, where the principles of sustainability have been applied right down to the smallest details. The Nieuwland district was built in the period 1995-2002 and is the world record holder in the area of active solar energy. The electricity generated by some 12,500 m² of solar panels on more than 1,000 homes and other buildings is enough to meet 40% of the total demand of the households living in those 1,000 homes [28]. The experience gained in Nieuwland was then applied to Vathorst, the urban district currently in development with roughly 11,000 homes and all attendant facilities, such as healthcare, education, sport, culture, shopping centres

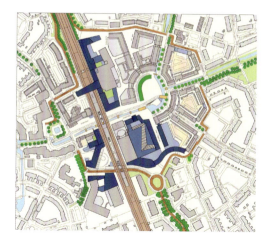

Figure 18: The city of Houten is a classical example of Transit Oriented Development (TOD). The urban lay out of Houten is designed for cyclists and pedestrians. Houten is well connected by train Source: Municipality of Houten

Figure 19: Artist impression of the redeveloped railway station of Houten. Immediately under the platforms a free parking for bicycles is situated. This underlines the principle of Transit Oriented Development in new town Houten. Source: Municipality of Houten.

Figure 20: Nieuwegein has renovated its town centre. The energy supply for heating and cooling for the town hall, theatre, library, housing and retail outlets is largely provided by heat pumps, together with underground thermal storage
Source: Municipality of Nieuwegein

Figure 21: In the Policy Strategy for Spatial Planning 2030 of Nieuwegein, sustainable development is one of the leading ambitions. It shows the main pipeline routes of the district heating network with a connection to neighbouring Utrecht, and the areas around the stops and corridors of public transport that are to receive more intensive housing
Source: Municipality of Nieuwegein

and its own train station. The focus over the coming years and decades will be on completing Vathorst and on the sustainable re-development of existing residential districts such as Soesterkwartier and Bergkwartier.[29]

The four other major towns in the Province of Utrecht, the municipalities of Houten, Nieuwegein, Veenendaal and Zeist each have specific climate programmes and ambitions.[30] These municipalities' goals in the area of climate, energy conservation and reducing CO_2 emissions are less ambitious and far-reaching than those of the Amersfoort and

Utrecht municipalities. Nevertheless, all four of these municipalities have realised remarkable projects worth following or have such in preparation. The municipality of Houten is a world renowned new town, one of the satellite towns of Utrecht to meet the needs of the growing Utrecht region. From the start, in the 1970s, Houten is a classic and successful example of Transit Oriented Development (TOD). The urban design of Houten is entirely oriented towards cycling. The car infrastructure has been made subordinate to this. The new centre is closely linked with the modern transport hub for passengers by train, bus and taxi, and readily accessible too by cyclists and pedestrians. Its TOD role will be further reinforced by the track widening along part of the railway link between Utrecht and 's-Hertogenbosch.[31] The new town has already started to retrofit its oldest residential neighbourhoods in order to make 8,000 houses more energy self-sufficient and healthier.

Nieuwegein is situated next to Houten, but actually its opposite with an urban layout mainly planned around car use. But like Houten, the municipality of Nieuwegein would like to become much more of a cycling town. The most notable project is its renovated town.centre, This is made up of the town hall, theatre, library, housing and retail outlets. The energy supply for heating and cooling the town centre is largely provided by heat pumps, together with underground thermal storage. Sustainability, climate programmes and ambitions are well integrated in the Spatial Policy Strategy 2030 of Nieuwegein. Its plans show the main pipeline routes of the district heating network with a connection to neighbouring Utrecht, and the areas around the stops and corridors of public transport that are to receive more intensive housing.[32] Between Nieuwegein and the A27 motorway, there is to be a sustainable industrial district and a 13 MW windfarm, providing a quarter of the provincial target.

Sustainability is not specifically mentioned in either the Strategic Plan 2025 or the Spatial Policy Strategy 2025 of the Veenendaal municipality, although the documents do include the usual spatial planning goals and aspirations. [33] The Veenendaal urban development 'Buurtstede' with 1,250 homes, the first part of a larger development of 3,200 homes in Veenendaal East, is being built with a sustainable energy system which makes use of a combined heat and power plant, underground thermal storage at a depth of 85 metres and heat pumps. The heating or cooling is distributed to and from the homes via the pipes of the distribution system. The energy system

also provides the necessary heat for warm tap water, together with the heating to five exiting apartment blocks nearby. One innovative element is that the Veenendaal municipality, two local housing associations and two project developers have joined forces to establish a local energy company that runs the energy system. [34]

Zeist houses the office of the World Wide Fund for Nature (WWF) of the Netherlands. This renovated laboratory and office building dates from 1954 and in 2006 was converted to the first building in Europe that supposedly emits no CO_2. [35] In the recently produced Spatial Policy Strategy 2020 of Zeist, sustainability is one of the principal themes, but it lacks any relation with climate programmes and ambitions. [36] The main aims of the municipality are the sustainable redevelopment of the surroundings of the Driebergen-Zeist public transport hub [37] and the sustainable and energy efficient redevelopment of Kerckebosch, one of the older residential neighbourhoods with 1.250 houses. [38]

The A12 Zone Connecting Utrecht, Houten and Nieuwegein

An overview and discussion of the most promising projects and activities in the field of sustainable spatial development and design across all the individual municipalities shows that these projects and activities surpass the administrative borders of the municipalities. The overview shows that a large proportion of these projects and activities is closely related to the central location and the national motorway, railway and waterway hub. To be able to accommodate the constantly growing demand for mobility in the Netherlands and the Province of Utrecht, central government, the Province of Utrecht and the six major towns of Utrecht are investing in various forms of infrastructure to meet future needs. This involves building the A2 and A12 motorways underground, so that the now divided urban areas are better connected, as well as expanding the light railway between Utrecht, Nieuwegein, Leidsche Rijn and the Uithof, the university campus, and improving the areas around the stations in Amersfoort, Utrecht, Driebergen-Zeist, Houten and Veenendaal.

Within the foreseeable future the underground section of the A2 motorway (Eindhoven-Amsterdam) will provide a barrier-free connection between the existing city (Utrecht) and Leidsche Rijn situated to the west, the largest urban development area in the Netherlands with more than 30,000 homes and 80,000 inhabitants forecast for 2025. A more urban-style underpass is envisaged for the A12 motorway (Arnhem-The Hague) for 2025-2040. The zone on both sides of the A12 offers good opportunities to develop an essentially mono-functional, extensively used, urban fringe area into a multi-functional, dynamic commuter area at the centre of a continuous metropolitan region. An area which is no longer only easily accessible by car, but also by tram and bike. The zone makes a substantial contribution to the economic strength of the region in the centre of the country and its positioning as a culture and knowledge-based region. The area lends itself well to the planned demands of the future. It is expected that in 2040 people will want to live and work in mixed urban areas, with spaces to meet and with multimodal accessibility. Some 2,500 to 7,500 additional jobs will be created, and there will also be room for 10,000 to 20,000 homes and a number of regional facilities.

Figure 22: The A12 zone in the Policy Strategy for Spatial Planning of the City of Nieuwegein. The A12 zone aims to link the municipalities of Utrecht, Nieuwegein and Houten. Source: Municipality of Nieuwegein

Figure 23: This visualisation of the A12 zone illustrates that this zone is multifunctional and focussed on urban living and urban lifestyles. This is in sharp contrast with the present situation with its outdated office buildings. Source: Stuurgroep A12 zone

There are four guiding principles underlying the development of the A12 zone which is intended to link the municipalities of Utrecht, Nieuwegein and Houten. These are: Utrecht-like urbanity, meeting, sustainability and green/blue. Utrecht-like urban living represents the link with the essence of Utrecht, the qualities on which the success of the Utrecht region is based. Key concepts here include high density, mixed use, green corridors, the human dimension and meeting spaces. Meeting stands for the new way of working in the heart of the Netherlands. At the intersection of the A12 and the A2 between the urban centres in the region, in a compact and mixed urban area with tram, car and bike on the doorstep, a bakery in the neighbourhood and a pavement cafe around the corner. Sustainability is first and foremost about a more intensive and multifunctional use of existing locations, the choice of the location, the spatial planning and design of the zone, the economic basis as well as how the residents and visitors to the area act. The area will be designed such that users are continually invited to act in ways which are as sustainable as possible. Key concepts here are tram use, bike, CO_2 neutral, energy generation and climate resilience. As with sustainable economic growth, there is a new way of working and economic activity in low environmental categories. Green/blue refers to the specific features which make the region so attractive, such as the residential area and maximum use of the natural features already present in the A12 zone, the linking themes being the special elements of the Hollandse Waterlinie and the strength of the water corridors running through the area that were once flooded as defences. By connecting the Green Heart of the country with the greatly valued landscape features in a way which is environmentally-friendly, the green/blue concept can bring added impetus to the region.[39]

Conclusion

The Utrecht region has made considerable steps in planning low carbon, sustainable and liveable cities. The Province of Utrecht and the six larger towns and cities in the Utrecht region are doing their very best in translating very tough climate and energy ambitions into special policies and a low carbon and sustainable build environment. The Province of Utrecht has wisely transformed climate issues into economic challenges and spatial policies. The cities of Amersfoort, Houten, Nieuwegein, Veenendaal, Utrecht and Zeist are doing the same, with smaller budgets and mixed success. The effort needed to meet the proposed reductions are greatly underestimated. Becoming a CO_2 neutral municipality by 2030, for instance, means an average reduction of 5% CO_2 every year. The Energy Report of the WWF demonstrates that this can be done and that by 2050 almost all the energy we need (95%) can come from renewable sources. The report shows that such a transition is not only possible, but also cost effective, providing energy that is affordable for all and producing it in ways that can be sustained by the global economy and the planet.[40]

Climate and energy ambitions have spatial impacts and consequences. In order to actually fulfil these ambitions, we need to plan and built our cities in a more compact way and more based on public transport and high speed trains than on cars. It is generally accepted that we require almost a complete retrofit of the build environment, a transformation of the energy infrastructure, carpeting roofs with solar cells, harvesting geothermal energy and building wind farms in almost every possible location. And planning low carbon, sustainable and liveable cities requires a transformation of the planning profession.

Acknowledgement

This article was prepared in association with and further to contributions and comments from Maarten Piek and Zjèf Bude from the Ministry of Infrastructure and the Environment, Hans Mertens, Hans Rijnten, Kato Marijs, Michiel Linskens and provincial executive of the Province of Utrecht Remco van Lunteren, Jeroen de Boer of the Municipality of Amersfoort, Marco Harms of the Municipality of Houten, Alex de Bree, Hanneke Peeters and alderman Hans Reusch of the Municipality of Nieuwegein, Cees Jansen, Cees van der Vliet and Arno Harting of the Municipality of Utrecht, Fenna Aarts and alderman Marco Verloop of the Municipality of Veenendaal and Erica Gielink and alderman Joke Leenders of the Municipality of Zeist.

Endnotes

1. The Administrative Agreement between the State, provinces, municipalities and water boards: 'Bestuursakkoord 2011-2015', Vereniging van Nederlandse Gemeenten, Interprovinciaal Overleg, Unie van Waterschappen en Rijk, April 2011.

2. 'The Netherlands 2020, Boundless Policies towards Low Carbon Regions and Cities', Martin Dubbeling and Michaël Meijer, in ISOCARP 05 Low Carbon Cities, September 2009, page 58-79.

3. The draft National Policy for Infrastructure and Spatial Planning, 'Keeping the Netherlands Competitive, accessible, liveable and safe': 'Ontwerp Structuurvisie Infrastructuur en Ruimte, Nederland concurrerend, bereikbaar, leefbaar en veilig', Ministry of Infrastructure and the Environment, June 2011.

4. The Administrative Agreement between the State, provinces, municipalities and water boards: 'Bestuursakkoord 2011-2015', Vereniging van Nederlandse Gemeenten, Interprovinciaal Overleg, Unie van Waterschappen en Rijk, April 2011, page 38.

5. The Energy Report: 'Energierapport 2011', Ministry of Economic Affairs, Agriculture and Innovation, June 2011, page 2.

6. The Energy Report: 'Energierapport 2011', Ministry of Economic Affairs, Agriculture and Innovation, June 2011, pages 47-49.

7. The draft National Policy for Infrastructure and Spatial Planning: 'Ontwerp Structuurvisie Infrastructuur en Ruimte, Nederland concurrerend, bereikbaar, leefbaar en veilig', Ministery of Infrastructure and the Environment, June 2011, pages 5-11.

8. The draft National Policy for Infrastructure and Spatial Planning: 'Ontwerp Structuurvisie Infrastructuur en Ruimte, Nederland concurrerend, bereikbaar, leefbaar en veilig', Ministery of Infrastructure and the Environment, June 2011, page 6.

9. The ex ante evaluation: 'Ex-ante evaluatie Structuurvisie Infrastructuur en Ruimte', PBL Netherlands Environmental Assessment Agency, June 2011, pages 28-29.

10. The preliminary draft of the 2013-2015 Provincial Spatial Planning Policy Strategy: 'Provinciale Ruimtelijke Structuurvisie 2013-2025 en Verordening (voorontwerp)', Province of Utrecht, July 2011, page 9.

11. The Utrecht 2040 Mission 'Sustainable and attractive': 'Utrecht 2040, samen zorgen voor een duurzame en aantrekkelijke regio', Provincial Council of Utrecht, Oktober 2010, page 30.

12. The 2011-2015 Coalition Agreement of the Provincial Council of Utrecht: 'Focus Vertrouwen Oplossingsgericht, Coalitieakkoord tussen de fracties van VVD, CDA, D66 en GroenLinks in de Provinciale Staten van Utrecht 2011-2015', April 2011, pages 8-19

13. The draft National Policy for Infrastructure and Spatial Planning: 'Ontwerp Structuurvisie Infrastructuur en Ruimte, Nederland concurrerend, bereikbaar, leefbaar en veilig', Ministery of Infrastructure and the Environment, June 2011, pages 57-59.

14. Report: 'Utrecht Roadmap To a Third Industrial Revolution', Province of Utrecht and Office of Jeremy Rifkin, 2010, page 9. The brochure '&U Ondernemen met nieuwe energie', Province of Utrecht, November 2010, summarizes the Utrecht Roadmap.

15. Article: 'Heel Europa kan profiteren van onze kennis, Utrechts klimaatbeleid zet de toon', in Milieu 2011-1, pages 6-8.

16. The preliminary draft of the 2013-2015 Provincial Spatial Planning Policy Strategy: 'Provinciale Ruimtelijke Structuurvisie 2 013-2025 en Verordening (voorontwerp)', Province of Utrecht, July 2011, page 9.

17. The preliminary draft of the 2013-2015 Provincial Spatial Planning Policy Strategy: 'Provinciale Ruimtelijke Structuurvisie 2013-2025 en Verordening (voorontwerp)', Province of Utrecht, July 2011, pages 22-25.

18. The 2009-2011 Amersfoort Action Climate Plan 'Klimaatactieplan 2009-2011', Municipality of Amersfoort, December 2009.

19. Policy document 'Amersfoort, a city that cares about the future': 'Amersfoort: Stad met hart voor de toekomst, Een programmatische aanpak voor de duurzame ontwikkeling van Amersfoort', Municipality of Amersfoort, March 2011.

20. Planning and implementation programme 'Utrecht's Energy': 'Programma Utrechtse Energie 2011-2014', Dienst Stadsontwikkeling, Municipality of Utrecht, January 2011, en 'Uitvoeringsprogramma Utrechtse Energie 2011-2012', Dienst Stadsontwikkeling, Municipality of Utrecht, January 2011.

21. 2010-2014 Coalition Agreement of the City Councils of Utrecht and Amersfoort: 'Groen, Open en Sociaal', Collegeprogramma Utrecht 2010-2014, Municipality of Utrecht, May 2010, pages 12-13 and 21. 'Verbonden, Slagvaardig, Duurzaam', Collegeprogramma Amersfoort 2010-2014, Municipality of Amersfoort, April 2010, updated January 2011, pages 14-15.

22. Planning programme 'Utrecht's Energy':
    'Programma Utrechtse Energie 2011-2014',
    Dienst Stadsontwikkeling, Municipality of
    Utrecht, January 2011, page 8.

23. Presentation: 'Ruimtebenutting in
    herstructurering, 86 jaar warmtelevering in
    Utrecht, Arno Harting, Municipality of Utrecht,
    November 2009, pages 9-12.

24. Presentation: 'Utrechtse historische binnenstad
    verdient "A++", maar hoe ? De energieleverende
    monumentale binnenstad', Arno Harting,
    Municipality of Utrecht, November 2010.

25. The Utrecht Spatial Policy Strategy 2015-2030:
    'Structuurvisie Utrecht 2015-2030', Dienst Stad
    sontwikkeling, Municipality of Utrecht,
    July 2004.

26. The Amersfoort Spatial Policy Strategy 2030:
    'De Koers voor de Structuurvisie Amersfoort
    2030', Municipality of Amersfoort,
    February 2011, page 5.

27. The Amersfoort Spatial Policy Strategy 2030:
    'De Koers voor de Structuurvisie Amersfoort
    2030', Municipality of Amersfoort,
    February 2011, page 11.

28. 'Nieuwland 1 MegaWatt PV Project,
    Amersfoort', Jadranka Cace and Emil ter Horst,
    Horisun, 2008, page 1.

29. The Amersfoort Spatial Policy Strategy 2030:
    'De Koers voor de Structuurvisie Amersfoort
    2030', Municipality of Amersfoort,
    February 2011, page 9.

30. The climate programmes of the municipalities
    of Houten and Nieuwegein:
    'Klimaatprogramma 2009-2013, Nieuwegein
    werkt aan een beter klimaat!', uitvoerings-
    programma, Municipality of Nieuwegein,
    June 2009. 'Klimaatbeleid 2009-2012,
    Uitvoeringsprogramma', Municipality of Houten,
    November 2008.

31. The Spatial Policy Strategy of the
    municipality of Houten and the Masterplan for
    the Centre of Houten: 'Structuurvisie Houten
    Centrum, Municipality of Houten', 2001, and
    'Masterplan Houten Centrum 2003-2015',
    Municipality of Houten, September 2003.

32. The Spatial Policy Strategy of the Municipality
    of Nieuwegein: 'Nieuwegein verbindt,
    structuurvisie 2030', Municipality of Nieuwegein,
    December 2009, page 74-77.

33. Strategic Plan 2025 and the Spatial Policy
    Strategy 2025 of the municipality of Veenendaal:
    'Strategische visie Veenendaal 2025',
    Municipality of Veenendaal, November 2005.
    'Visie op Veenendaal', Structuurvisie Veenendaal
    2025 (versie 1.1), Ruimtelijke visie en
    verkeersbeleid, Municipality of Veenendaal,
    November 2009.

34. Website: www.devo-veenendaal.nl/
    energiesysteem/hoe-werkt-het.

35. Website of RAU Architects, the architect of the
    World Wide Fund for Nature office building:
    www.rau.nl

36. The Spatial Policy Strategy of the
    Municipality of Zeist: 'Structuurvisie Gemeente
    Zeist 2020, Zeist schrijf je met een Q', ontwerp
    structuurvisie, Municipality of Zeist, October
    2010, pages 125-128.

37. Websites: www.stationsgebieddriebergenzeist.
nl and www.urgenda.nl/projecten/
regioprojecten/stationsgebied-driebergen-zeist.

38. Website: http://www.kerckeboschinbeweging.nl.

39. Visualisation of the A12 zone
'Verstedelijkingsperspectief A12 Centraal, rode
draad voor de langere termijn ontwikkeling van
de A12 zone in de Utrechtse regio', Stuurgroep
A12 zone, April 2011, pages 7 and 8.

40. 'The Energy Report, 100% Renewable Energy
by 2050', Stephan Singer (editor in chief), World
Wide Fund for Nature (WWF), Ecofys and
OMA-AMO, January 2011.

WikicitY Open Planning for a Liveable Amsterdam 2004-2011

Zef Hemel

The recently published Structural Vision: Amsterdam 2040 *is the 10th major plan for the Dutch capital. The first – the legendary General Extension Plan – appeared in May 1935, more than 75 years ago. Since then the city has, on average, produced a new integrated vision for the future for the whole of its territory every seven years. The Structural Vision: Amsterdam 2040 continues this Amsterdam tradition of making coherent plans in a democratic manner, but it differs from its predecessors in one important regard: rarely has a long-term perspective for Amsterdam been so emphatically developed from the bottom up, proceeding from a multitude of interests and drawing on contributions from every section and stratum of society. Thanks to an open approach and making full use of 'the wisdom of crowds', many people have contributed to the conception of a liveable, sustainable and thriving city, something which would have been unthinkable without such a breadth of input.*

Figure 1: Utrechtse straat Amsterdam

More than two million people inhabiting the Amsterdam region do love street life. In the city's modal split almost forty percent of journeys are now by bike. Mixed use, place making and lively streets are the secrets of Amsterdam's postmodern planning. Developing a livable city in the Dutch context means, above all, public participation. Ordinary people know best what livability needs

Introduction

The Structural Vision for Amsterdam took shape between 2008 and 2010, in the space of barely two years. Via a special website, binnen30minuten.nl – 'within 30 minutes', which is indicative of the city's radius of influence as well as its accessibility from the surrounding region within half an hour – everyone was welcome to contribute and share ideas and suggestions with regard to the city. The site generated more than 2,000 ideas and prompted hundreds of discussions. Almost 8,000 people visited the 'Free State of Amsterdam' exhibition in the Tolhuistuin ('Tollhouse Garden'), where for a period of six weeks in the autumn of 2009 the citizens could personally programme the future of the city. About 2,000 schoolchildren allowed their

fantasy to run free as they imagined a better and more pleasant city, while some 200,000 people watched the documentary *Amsterdam Makeover 2040* on Dutch national television. At the request of the neighbouring municipalities the Structural Vision integrated regional characteristics. When the vision was published, almost 800 citizens participated in a conference about the future of the metropolis. This hands-on development of a scenario for the future by the members of the metropolitan society was by no means incidental; it was a deliberate choice. It stemmed from the idea that spatial planning, even in Amsterdam, had ended up at a dead end and needed to be reinvented.

Structural Vision: Amsterdam 2040

Waterfront

	live/work mix
	work/live mix
	work
	projects in planning stage or recently completed

Roll-out of centere

	live/work mix
	work/live mix
	limited qualitative impulse for major streets and squares
	qualitative impulse for major streets
	qualitative impulse for squares
	Former naval base
	qualitative impulse for a city park

Southern flank

	Zuidas
	live/work mix
	work/live mix
	work
	projects in planning stage or recently completed

Metropolitan landscape

①	Amstel wedge
②	Amsterdamse Bos Wedge
③	Gardens of West
④	Bretten Zone
⑤	Zaan Wedge
⑥	Waterland
⑦	Diemen Wedge
⑧	IJmeer Wedge

[*] For the Port-City study area, the map represents scenario 3, with the exception of Buiksloterham. Future studies could result in adaptations anywhere in the Port-City study area.
Potential developments on the southern shores of the Gaasperplas lake were investigated in the 'Gaasperplas Reconnaissance".

^{**} If the Port-City plans reveal that a connection is necessary, then this will be realized as a tunnel.

^{***} High Quality Public transport

 City of Amsterdam

General

	aboveground expansion of motorway capacity
	underground expansion of motorway capacity
	high-speed railway line
	aboveground HQPT *** (bus/tram/metro)
	underground HQPT *** (bus/tram/metro)
⊕	international public transport hub
⊙	main public transport hub
○	secondary public transport hub
❶	Schiphol/Almere Regiorail option
❷	East/West metro line option
	nieuwe ferry link
	underground connection **
P·R	P+R facility
≪	sea lock
	2nd ocean liner terminal
⚓	temporary berths for inland shipping
☆	intesification of the RAI precincts
	high-class retail area
	intesification of port
	urban support enterprises
◎	qualitative impulse for borough centre
	marina
	possible zone for port expansion
	water- or groundwater related project
✈	2nd Schiphol Airport terminal
	option for Olympic Games site
	study area *
	regional cycle route
◉	Defence Line of Amsterdam
	beach
✳	metropolitan place
✪	recreational programme
	proposed nature development
	waterside development
	qualitative implse for a city/wedge transition
	Sports Axis
	Compass Island and cycle bridge

Figure 2: Structural Vision Amsterdam 2040
The map of the tenth Structural Vision of Amsterdam envisions a story. It integrates four 'thrusts', each one an inspiring narrative of the future of the Dutch capital. The narratives were developed by studying long term spatial trends, and were enriched through the contributions of thousands of citizens during a two year process of intense participation. The thrusts were called Faith, Hope and Love. Faith stands for: believe in the power of an extending city center. Hope: reliance on the economic power of the two thrusts of the waterfront and the southern flank Love: cherishing and celebrating the surrounding landscape

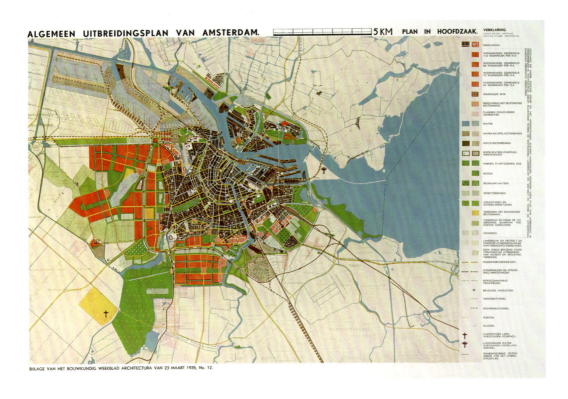

ALGEMEEN UITBREIDINGSPLAN VAN AMSTERDAM.   5 KM   PLAN IN HOOFDZAAK.   VERKLARING

BIJLAGE VAN HET BOUWKUNDIG WEEKBLAD ARCHITECTURA VAN 23 MAART 1935, No. 12.

Figure 3: General Extension Plan
Highly praised by Siegfried Giedion in his 'Time, Space and Architecture' (1941), The General Extension Plan
of the City of Amsterdam (1935) was the first long term spatial plan for Amsterdam and its environs. The plan
looked forwards to the year 2000. It was a highlight in optimistic Modernist planning, developed in the years of
the Great Depression. It was based on extensive scientific surveys

Adaptive Planning

What is planning? 'Planning is what planners do.' Such a definition does not offer much of a foothold. 'Planning is concerned with making decisions and informing actions in ways that are socially rational,' John Friedmann noted in 1987. Friedmann understood that the idea of planning is elusive. 'There are many forms of planning and many specific applications.' He mentioned decision-making and action based on societal guidance as ingredients of a definition. But if planning has to be reinvented, then where should one begin? Planning is essentially about the way we relate to other people. We asked ourselves how we could activate people and encourage them to work together towards a common goal. That demanded shared meaning. Planning, we ascertained, is for at least 80 per cent about communication.

What planners do is nothing less than build on a civil society. In retrospect, that is also the lesson which can be drawn from the Amsterdam experiment: the more open the planning, the less the planners need to grasp for their instruments. In other words, the more human the planning, the less rigid it will be. Moreover, the great advantage of an open, inter-relational planning process is that it becomes more flexible and can adapt more easily to changing circumstances. In an environment of permanent, ever-increasing flux, adaptive planning is urgently required. Without flexibility and the ability to improvise, spatial planning will in the long run fade away. By making planning open and more communicative, it can be saved. And it must be saved, because without cohesion and societal cooperation there is no way forward.

Proceeding from this starting point, in late 2004 the City of Amsterdam's Physical Planning Department (DRO) instigated an internal process that was intended to inject new life into the planning discipline. The deadlock into which Amsterdam's planning machine had fallen tied in closely with the ossification of the DRO's own methodologies. While the task of urban design profited massively from the boom of the 1990s and the judicial-planning portfolio had been filled proportionately as a consequence of strong social opposition, the order book for the traditional research-focused, policy-based work of the spatial researchers shrank.

At around the same time, Amsterdam's City Council set about simplifying procedures in order to reduce process costs. The market had to be allowed greater leeway and whenever possible financial risks had to be shifted onto the shoulders of market forces. Slowness and viscosity in urban development were regarded as a problem, and from a municipal perspective the best way to deal with this was by leaving more to free-market forces. By doing this, or so people thought, it would also be possible to build more quickly and in greater volumes. Though complexity was mentioned as a reason, financial considerations and political objectives proved to be the principal factors. The administration had promised to build at least 20,000 new dwellings within four years. When it looked as if this would fall short of expectations, the planning had to become quicker, more efficient, cheaper and more rational. However, this bore little relation to what was actually going on: the rationality of the planning was already far too great; the planning had to become more communicative. The planners practised implementing the new, communicative planning for two years. Their efforts were in the first place aimed at achieving results more quickly. An attempt was made to gain support for ideas through enticement and persuasion, rather than by presenting data. Presentations had to be shorter and more attractive, and a new cartography was born. The goal was broadened: time gains aside, the planners wanted to inspire people, inducing them to share their thoughts, to activate them. Towards the end of 2005, the idea of establishing platforms that would be open to everyone and which would permanently share insights with third parties was in the ascendant. These interfaces, or so it was thought, were meant to mediate between the world of scarce resources – the unruly practicalities – and that of future cohesion, i.e. a shared vision. The first platforms were established in the autumn of 2006: first South-wards, then Westwards, then Eastwards[1], followed a year later by the RADAR and ROER (rudder) consultative bodies[2].

Figure 4: Destination Amsterdam
Last slide of the story 'Destination AMS' (2006-2007). Over two years the story of the future of Amsterdam was told more than sixty times. It consisted of twenty chapters. Each chapter added new insights and combined profound analysis with stirring ideas and revelations. The postmodern story started in the historic center and ended in the outskirts. Every time the story was told, people got inspired and added their own thoughts. Thus, the knowledge, wishes and ideas of thousands of people were aggregated. After two years the full story was ready. Now it could be used to develop realistic, convincing story lines

Storytelling

In late 2005, midway through the 'planning discussion', a planning story for the future was concocted. The departure of a colleague from the provincial planning agency was seized upon to test the provisional fruits of the planning discussion externally. This also presented an opportunity to do something with a recent experience: discussions with political parties on the eve of the municipal elections had brought to light that Amsterdam's politicians were lacking properly formulated spatial ambitions; there was no politically articulated perspective. The idea of the planners devising their own futuristic vision grew under the lee of the elections. It was based on all the ideas which had been generated over the course of the planning discussions and was aimed at stimulating ambition. The 'Bestemming AMS / Destination AMS' narrative was released in the midst of the election fever of early 2006.

To the astonishment of many, there was a great deal of interest in this story about the future. People who heard it passed it on.

april 2008
copyright DRO Amsterdam

Figure 5: Amsterdam Metropolitan Area
In only nine months a great story on the future of the Amsterdam region was developed, based on the tested method of storytelling. In December 2007 the assembled administrations of thirty six municipalities decided to base their plans on this one story line and offered full support to intensifying their collaboration

Requests for presentations followed one after the other. The venues kept growing in size, from small conference rooms to gymnasiums, lecture halls, theatres, works canteens and eventually large conference centres. The planners told the 'Destination AMS' story more than 60 times. And the story itself kept growing, because at each presentation the audience provided new information and suggestions, and these were continually incorporated into the story. No presentation was the same and nothing was set in stone. Interestingly, the narrative tied in with a growing number of listeners' personal stories. Instead of a plan being formulated in the offices of a municipal department or urban development agency, a vision for the future was gradually created to which many people had contributed. It seemed that the story was absorbing all the knowledge, experience and insights from different parts of society, and was giving them back to the city. It felt, in short, like Wikipedia: thousands of people working on one story, chapters growing not from harmonious thought but

from constant scrutiny and emendation.
As time went on, this connection between personal stories and the story about the future metropolis spawned new initiatives. Projects were launched that related to the story or referred to it, some of them even arising from it directly. The story not only inspired people, but prompted them to identify with it. More and more people became 'collaborators'.

In the spring of 2007, administrators from the neighbouring municipalities, roused by the narrative, decided to create a regional vision for the future in conjunction with Amsterdam and the provinces concerned. Everyone became involved, ideas were amassed. This informal approach meant it was possible to seek agreement and coordination at an early stage. This integral scenario was ready barely nine months later. It was launched at a regional congress. It was decided to use this joint story about the future, which was endorsed by 36 municipalities and two provinces, as the basis for all the structural visions that were yet to be formulated. The agreement was marked by changing the name of the erstwhile 'North Wing of the Randstad'. During a congress on 14 December 2007, the assembled administrators renamed the 'North Wing' as the 'Amsterdam Metropolitan Area'. The participants decided to intensify regional cooperation even further.

Not long thereafter, Amsterdam's City Executive made moves to produce a new structural vision for the city's own territory on the basis of the regional vision for the future. In the eyes of the mayor and aldermen, this 10th structural masterplan for the city would have to provide a framework for 'a sustainable, attractive and accessible metropolis' in 2040. The planning work proper could now begin.

Soft Planning

The achievements in the planning process described above are far from set in stone. It is not the hard edges of planning – money, the actual plans, procedures, instruments – that determine success, but the 'soft' edges: the shaping of a vision, whipping up enthusiasm, getting people actively involved. Interestingly, within the City of Amsterdam's planning practices as outlined above, the story takes the place of the design, and in this the story serves as just that: 'An oral presentation of events, whether true or invented, told with the aim of entertaining and enthralling an audience.' The narrative element actually plays a pivotal role.

This raises the question of what it is that makes story-telling so successful. In psychology, five factors have been distinguished: these are receptivity, familiarity, trust, empathic witnessing, and recreating the self (Gergen and Gergen, 1986). I shall dwell briefly on each one in turn.

The first factor is receptivity: as soon as people hear a story, they become receptive. That is because story-telling is usually associated with pleasure, relaxation, sociability, or even togetherness. This was certainly borne out by the responses at the meetings. The stories were always received with great enthusiasm, and this enthusiasm proved to be infectious. As for familiarity, stories tend to strike a chord among listeners because of their anecdotal quality – far more so than with maps or designs, which may be impenetrable for laymen. Stories tend to reflect the experiences of ordinary people directly. The third factor is trust or confidence. Stories provide an opportunity to feel a sense of confidence. People tend to feel more confident about the future when numerous recognisable situations are placed in a wider context. That was one of the key qualities of the 'Destination AMS' story-based project. Various ongoing spatial developments were extrapolated into the future and placed within a single reassuring whole.

The fourth point is that the audience is essentially listening to someone's personal testimony. This personal testimony is far more likely to inspire trust and empathy than, say, a plan being presented by some official or administrator at a consultation evening for local residents. Finally, listening to stories creates opportunities for redefining the self. The audience is invited to identify with different roles and characters. As a result, stories tend to soften the us-and-them attitude that people naturally adopt when faced with an unknown future. Where planning is concerned, this is extremely important: stories are embedded in relationships with others. Because of this specific relational value, they can help to alter perceptions of a diversity of scenarios, making them seem more palatable or even making them look like interesting challenges. People lay themselves open to criticism and negotiation in a narrative process, and they are willing to modify their own convictions, so it is easier to reconcile a diversity of interests.

Good stories are infectious and spatial planning exists by the grace of good story-telling. Although this narrative element is often overlooked in the planning literature, it seems crucial to its success. Narrative practices such as those employed in Amsterdam present opportunities to create a public space that incorporates a sense of solidarity and trust on the one hand, with respect and understanding for the need for different perspectives on the other. Good stories confront us with our moral responsibilities and encourage us to act collectively. They provide the best safeguards against 'blueprint thinking' and undue faith in a 'makeable society'. But none of this potential can be realized unless stories are first incorporated into our planning procedures.

The critical success factors were determined by experiment, proceeding from the experience gained in the aforementioned platforms. Until then a great deal of attention had been devoted to the set of instruments or toolkit, the organization and modus operandi. Behaviour and attitudes are, however, just as important. Nine practical rules were formulated, and these boiled down to the following: get down to work immediately and establish a platform; start small and exclude nobody; all forms of manipulation (whether power, money or competences) are forbidden; focus on the content and share stories; be succinct in presentations and listen attentively; rein in the emotions, remain curious and never give up.

In Amsterdam stories have been jointly developed by many parties ever since, within the abovementioned platforms that explore the future of an area or sub-sector and place it on the agenda. These platforms are driven by content and have swiftly developed into consultative bodies where knowledge is continually shared, visions shaped and lessons drawn from real-life experiences. Everyone is welcome to participate. That does not alter the fact that there is constant attention to maintaining a healthy balance of power. Finance, instruments and legislation are emphatically consigned to the background; they are subservient to communally formulated goals rather than leading, let alone being employed to limit the possibilities. This is how 'story-telling' has been fruitfully integrated into Amsterdam's planning practice over the last five years.

The Free State

In early 2008 a start was made with the preparations for the Structural Vision. An atlas was compiled to serve as the agenda for a great many discussions. Conditions and tasks from the so-called regional development scenario were employed as guidelines and appeared as

Figure 6: Maquette of Amsterdam South-East Bureau Studio Klok. The Amsterdam based designer Arjan Klok was one of the nine design offices who were asked to develop an open plan in 'The Free State of Amsterdam'. Klok chose a radical participatory approach. Over six weeks, people visiting the exhibition could buy a piece of land (like their ancestors did in the seventeenth century), and build their own house, company or shop. It led to fierce discussions on mixed use planning, participatory approaches and the making of lively neighborhoods

such in the keys to the maps. The region-wide, metropolitan ambition from the development scenario was adopted as the guiding principle.

The majority of the discussions were conducted a year later, in March 2009, and many of these took place within Amsterdam's bureaucratic apparatus, between municipal departments and with the city boroughs. The outcomes were translated into a quartet of spatial developments – these were in fact cast as narratives – which later became known as developmental directions or 'thrusts': a densely developed inner-city milieu that continues beyond the city's orbital motorway, extending into the post-war city; a regional waterfront with dense, functionally mixed

development along the River Zaan and IJ waterway all the way into the IJmeer; a curved Southern Flank between Schiphol Airport and the Academic Medical Complex, with offices and stacked, high-rise living on either side of the 'bundles' of infrastructure; and the integration of the metropole's circumjacent man-made landscape with its polders, parks and meadows. These four thrusts were in part derived from the 'planological discussion', while to a certain degree they also seemed to derive from the 'Destination AMS' directly. As a story about the future, a dream in the making, they did not prescribe anything in advance, but they did offer sufficient foothold to develop a new, grand narrative about Amsterdam's development into a sustainable and

Figure 7: Maquette of Gaasperplas Aquatic Free State Bureau Alle Hosper. The contribution of the Haarlem based landscape architects of Alle Hosper for 'The Free State of Amsterdam' consisted of a complete restructuring of post war neighborhoods in the Southeastern part of Amsterdam with the help of a new system of water management. Dwellings owned by the housing corporations were sold. With the proceeds the existing artificial lake in the West was extended; the new owners/present inhabitants, mostly elderly people, were allowed to adapt their dwellings to their personal needs. The huge hospital in the area was decentralized. A vibrant neighborhood, surrounded by lakes and waterways, was made possible by these interventions

liveable metropolis. It was now the moment to involve the whole of the city in the forward-looking discussion.

An interactive website was launched, so that citizens could make known their wishes with regard to their city. Via 'binnen30minuten. nl' they could also comment freely on each other's ideas. Over the course of 2009, more than 2,000 ideas were collected in three consultative rounds. The devisers of the ten best ideas were also invited to meet the alderman for a face-to-face discussion. The campaign's grand finale was a large-scale event in the autumn. In September 2009, at the end of the City Council's four-year term in office, the planners presented the 'Free State of Amster-

dam'. This ambitious exhibition programme addressed the future of the Amsterdam Metropolitan Area. Colossal scale models were exhibited in the Tolhuistuin (Tollhouse Garden) for a six-week period. The day after the opening, *The New York Times* characterized it as 'Amsterdam's latest buzz-worthy exhibition'. The 'Free State' called upon the city's inhabitants and visitors to share their thoughts about the city. Nothing was predetermined and they could talk about the future in all openness.

Even the nine scale models, most of which were realized at a scale of 1:1000, refrained from establishing the future in fixed outcomes; the models were starting points for novel possibilities. They formed the core of the exhibition and were the response to a commission granted to nine urban planning bureaus based in Amsterdam and Rotterdam to devise future scenarios for specific sections of the city. These bureaus were asked to render the degrees of freedom in their proposals as broadly as possible and embody this in 'living' scale models. They were asked to reveal the potential outcomes of various spatial strategies to the public in a scale model. As few aspects as possible were predetermined. The idea was that engagement and individual responsibility are typical of the urban development of the 21st century, alongside freedom, changeability and the capacity to improvise. Building on a new civil society is the modern-day task of the planning discipline.

Open City

The exhibition was accompanied by a programme of debates. On no fewer than 29 evenings, citizens could unfold their thoughts freely. All these discussion evenings were open to the public, but were deliberately assigned to interest groups and organizations to allow them to present their own programme, focused on the future of the city, with their own special guests and a broad-based audience. The organizations and groups approached included political parties, the Chamber of Commerce, urban planning bureaus, homeless people, philosophers, expats, students, shopkeepers and secondary school students, and they all took up the invitation. This programme component took the form of 'story-telling'. Gathered around the scale models, people could tell their own stories. The more personal the stories, the more exciting people found them. Night after night, all these narratives, with their traces of rhetoric and persuasion, provided new knowledge, but also inspiration and mutual understanding. Thanks to the interchange of all those personal experiences, insights and desires,

these evenings were visionary and practical in equal measure.

A free supplement was distributed in a print run of 100,000 with *Het Parool* newspaper, to encourage the city's citizens to visit the 'Free State' and actively participate in the programme. 'Dreaming about the city' was produced by the editorial staff of this Amsterdam-based daily newspaper.

Almost 8,000 people responded to the call, including 2,000 schoolchildren who visited the exhibition in the context of 'Looking at Art' – a programme that offers professional guided tours of the city's museums to Amsterdam primary schools. This programme was extended to include the Free State. It brought children aged between 10 and 12 years into contact with urban scale models for the first time, and they could observe how the city is conceived and deliberately designed. They effortlessly generated ideas for better cities.

Openness was particularly evident at the exhibition space itself. The choice of venue did not fall on the municipal information centre for space, building and living. After months of hunting, the right location presented itself: the Tolhuistuin, or 'Tollhouse Garden'. Situated on the banks of the IJ waterway and directly opposite the Central Station, there was a venue in a park which had been hermetically sealed to Amsterdam's inhabitants since 1942, and a large space was available in the temporarily vacant, former company canteen. The site was eventually transferred to the city on 6 June 2009, just three months before the opening of the 'Free State'. Offering a splendid view across to the historical city and the city in the process of renewing itself, we had happened upon the ideal setting for an exhibition of scale models which addressed the future of the metropolis.

The opening was preceded by the transmission of the documentary, *Amsterdam Makeover 2040,* on Dutch national television. Broadcast, the film was watched by more than 200,000 people. It placed Amsterdam's spatial issues in a global, continental and national perspective. Produced in the context of the International Architecture Biennale Rotterdam (IABR), which took the 'Open City: Designing Coexistence' as the theme for its 2009 edition, the documentary's key theme was open versus closed cities within configurations of urbanized mega-regions.

On the Friday prior to the opening, there was an exhibition preview for 300 schoolchildren from Amsterdam-North. A meal in the garden, prepared using ingredients cultivated within the region, was combined with an opportunity to see the scale models. On the day of the actual opening, a special train used the Amsterdam/Paris high-speed rail link to carry the Rotterdam Biennale's guests to the exhibition site on the far side of the IJ waterway. The German philosopher Peter Sloterdijk delivered the opening speech for an audience of more than 400 invited guests.

A week after the opening, a two-day International Urban Planning Congress, entitled 'Morgen/Tomorrow', was staged at the Westergasfabriek.

Under the rallying-cry of 'Cities can save the world', the conference offered a programme of lectures and workshops, in which the flows of water, energy, waste, ICT, food and mobility were considered in their mutual interaction, for more than 400 participants. Besides general presentations about Chicago, Pittsburgh, London, New York, Berlin, Moscow, Mumbai and Tirana, the outcome included a whole raft of examples of local practices of metabolism which can mitigate and positively influence global problems.

Figure 8: Schoolclasses visiting Free State
Some two thousand school children from primary schools all over Amsterdam paid a visit to the 'Free State of Amsterdam'. For the first time in their lives they were confronted with scale models of their own neighborhood. Each excursion ended with an open question: what would you like to add to your city? Dreaming was part of the idea of freedom in 'The Free State'

Figure 9: Visitors creating their ideal neighbourhood
All the scale models in 'The Free State of Amsterdam' were in some way flexible. Blueprint planning was forbidden. Sometimes people could add new things. Instead of designs, some models showed mainly strategies; a few models were even growing in an organic way during the exhibition. With the help of chemicals one model transformed whole neighborhoods by 'crystalizing' trees and plants. After six weeks people could admire the results. In a closing session, many of them celebrated the transformations and gave their personal best wishes

Figure 10: Keynote speaker P.K. Das (Academy of Architecture Mumbai) at the Congress Morgen/Tomorrow
The congress Morgen/Tomorrow started just one week after the opening of 'The Free State of Amsterdam'. Some
400 people attended the two-days meeting in the 'Westergasfabriek'. Leader of the Green Party in the European
Parliament and former mayor of Frankfurt am Main, Daniel Cohn-Bendit, presented the opening lecture and gave
his own definition of an 'open city'; former mayor of London, Ken Livingstone, spoke of sustainable cities. These
politicians were followed by keynote speakers from cities all over the world. One of them, the Indian architect and
planner P.K. Das, told the audience about his participatory approach towards improving public space along the
coastline of Mumbai

An Aggregated Structural Vision

All these events contributed to the narrative of Amsterdam's *Structural Vision*, which was completed in December 2009. All the material from the website, the fruits of the 'Free State' event and the congress were collated and aggregated by the city's planners. Aggregation is the operative word here, because selection would have meant too many insights being lost; it is the very multiplicity of ideas and stories that makes a structural vision diverse,

robust and convincing, and diversity does full justice to the big city's complexity. Aggregation was also called for in order to honour the many different perspectives in a situation of uncertainty, a means of reducing the possibility of mistakes. After all, nobody is able to predict the future and there is nobody who can single-handedly manage the city's development.

In *The Wisdom of Crowds* (2004), James Surowiecki demonstrates how diversity, autonomy and decentralization are preconditions for propagating collective intelligence. Large groups of people will come up with better and

Structural Vision: Roll-out of centre

Figure 11: Structural Vision – Roll out of City Centre

The success of Amsterdam over the last years can be attributed to the reappraisal of the world famous historic center and its surrounding neighborhoods. Urbanity, mixed use and lively places can be found mostly here. The big question is if it will be possible to extend this area of liveliness to other parts of the city. Extension is also needed since the seventeenth century 'grachtengordel' has become part of UNESCO's List of World Heritage in 2010. High rise is now excluded from the monumental ensemble and its surroundings within a distance of at least two kilometers. Will it be possible to transform these cars based, post war areas into lively, high density, mixed used neighborhoods?

more robust forecasts and make more intelligent decisions than even the most skilled decision-maker. Intelligence is formed by mixing expertise with other forms of knowledge. One-sided manipulation, such as 'group think', is fundamentally unacceptable. 'The smartest groups, then, are made up of people with diverse perspectives who are able to stay independent of each other.' Moreover, the closer to a problem someone is, the more likely he or she is to have a good solution to it. 'Decentralization's great strength is that it encourages independence and specialization on the one hand while still allowing people to coordinate their activities and solve difficult

problems on the other,' writes Surowiecki. It is also better to organize urban development from the bottom up. By developing the Structural Vision with the help of thousands of people, Amsterdam has managed to tap this collective intelligence.

The four developmental thrusts provided the storylines in which the panoply of insights could be processed. Much attention was devoted to the text's readability. The accompanying maps – wherever possible even richer and more detailed than usual – had to seduce first and foremost, but they also had to be legible and at the same time overwhelm the

reader. The selected cut-outs were regional. They were angled slightly in order to depict all the municipalities and to position Zuidas, Amsterdam's 21st-century commercial and residential development, at the midpoint of the map, while the 19th-century defensive ring of the 'Defence Line of Amsterdam' was chosen as the boundary for the fleshed-out scenario, because it is situated at an ideal cycling distance from Amsterdam. Each of the narrative threads played out within this footprint.

One of the spatial trends is that Amsterdam's metropolitan centre is being used more and more intensively and is expanding ever further. Almost all the neighbourhoods within the A10 orbital motorway now display city-centre traits. Living within the ringroad is highly desirable, the parks and monuments are attracting more and more visitors, and for creative and knowledge-based enterprises this area is the ideal business location. However, because of its negative impact on the areas of exceptional value, such as the city centre's protected cityscape and the section of the historical ring of canals that was inscribed on UNESCO's World Heritage List in 2010, high-rise construction is not permitted here. The scarcity of space means that people are always forced to search a little further afield.

Now that the city-centre milieu is spreading out across the IJ waterway and towards Zuidas in the south, high-rise construction will be encouraged in such areas from the viewpoint of optimum land use.

A second spatial trend is the rediscovery of the waterfront. The IJ waterway and the IJmeer expanse of water have a particularly high experiential value and offer many possibilities for recreation. The waterfront and shorelines also offer countless opportunities for urban development, especially in the obsolete port precincts and industrial zones. Due to all these developments, the IJ waterway is becoming increasingly central within the metropolitan footprint, while it continues to rank among the busiest inland shipping routes in the Netherlands.

The third trend is the internationalization of the Southern Flank, which involves a succession of massive projects: the expansion of Schiphol Airport, the development of Zuidas, and the intensification of the residential and business areas in Amsterdam-Southeast. Station Zuid, at the heart of Zuidas, will become one of the most important public transport hubs in the Netherlands. In the near future, all high-speed trains – whether from Paris,

Structural Vision: Waterfront

Waterfront		General			
	live/work mix	═══	aboveground HQPT ═ (bus/tram/metro)	🏛	marina
	work/live mix	✕✕✕	underground HQPT ═ (bus/tram/metro)	◼	possible zone for port expansion
	work	○─○	international public transport hub	◼	option for Olympic Games site
	projects in planning stage or recently completed	○─○	main public transport hub	◼	study area
	qualitative impulse for a city park	●─●	secondary public transport hub		regional cycle route
	Former naval base	─△─	nieuwe ferry link		beach
		-------	underground connection		metropolitan place
	For the Port-City study area, the map represents scenario 3, with the exception of Buiksloterham. Future studies could result in adaptations anywhere in the Port-City study area.	P+R	P+R facility	✿	recreational programme
		⚓	sea lock		proposed nature development
	If the Port-City plans reveal that a connection is necessary, then this will be realized as a tunnel.	⚓	2nd ocean liner terminal		waterside development
		↓	temporary berths for inland shipping		Compass Island and cycle bridge
	High Quality Public transport	↻	intesification of port		
		◪	urban support enterprises		
		◻	qualitative impulse for borough centre		

Figure 12:Structural Vision – Waterfront
From the historic wind mills in the West to the modern polder landscape of Almere new town in the East, the Amsterdam waterfront stretches over a distance of more than twenty miles. Brown fields in the far West become high density working estates; artificial land - islands included – in the East become high density housing estates. All will be made accessible by ferry boats and a tunnel for public transport under the IJmeer lake. In this new regional waterfront Amsterdam Central Station will become the new transport node of trains, trams, busses, bicycles and ferries

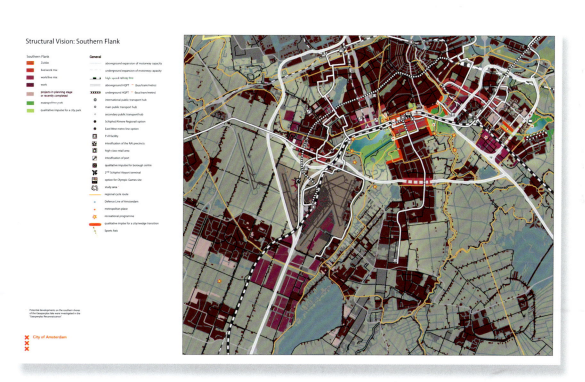

Structural Vision: Southern Flank

Figure 13: Structural Vision – Southern Flank
An eight minutes' drive from Schiphol Airport will bring you to the Zuidas (South Axis) in the southern part of the city. Zuidas will be built above a landscape of motorways, railways and metro lines. The coming years it will become the major metropolitan center in the Netherlands - destination of all the high speed trains coming from London, Brussels, Paris, Berlin, Cologne and Frankfurt. High density mixed use neighborhoods will support new public facilities

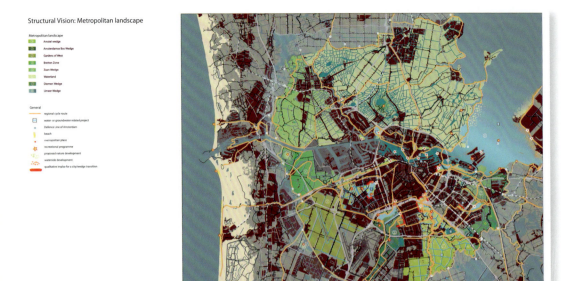

Structural Vision: Metropolitan landscape

Metropolitan landscape
- Amstel wedge
- Amsterdamse Bos Wedge
- Gardens of West
- Bretten Zone
- Zaan Wedge
- Waterland
- Diemen Wedge
- Linear Wedge

General
- regional cycle route
- water- or groundwater related project
- Defence Line of Amsterdam
- beach
- metropolitan place
- recreational programme
- proposed nature development
- waterside development
- qualitative impulse for a city/wedge transition

✕ City of Amsterdam

Figure 14: Structural Vision – Metropolitan Landscape
Planning in Amsterdam over the last seventy-five years has created a green belt which lends itself excellently to a whole range of new uses: food production, recreation, biodiversity, water management, cleaning the air. New towns surrounding the green belt together with the city in the middle must collaborate on the future of this unique Metropolitan Landscape. It can be spoiled, but it can also thrive

Brussels, London, Frankfurt or Berlin – will stop here. The main driver of development is the large bundle of infrastructure that links Amsterdam with the other cities in the Randstad conurbation, with the airport and with the rest of the Netherlands.

The fourth spatial trend is interweaving the metropolitan landscape and the city. This landscape penetrates far into the city in the form of wedges of greenery, which increase the city's appeal and presents Amsterdam with the possibility of densification within the existing urban footprint while still remaining liveable. This means that the city is heavily dependent on its immediate surroundings. The ambition of the Structural Vision is to keep the green wedges green, improve their accessibil-

ity, utilize them for the purification of water and the supply of clean air, and make them more attractive for recreational use.

Civil society

In the months that followed, City Council elections were held and political negotiations ensued to form a stable coalition for the governing City Executive. The elected councillors assumed their seats in early May 2010. After everyone had been briefed and shown the ropes, the City Executive could prepare for the final debate. Almost a year later, on 17 February 2011, the Structural Vision was unanimously adopted by the City Council.

To celebrate this, but also to emphasize that the task was far from complete, a major conference about the new Structural Vision, which had just rolled off the printing presses, was organized three months later. Everyone who had contributed over the preceding years was invited to participate: city-dwellers, experts, politicians, entrepreneurs. Almost 800 citizens took up the invitation. Plenary lectures were once again alternated with a diversity of workshops. People were activated. Thanks to the diverse mix of participants, the atmosphere was lively and open, and the message resounded once again: It is not us, but you together who will decide the future of the city. The future is open, but no longer is it undecided. After all, there is now a shared vision. Building on a civil society is like Wikipedia. It will continue.

Endnotes

1. Southwards, Westwards and Eastwards were the names of the three different consulting platforms, in which participants (mostly professional planners, but all parties were welcome) shared insights on the future planning and development of, respectively, the southern, western and eastern sides of the Amsterdam Metropolitan Area, those being areas outside Amsterdam, the centre-city. In the platform Westwards, for example, plans and initiatives affecting the area in between Amsterdam and the North Sea were discussed.

2. RADAR is the name that was given this specific consulting platform and was not meant as an acronym, merely as a reference to a radar: how to 'stay on track' or 'guiding'. The other consulting group was called ROER which means 'rudder' and has the same sort of meaning.

References

Ahrend, Hannah (1958) *The Human Condition*. Chicago.

Bruner, Jerome (2003) *Making Stories: Law, Literature, Life*. Harvard.

Friedmann, John (1987) *Planning in the Public Domain. From Knowledge to Action*. Princeton.

Gergen, Kenneth, and Mary Gergen (1986) *Social Psychology*. New York.

Hajer, Maarten, Jantine Grijzen and Susan van 't Klooster (eds) (2010) *Strong Stories. How the Dutch are reinventing spatial planning*. Rotterdam.

Nye, Joseph (1990) *Soft Power. The Means to Success in World Politics*. Harvard.

Shirky, Clay (2008) *Here Comes Everybody. The Power of Organizing Without Organizations*. Penguin.

Surowiecki, James (2005) *The Wisdom of Crowds*. New York.

02

STUDIES
AND
STRATEGIES

Beyond Cities: Is an Urban Planet even Possible?

Jeremy Dawkins

The fate of the planet seems to hang on how well mass urbanisation is planned and managed over the next few decades. An ISOCARP Urban Planning and Advisory Team, meeting in Singapore in July 2010, developed a fresh analysis of rapid urbanisation and proposed radically new approaches to achieving sustainable urban regions (ISOCARP, 2010). This article outlines the team's findings, including the likely patterns of land use in the sustainable urban regions of the future, and presents the team's ten 'practical solutions' – realistic but meaningful first steps which can be implemented immediately, everywhere.

The team was commissioned by the Philips Center for Health and Well-Being, whose generous support is gratefully acknowledged. The members of the team were Jeremy Dawkins (Team Leader), Martin Dubbeling (UPAT Raporteur), Antonia Cornaro, Nadya Nilina, Francisco Pérez, Dr Awais Piracha and Luc Vrolijks. Tragically, Luc suffered a fatal stroke on 1 August 2011, depriving us of a highly valued friend and colleague, Yvette of a generous and loving partner, and the world of gifted architect, planner and urban designer. We express our condolences to his family and friends and to all of the ISOCARP community who knew him.

The report is available at www.isocarp.org/fileadmin/user_upload/network/ISOCARP_UPAT_final_20110114.pdf.

An 'urban' life – a life of personal, social and economic opportunity – is ultimately the right of everyone[1]. But does it require continued rapid *urban*isation? If so, can the world survive a doubling of the urban population in the next half century?

Rapid urbanisation still means the further widening of social inequalities, the wholesale loss of fertile land, massive increases in the consumption of fossil fuels and accelerating depletion of natural capital[2]. To envisage a doubling of the urban population – from three billion out of a global population of six billion today to six billion out of a global population of nine billion some time after the middle of the century– is to contemplate irreversible climate change and the collapse of humanity's life-support systems.

Fortunately, we are at a point when 'rural' no longer means toiling subsistence, and when an interactive 'urban' life can be enjoyed anywhere. So personal fulfilment no longer literally entails a 'civic', 'civilised', *city* life – the people of the world now have many opportunities even in relatively remote locations, and continued urbanisation is no longer necessary to fulfil the reasonable aspirations of the non-urban half of the world's people.

Thus, one way to avoid global collapse would be to halt or even reverse urbanisation by equalising access to educational, cultural, technological and economic resources across all urban and rural areas. For much of the second half of the twentieth century, something like this was the stated aim of the Chinese government. However, few would think that such an aim would be remotely feasible: China's current experience is more likely to indicate a future of vast, continuous, urbanising regions wherever populations and economies are growing rapidly (Buijs, 2010; Mars and Hornsby, 2008).

The alternative response to rapid urbanisation is to transform both the processes of urbanisation and the kinds of urban areas that result. This raises new questions. Can rapidly urbanising regions create (rather than destroy) natural capital? Can they generate (rather than deplete) energy? Can they increase (rather than reduce) fairness and equality of opportunity? If so, what radically new forms of planning and governance would be needed to achieve these outcomes?

The Urban Planning Advisory Team (UPAT) which met in Singapore from 23 to 31 July, 2010, had the exciting opportunity to sketch answers to these fundamental and challenging questions. ISOCARP's generous partner in the project was the Philips Center for Health and Well-Being, which has established a Liveable Cities Think Tank to identify the pathway to liveable cities. The UPAT process and its outcome are fully described in the report *Liveable cities in a rapidly urbanizing world* (ISOCARP, 2010), available at http://www.isocarp.org/fileadmin/user_upload/network/ISOCARP_UPAT_final_20110114.pdf.

This article outlines the findings of the Singapore UPAT in four sections:

1. A new paradigm for planners: the 'non-city rapidly urbanising region'
2. Harnessing the creativity of rapidly urbanising regions
3. Possible outcomes: Radically new land use patterns and densities
4. Possible outcomes: What are some practical first steps?

A New Paradigm for Planners: The Non-City Rapidly Urbanising Region

Rapid urbanisation is eating the future

Rapid urbanisation, particularly in Asia, Africa and Latin America, is creating entirely new kinds of urban environments, generally with the following characteristics:

- Vast, dense, diverse, uneven and fragmented nodes and corridors of industrial complexes, commercial clusters, urban services and housing estates, associated with ports and highways, poorly connected by retro-fitted arterial roads and railways...
- ...driven spontaneously by export opportunities, rapidly increasing domestic consumption and the aspirations of the rural population...
- ...resulting in economic growth and rapidly rising standards of living, accompanied by loss of habitat and natural resources, rapid consumption of natural capital, pollution, congestion, inequalities, inefficiencies, corruption and exploitation.

The quality of life in these new urban regions could, at one end of the spectrum, condemn ordinary people to deprivation and exclusion, or, at the other end, foster fulfilment of human potential – depending on how these regions are planned, managed and governed. The challenge is to imagine how these new urbanising regions can provide people with the most humane and sustainable environments for urban living.

If urbanisation continues in anything like the present patterns, we will need the resources of four or five planets by mid century. To make this project meaningful, we must assume that drastic changes will have been forced on the world through the collapse of ecosystems, and that strong global action will have taken place. Our (heroic) assumptions include the following.

- Strong global action to establish a high price on carbon.
- Strong global action to price natural capital at its real value. (Perhaps the best work in this regard has been done by the Economics of Ecosystems and Biodiversity Study (TEEB)[3] (TEEB 2009, 2010, 2011).)
- Therefore we assume that rapidly urbanising regions are powered by low-carbon energy and that 'free' environmental goods and services are accurately valued and managed conservatively as capital assets.
- We assume that urban development has become 'light-weight', in that the extremely resource-demanding construction of the present is replaced with durable but light-weight and adaptable structures using recycled materials to the maximum, and that heavy industry moves from carbon (heat) processes to hydrogen (electrical/chemical) processes, both transformations having been driven by real values being attributed to natural capital.[4]
- We assume that there are high levels of social mobility, openness and transparency in a fully digital world.
- We must also assume that strong and enlightened leadership provides holistic, long-term strategies and science-based policies for urbanising regions (see section *The regional commission: working around dysfunctional boundaries and layers of governments* below).

These assumptions become the *preconditions* for liveable, sustainable urban environments.

Rapid urbanisation does not result in 'cities'

Urban growth in its traditional form is unlikely to play a significant role in accommodating the next three billion people in urban environments. These people will be living in the 'city', but not in planned, incremental extensions of existing cities nor in newly-planned cities. Rapid urbanisation, spreading around growth zones, ports, airports, mining districts and transport corridors, will be urban but 'non-city': fast, extensive, less structured, more dynamic, more spontaneous and in some ways more innovative than more familiar forms of urban growth.

Where this leaves traditional forms of planning was one of the critical questions addressed in this project. We concluded that contemporary planning approaches and the use of familiar models of urban form (for example, the metropolitan region with core, sectors, corridors and subregions) cannot be applied to these 'non-city' rapidly urbanising regions. *Attempts to apply these models are likely to fail in both diagnosis and prescription.* More importantly, such attempts are likely to fail to capitalise on the potential of these regions to generate new models, new approaches and new solutions.

Figure 1: The UPAT team at work
From left to right: Martin Dubbeling, Awais Piracha, Nadya Nilina, Luc Vrolijks, Francisco Pérez, Antonia Cornaro and Jeremy Dawkins

In short, many of the models and techniques developed for the management of traditional cities and for traditional forms of urban governance are largely irrelevant in guiding rapid mass urbanisation. City planning, developed in different times and circumstances, cannot claim to be able to deliver the kinds of transformations described below. If misapplied, it may fail or, worse, actually impede the rapid, spontaneous and creative initiatives required.

Some of the characteristics of the new urban regions can already be seen in the older example of rapid post-war urbanisation around Tokyo – for instance multiple nodes and corridors of development, generated by expanding industrial complexes and/or by lines and nodes of communication, generally retrofitted with highways and rapid transit – and even in ex-urban development in the US. The full form of this kind of urbanisation, however, is seen in the examples of Shenzhen in China and the Eastern Seaboard in Thailand. It is this form of urbanisation which is most likely to take place over vast areas in China and India and parts of SE Asia, Africa and Latin America.

These new urbanising regions may be a form of 'city' and are likely to be referred to as cities. In fact they are not 'cities' in anything like the classical sense of the word. Whereas the traditional image of the city, in all cultures, reflects some form of monarchical power – a single centre of wealth and authority, a centre of advantage and accessibility at the crossroads – the rapidly urbanising regions do not form into patterns resembling contained cities with concentric structures and with networks radiating from a centre. It could therefore be a serious impediment to the effective management of these regions if the planners and administrators imagine that they are building 'cities': 'non-cities' call for a clever form of 'non-planning' from the politicians, urban managers and planners.

Rapidly urbanising regions need to be seen as a new paradigm in the production of the human habitat. If planners adhere to a traditional model of the structured city, they may fail to appreciate – and fail to address, and/or take advantage of – the following attributes of this new phenomenon.

- Rapidly urbanising regions extend dynamically, and even unpredictably, across large areas, ignoring all levels of governmental boundaries, and stretching for 100 or 200 km or more. In the case of the Beijing-Shanghai corridor, the dense rapidly urbanising region extends some 1500 km (Mars and Hornsby 2008).
- Rapidly urbanising regions are discontinuous, leapfrogging over constraints and responding to dispersed opportunities in the landscape including, for instance, pre-existing settlements, major infrastructure such as ports, emerging industries and natural resources. They are flexible and dynamic, and can be more resilient than traditional cities (Webster, 2004).
- Rapid urbanisation creates a kaleidoscopic mosaic of fragments and corridors, with the same growth patterns and 'daily urban systems' tending to be reproduced at all scales, from the crossroads and the village to subregions and regions.
- Rapidly urbanising regions are poorly connected, making many journeys long, uncomfortable and/or expensive.
- Rapidly urbanising regions are segregated: land uses are typically separated into estates and districts at both the local and regional scales, and people are typically separated into sectors by income and occupation; neighbourhoods and quarters are typically separated by transport corridors and other forms of infrastructure.
- Rapidly urbanising regions are wasteful and inefficient in the use of resources and excessively damaging to the environment – responding to short term and local interests rather than strategic and regional priorities.

Jeremy Dawkins

- Rapidly urbanising regions are seldom governed as a whole, and when they are there is little or no opportunity for citizen participation at the local level.
- All of these characteristics are the result of large movements of people and rapid economic growth overlying existing natural, social and administrative landscapes.

We concluded that the dynamism of these rapidly urbanising regions may be able to produce a human environment which is not only liveable and sustainable but which will provide models for the transformations also required in the mature cities of fully urbanised countries. There is, however, a very big IF attached to this possibility: it requires new concepts and new planning tools, it requires strong global action on energy, climate change and biodiversity, and it will only happen if the rapidly urbanising region is governed by enlightened regional leaders with an open-ended mandate (see section *The regional commission: working around dysfunctional boundaries and layers of governments* below). Assuming all this, what could these regions be like, in a generation or two?

To begin to answer this question, the UPAT team investigated non-city rapid urbanisation at three scales, from regional to local. While merely schematic, the following three kinds of rectangular territories enable us to investigate and describe the nature and planning of these new kinds of places.

'10x100': the 10 km by 100 km 'slice' or transect

This is a large area of 1000 square kilometres (1000 km^2), and therefore indicative of the scale at which rapid urbanisation takes place, with towns, industrial areas, ports and transport corridors expanding from one end to the other. It reflects the often linear nature of rapid urbanisation. It may ultimately accommodate 10 million people. (By way of comparison, Singapore with its islands has an area of about 700 km^2, with a population of 5.2 million.) This is the scale at which natural resources, major transport corridors, transit systems and major infrastructure such as ports and airports are planned.

'10x10': the 10 km by 10 km subregion

This area of 100 km^2 could in classical terms be seen as a city of one million people. As in Singapore, public housing, public transport, traffic management, water management, major commercial and recreational precincts are largely planned and implemented at this scale.

'1x1': the one-square-kilometre urban living area

This is the scale of communities and urban life in all its shapes and forms. Each 1x1 urban living area will be different, but most will have dwellings for a population of around 20 000 to 40 000 people, together with natural areas, open space, water bodies, small scale agriculture, industry, storage, offices, shops, schools, health services, transport interchanges and civic and cultural facilities.

These three scales, admittedly abstractions and simplifications, enable the focus to move from the whole region to the subregion to the neighbourhood (while also recognising that many of the challenges may well be at the intermediate scales). One thousand 1x1 urban areas do not add up to an urban region, just as the region cannot be divided into ten 10x10 subregions; across the 1x1 urban living areas, land uses come in many sizes and may be distributed very unevenly. Nevertheless:

• The rebuilding of natural capital, the optimisation of local energy potential and the social fairness of the urban environment all have to be implemented and safeguarded at the regional scale or larger;
• Natural resources, land use and infrastructure should be integrated at the subregional scale; and
• There should be a fine grain of diverse land uses and transport modes within a walking catchment of a few square kilometres.

The hypothetical 10x100 rapidly urbanising region (1000 km²) is notionally made up of ...

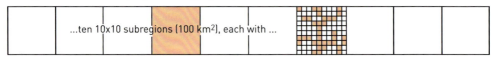

...ten 10x10 subregions (100 km²), each with ...

...one hundred 1x1 squares, 35 of them being *urban living areas*.

Figure 2: The three scales adopted for the investigation of rapidly urbanising regions

Jeremy Dawkins

Harnessing the Creativity of Rapidly Urbanising Regions

Overlapping mosaics

Planners are, of course, familiar with maps and plans, including those showing intended land use patterns, or urban designs, or blueprints, or structure plans, or regulatory land use allocations. A very different kind of spatial language is required in rapidly urbanising regions, closer to natural patterns and processes, often having fuzzy boundaries and anticipating unpredictable patterns of growth and change. The image is one of patchworks or mosaics – a fluid jigsaw puzzle that reflects the natural world and the complexities of the human habitat.

The first layers of spatial representation seek to understand the overlapping mosaics of natural resources and opportunities which will strongly influence urbanisation, including:

- The distribution of ecological communities and habitats, including critical areas and corridors;
- The landscape which sustains ecological diversity and delivers access to resources, recreation and nature;
- The hydrological component of the landscape, crucially important for managing local water sources and building resilience;
- The potential for renewable energy sources (wind, water, ocean, solar, agricultural and aquacultural, biomass, geothermal, heat storage, energy storage, kinetic potential, etc);
- The suitability of the topography and soils for different agricultural, built and natural purposes;
- Climate and environmental risks;

- The cultural landscape, including cities, towns, villages, historic areas, places of cultural significance and meaning, landmarks, visual landscapes, natural heritage areas, etc;
- The potential arterial routes and catchments for all modes of the transport network.

Some of these layers are fixed, some fluid; some are sharp and some fuzzy; some are non-negotiable while many are amenable to planning, design and mutual optimisation. As mapping and analysis moves to strategic planning and design, layers are continually added for the large-scale components of the 10x100 region, including ports, airports, commercial centres, regional hospitals and educational campuses, heavy industry, agriculture, aquaculture, mining, forests and natural areas, regional parks, transport corridors, energy resources, etc.

Some of these uses require land to be irrevocably committed while for others the land allocation can be contingent and responsive to how development unfolds. In every case, the regional strategy must be explicit yet at the same time capable of being implemented in many ways – the strategy is nothing like a master plan. Likewise, decisions on elements of the regional structure should be made *as soon as necessary, and as late as possible,* to be informed by the best information and the latest patterns of development. In addition, land allocation should be based on smart combinations and multiple uses, for instance locating a highway so that it serves as a flood protection barrier, and creating recreational areas on new offshore islands that protect the coast from erosion and storm surge.

If the 10x100 region is notionally made up of one thousand 1-km^2 square segments, it is apparent that these segments are highly varied, with many being mono-functional, making up airports, ports, road and rail infrastructure, heavy industry, forest, natural areas, water bodies, farms, regional parks and the like. Others will be a complex combination of, for instance, commercial centres, health facilities, educational campuses and sports grounds. Many of the 1x1 *urban living areas* – about 350 of the thousand segments – will be areas where most of the population live, work, shop, study, play sport, etc.

Over time, governed entirely by opportunity, demand and circumstance, the details of the urban living areas will be sketched in and progressively planned in detail. Within any single neighbourhood, there should be many opportunities:

- For a choice of lifestyle, employment, expression
- For growth, development, prosperity
- For living and working in healthy buildings and enjoying space, light, fresh air
- For child care, education, health and community services, parks, nature
- For variety—quiet, active, dense, loose, high, low, upper and lower social groups
- For influencing community decisions
- For belonging, contact with the earth, a connected social environment.

The 1x1 urban living areas will be fine grained, often with land uses tiered at the different levels of thin, tall buildings, and allowing people of diverse occupations and incomes to live and work in the same neighbourhoods, to shop in the same centres and to send their children to the same schools. Again, land planning should be based on smart combinations and multiple uses, for instance green roofs to cool down buildings, to retain rain water, and to provide opportunities for local parks and food gardens; street trees that provide shade, produce food and retain rain water; and a park on top of a highway, filtering the air, reducing noise and providing amenity for residents.

Food production must become a visible layer within the city. Producing food is partly a

professional activity, partly something that inhabitants do; it takes place in different shapes and forms, from high-tech hydroponic glasshouses on the roofs and facades of office buildings to collective gardens to provide high quality slow-food, and has many social and environmental benefits. Notwithstanding, agriculture cannot compete for private urban land. It can be a significant activity in the public landscape framework, and it can be an interim use on infrastructure reservations and other land banks. Its more complete integration with the urban environment requires a high level of control, in which a public authority is able to allocate land on the basis of more than monetary consideration. Many 'smart combinations' are possible, including crops on industrial buildings (providing insulation to the building and using CO_2, grey water and compost produced in the building), urban landscape that is not only attractive but also productive, and other technologically advanced approaches.

In the rapidly urbanising regions, the landscape is under tremendous pressure. Natural resources rapidly disappear, farms become housing projects, trees vanish, watersheds become polluted, streams are reduced to drains, and the green pattern gets more and more fragmented. All experiences indicate that 'once it is gone, it is gone', and it is very difficult to remake landscape in a dense urban area. This means that early protection and landscape development based on a landscape ecology approach are needed to maintain and nurture a landscape framework that enables and supports a liveable city. One example is the city of Almere, made on reclaimed polder land in the Netherlands. The first activity undertaken was to plant and develop a main framework of 'forest-strips' to provide all inhabitants easy access to nature. Over 30 years, this resource has grown into one of the key assets of the city. While the scale is completely different, a similar strategy can be successful at the 10x100 level: early identification of a landscape ecological framework – protecting and enhancing it – and providing access for the people.

Overlapping networks

Threading through and connecting these overlapping mosaics will be many networks, including wildlife corridors, green wedges, parkways, waterways, roads, railways, light rail, cycle paths and infrastructure corridors. In a traditional metropolitan strategy, these elements are the bones or skeleton of the region and tend to be fixed once the initial planning has been completed. In theory the same approach is applied to non-city rapidly urbanising regions, but in practice the planning of these networks tends to follow rather than lead development, and is then too static to accommodate the dynamic changes that take place under conditions of rapid urbanisation. The result can be highly inefficient, and expensive or impossible to correct.

Just as a new kind of spatial language, of patchworks or mosaics, is required for land use patterns, so a new spatial language is needed for layers of loose networks laid over the regional mosaics, representing green corridors, parkways, drainage, railways, roads, transit, pipes, wires, etc. The equivalent of the land use *mosaic* is the network *fishnet*. Layers of 'fishnets', of all sizes and complexities, represent loose grid systems. Compared to a typical planned grid, they have more connections, they have redundancy, and they are adaptive. This approach responds to the uncertainties of rapidly urbanising regions – uncertainties which it is desirable not to try to prevent, since this is also the source of the region's innovations and resilience.

The design of networks early in the process of urbanisation is intended to reflect the main structures and protect connections for later development. It is this which gives the networks the character of fishnets: stretched

in some places, dense in others, linear, square, multidirectional, but always connected. The design of the 'fishnets' is based on likely development scenarios, natural conditions, the protection of streams and waterways and a host of other considerations. A 'fishnet' has to be robust in its main shape, but allow nodes to develop in quite different ways, allowing for a network that can absorb a large degree of uncertainty. A fishnet is a finer network than is ultimately required. While some of the links in the network will be strengthened and 'promoted', many links will never be implemented: the course of dynamic development will determine which is which.

As in the case of major elements of the regional mosaics, some of the links in a 'fishnet' (of roads or green corridors, for instance) will need to be irrevocably committed while others can remain indicative or strategic, their final form responding to the way in which development unfolds. The fishnet is another instance of the principle that the best regional planning is strategically certain, and tactically flexible.

People move to cities for opportunities, including greater mobility. The transport systems of non-city rapidly urbanising regions, including footpaths and cycle paths as well as cars and transit, will continue to offer the population very high levels of mobility (powered entirely by non-carbon/renewable energy)[5]. Transport requires hierarchy – from local to international – with a seamless integration of all modes, each doing what it does best. The rapidly urbanising region needs to avoid dependence on cars, even though in the early stages of urbanisation large roads are cheaper and easier to build than mass transit. These regions, therefore, need to deliver fast, frequent and comfortable public transport services as early as possible, integrated with all other modes from the outset. It is essential that land use patterns and densities be designed and programmed to achieve this outcome.

The regional commission: working around dysfunctional boundaries and layers of governments

Administrative boundaries in city regions can seriously impede desirable policy making – for instance when a city's growth occurs beyond its boundaries; when the distribution of the population and the location of major destinations are determined by the exercise of local powers irrespective of (or in opposition to) natural resources, trade areas and transport services; when competing transport agencies refuse to work to regional objectives; when responsibilities for watersheds and catchments are randomly divided; or when revenues and responsibilities are vertically and spatially distorted.

All of these impediments to effective urban management are much greater in non-city rapidly urbanising regions, where there will be layers of local, rural, municipal and regional governments and special-purpose agencies and districts already in place. Do rapidly urbanising regions need a new form of government? Should a new regional government replace all the existing governments, sweeping aside all these boundaries, as is often advocated?

We concluded that it is best to leave most or all of these government structures in place. Firstly, there is the practical reality that structural reform on such a scale creates enormous problems of conflict, re-integration and adjustment, lasting for years, even decades. Secondly, and even more importantly, notwithstanding parochialism and narrow mandates, existing government structures have expertise, local knowledge and essential functions to perform, and will be needed to implement regional strategic plans and policies.

The imaginative alternative to restructuring is the superimposition of a regional leadership body – an expert commission, or a council of elders – which has the necessary authority to guide the region, but of a different kind. It is not endowed with legal powers and resources, since any such powers and resources would have unavoidably been removed from existing agencies. Instead, it has high public standing, as a small, stable group of wise and experienced men and women, operating transparently, and guided by community engagement and excellent science.

This 'regional commission' has an open mandate (unconstrained by statutory functions and funding) and is thus better able to exercise persuasive moral authority than any normal government body. It exercises and strengthens this moral authority in articulating a credible, compelling, public vision for the urban region, in maintaining a strategic focus on the long term interests of the whole region, and in providing agencies and the public with a constant flow of independent data, assessments and forecasts.

Jeremy Dawkins

Possible Outcomes: Radically New Land Use Patterns and Densities

A further challenge was to quantify the allocation of land across a future, sustainable urban region. This is not easy or simple to do (and is seldom done), for several reasons. Firstly, there is no master plan and no prescriptive land use regulation beyond strong regional policies relating to 'mosaics' and 'fishnets', so patterns of land use will fluctuate markedly over time in response to opportunities, constraints and demand. Secondly, even well-managed rapid urbanisation retains its spontaneity, so the filling in of the 'mosaics' and 'fishnets' is piecemeal and opportunistic, resulting in diverse patterns from place to place. In short, land use allocations such as those listed below cannot be seen as either 'plans' or predictions for any given time or place.

Nevertheless, it is essential to attempt to describe a desirable future pattern of land use allocation. Without such an attempt to quantify intended outcomes there are no guidelines, no benchmarks against which to measure outcomes, and no aspirations. The following tables should be understood in that spirit.

The **10x100 region** (the transect) might have the following characteristics. As noted above, the figures are not prescriptions or predictions. They are indicative of the broad shape of the possible/desirable/sustainable future non-city rapidly urbanising region.

Area	1000 km^2
Population	10 million people
Population density	10 000 people/ km^2 = 100 people/regional ha
Dwelling density	40 dwellings/regional ha

The 1000 km^2 area is allocated as follows:

Nature, farming, broadacre open space	25%	250 km^2
Large scale commerce and exchange	10%	100 km^2
Large scale industry and production	10%	100 km^2
Large transport infrastructure	15%	150 km^2
Water and waste processing	5%	50 km^2
1x1 urban living areas	35%	350 km^2

Notes on areas used for indicating densities

I A density expressed as 'people per regional hectare' (abbreviated as people/regional ha) is the population divided by the entire area of the region in hectares.

II In the tables below, density expressed as 'people per urban living area hectare' (people/urban living ha) is the population divided by the area of the 1x1 urban living area, which generally excludes areas allocated to regional infrastructure and other major elements.

III In the tables below, density expressed as 'people per site hectare' (people/site ha) is the population divided by the area of the actual residential site(s) while excluding the rest of the land in the urban living area (non-residential uses, streets, parks, etc).

If the 10x100 transect is thought of as being made up of one thousand 1-km^2 squares, around one in three is allocated to nature, farming, broadacre open space and water, another one in three is allocated to large-scale commerce, industry and transport, and only about one in three is an urban living area. As indicated in the above table, the 1x1 urban living areas notionally comprise 35% of the area of the region. While there will be a great deal of variation between the 1x1 urban living areas, the typical or average 1x1 urban living area might have the following characteristics.

Area	1 km^2 = 100 ha = 1 000 000 m^2
Population	30 000 people
Population density	300 people/urban living area ha, 600 people/site ha
Dwelling density	120 dwellings/urban living area ha

The 1 km^2 area is allocated as follows:

Nature, water, agriculture, etc	15 ha footprint	15%
Parks and active recreation	10 ha footprint	10%
Roads and transport infrastructure	25 ha footprint	20%
Housing for 30 000 (12 000 dwellings)	1 000 000 m^2 floorspace }	
Employment areas (10 000 jobs)	200 000 m^2 floorspace }	45%
Civic, educations, retail and services	300 000 m^2 floorspace }	
Landscaping around housing, etc	10 ha footprint	10%

This table shows that, in the 1x1 urban living areas, a notional 1.5 million square metres of floorspace (for housing, employment and retail and other services) is built on 55% of the land (the 45% of the land occupied by building footprints and 10% used for on-site access and landscaping). Thus floorspace of 1.5 million square metres occupies 55 ha or 0.55 million square metres of land, giving an average ratio of floorspace to site of about 3:1. A floorspace ratio of 3:1 is relatively high and is definitely urban rather than suburban, but it is not excessive, is entirely feasible, and can be achieved at high levels of resource and energy efficiency.

Having followed the patterns of land use through to the local level, it is now time to return to the overall regional scale. When land was allocated at the regional scale, in the first table above, the 1x1 urban living areas were treated as a single land use, occupying 35% of the whole area. It has now been seen that the 1x1 urban living areas include more of the non-residential uses such as parks, agriculture and commerce, and transport infrastructure such as local roads, already listed for the region. If these local land uses are reallocated at the regional scale, the overall characteristics of the region are as follows.

Nature, water, agriculture, local parks	33%
Large scale commerce and exchange	10%
Large scale production and storage	10%
Urban buildings and associated landscaping	20%
Transport infrastructure including local roads	22%
Water and waste processing	5%

Jeremy Dawkins

While such an urban land use pattern is radically different to the current norm, we concluded that land use allocations of this kind are not only feasible (under the heroic assumptions initially adopted) but also absolutely essential if continued rapid urbanisation is not to precipitate irreversible climate change, the collapse of life support systems and disastrous social and global conflict. To put that in another way: if the above radically new patterns of urban land use are *not* feasible, nor is an 'urban planet'.

Possible Outcomes: What Are Some Practical First Steps?

The Urban Planning and Advisory Team was challenged to develop simple, practical and original solutions that improve the quality of people's lives in sustainable cities in South East Asia. These solutions were to be readily implementable and capable of being translated into reality within a few years and replicated in communities worldwide.

The team regarded this as an exciting and very challenging assignment: to first identify the 'big picture' long-term transformations which are required of cities and urbanising regions, and then to imagine the first practical steps towards those goals. The 'practical solutions' would need to be relatively simple and capable of immediate implementation everywhere, yet at the same time be both original and real drivers towards the urban environments of the future.

The team developed ten such practical solutions. Each has a name, such as 'Regional leaders', 'Landscape first' and 'Map the energy', as listed in the table. The ten practical solutions are not ranked or prioritised,

and indeed they are not necessarily the top ten actions that should be taken: the team developed them because they are important, original and feasible, while recognising that many other important actions need to be taken at the same time.

Each of the ten practical solutions relates to a specific principle, listed in the first column of the table. A single sentence explains each principle, and then a note describes how each principle applies to rapidly urbanising regions.

The first four practical solutions, on the green background, relate primarily to the scale of the '10x100' region. The next six practical solutions, on the yellow background, relate primarily to the '10x10' subregion and the '1x1' urban areas. All ten practical solutions may be most likely to emerge in the dynamic and innovative conditions of rapidly urbanising regions. They are equally applicable to mature cities, rapidly expanding cities and even shrinking cities, since these and similar 'practical solutions' are likely to be essential ingredients in responses to the great global challenges.

Fundamental principle	'Practical solution'
Strong regional governance Stable, credible, passionate regional leadership is essential to take responsibility for the urbanising region and the long term. Regional leadership must have sufficient legitimacy and credibility to transcend fragmented layers of government, short term and parochial priorities, competing interests and a lack of strategic responsibility for a rapidly urbanising region	**'Regional leaders'** Without attempting to remove or restructure layers of governments, the highest level of government appoints a small leadership council or regional commission comprising wise, expert and highly respected people who have the moral authority, and scientific resources, to define strategic regional priorities, to plan patterns of development and to persuade and educate the decision makers and the public.
Natural capital It is imperative that in future the natural systems of a region are understood, conserved and recovered as urbanisation proceeds. Maximising biodiversity in a rapidly urbanising region requires a landscape framework to be designed based on excellent science, before indiscriminate development takes over	**'Landscape first'** Define the regional landscape framework and plant it prior to urbanisation, to protect and recover biodiversity.
Local energy Urban areas should maximise the local generation of low-carbon energy, through the efficient use of local energy resources. All rapidly urbanising regions have a unique endowment of potential energy resources distributed unevenly across the region, which can be fully employed only if researched, mapped and protected ahead of development.	**'Map the energy'** First map the potential wind, wave, hydro, solar, biomass, geothermal and other energy resources, to prevent their sterilisation and to ensure that urbanisation makes the most of these resources.
Urban agriculture Food production, and agriculture generally, should be integrated throughout the urban environment. Minimizing the separation between food production and urban living reduces energy use, improves urban metabolism, enriches daily life and improves well-being	**'Productive landscapes'** Use food plants for urban landscapes, public gardens, street trees and interim uses of land banks.
Strategically certain, tactically flexible Liveable cities need strong strategies for the large scale patterns and networks, with greater creativity, flexibility and responsiveness at the smaller scale. The planning of rapidly urbanising regions is often typified by weak strategic regional frameworks but detailed local plans and rules, which are often used to simplify or standardise local development, usually by segregating land uses which might have negative impacts.	**'Mix to the max'** Planning controls should be based not on land use but on effects or performance, to encourage innovation and to allow every kind of low-impact use to become part of a rich urban living ecology.

The more urban, the more innovation

Cities generate innovation, through the intensity of interaction, the rate of change, and the market for creativity and art.
Rapidly urbanising regions need to support the arts and enrich the cultural landscape, in order to create environments which attract and foster creativity and build stronger communities.

'Budget for the arts'

A significant share of the urban budget allocated to the arts will enable artists to be engaged on all major project teams, and enable off-beat spaces to be made available for artists' studios and for other cultural production.

Mobility at all scales

From local high-quality pedestrian spaces to international bullet trains, liveable cities provide high mobility without compromising equity or environmental quality.
In the 1x1 urban living areas of rapidly urbanising regions, the quality of the pedestrian environment should come first, with all other modes, including private cars, performing their optimal role and interconnecting effortlessly.

'Node for all modes'

All modes connect seamlessly in a purpose-built interchange integrated into the heart of 1x1 urban living areas. *See the diagram Node for all modes.*

Actively engaged citizens

Liveable cities foster health and community connectedness by providing multiple destinations and opportunities within walking and cycling distance of where people live, work and play.
To counter the tendency in rapidly urbanising regions for important urban functions to be segregated and even inaccessible, the many destinations of 'daily life' should be co-located, and where possible integrated, in places of high accessibiliy

'Urban playground'

Plan the new retail centres to fully integrate commercial activities with public areas, social spaces, entertainment, sports and active recreation.
See the diagram Urban playground

Equity and social mix

Liveable cities improve life chances, health status and well-being by minimizing social division, exclusion and income inequality.
Wilkinson and Pickett provide compelling scientific evidence that 'equality is better for everyone' (2010). Whatever the level of inequality in income and opportunity in society, well-planned social mix in rapidly urbanising regions can improve levels of trust and well-being.

'People to people'

Intervene in many ways to ensure that each 1x1 urban living area has the broadest mix of employment types, income levels and cultural backgrounds, so that the area reasonably reflects the demographics of the whole region.

Corporate citizenship

Large corporations can play an increasingly creative role – through their products, their operations and their partnerships with governments and communities – to help make cities liveable.
In rapidly urbanising regions, corporations can be instrumental in driving innovation and raising standards, through their own developments and through direct relationships established with a local community for mutual benefit.

'Business to cities'

Corporations and large agencies each form a close relationship with a community by 'adopting' a 1x1 urban living area to better understand rapid urbanisation, to gain insight into daily life, to test innovations and to assist the local community.

Conclusion: Urban Planet in the Balance

The 'cities' issue is receiving historically high levels of attention. Urban planning stories are in the news – stories covering many dimensions of urban issues at all scales, from local to global. Planners are working with communities to find creative, integrated, strategic, sustainable responses to all of these issues.

It is hard not to conclude, however, that the fate of the planet will be largely determined by the scale and type of urbanisation which takes place in those parts of the world where the growth and movement of populations is greatest. Here, in East Asia, in the Indian subcontinent, in Africa and parts of Latin America in particular, rapid urbanisation is creating

a new paradigm for which there is not yet a recognised planning, urban management and governance response.

To have any significant impact at a global scale, any response will need to be radically different to the planning, urban management and governance practices of the past. The scale of the change can be seen from the desirable/necessary patterns of land use identified in the section *Possible Outcomes: Radically New Land Use Patterns and Densities*, above. Consider a part of a country (or, as is often the case, a region which is parts of several adjoining countries), where there are vast areas of rural lands, forest, mountains, and the like, within which is a 'non-city' rapidly urbanising region of 1000 km^2, growing towards a population of 10 million people. The Singapore UPAT found that within the *urban area*, within that urban region of 1000 km^2 – within what used

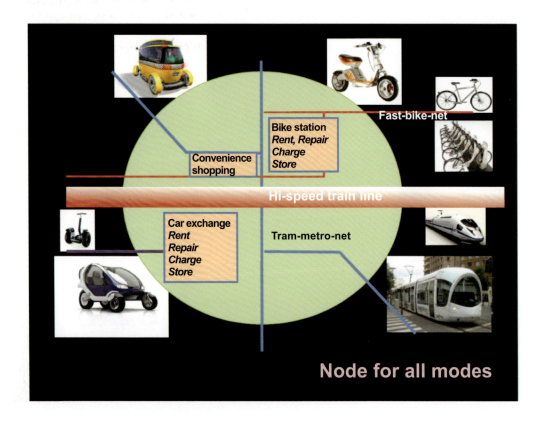

Bike station
Rent, Repair Charge Store

Fast-bike-net

Convenience shopping

Hi-speed train line

Car exchange
Rent Repair Charge Store

Tram-metro-net

Node for all modes

to be called the city – agriculture, conservation areas, regional parks and wet areas occupy fully 30% of the land and large scale commerce, industry and infrastructure occupy another 35%, while what we think of as 'urban' occupies only the remaining 35% of the land.

To achieve that unlikely outcome, the Singapore UPAT found that the management of a rapidly urbanising region would require, amongst other things, an adaptive strategic land use planning approach we called 'mosaics', an adaptive strategic network planning approach we called 'fishnets', and a radical governance approach we called 'regional commission'. Even then, any success would depend on strong global measures to (amongst other things) price carbon and value natural capital.

To make all this real, we were challenged to imagine ten 'practical solutions' which were steps towards these outcomes yet capable of being implemented immediately, everywhere. Our ten 'practical solutions' are presented in the section *Possible Outcomes: What Are Some Practical First Steps?*, above. We hope they will be considered systematically in many situations. For instance, to take just the first five of our proposals: the power of moral authority can often achieve much more than legal and financial resources, and should be tested wherever possible ('Regional leaders'); many projects could reverse the typical priorities whereby the green, conservation, landscape framework takes up the residual land and is implemented at the end ('Landscape first'); many planning projects could begin with an inventory of potential energy resources (Map the energy'); there are many opportunities

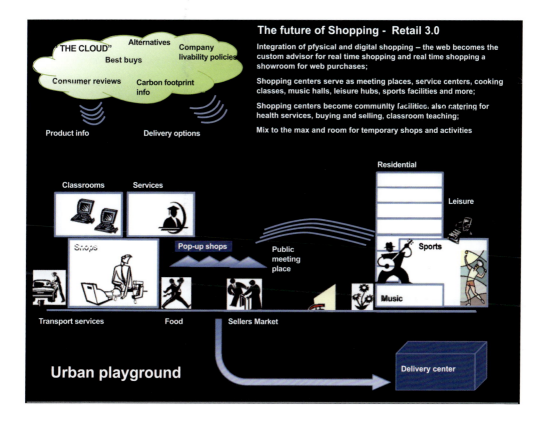

(usually missed) to introduce food production and agriculture into even dense urban
environments, something Singapore is actively
pursuing (Productive landscapes); and a much
richer and creative mix of uses, activities and
people can be achieved when the usual pattern of loose strategy but tight local controls is
reversed ('Mix to the max').

We gained a great deal from the intense UPAT
experience. We intend to investigate these
matters further, and in the meantime we will
seek to apply the findings in our work. To all
who have read this article, we say: comments,
criticism and ideas will be warmly welcomed.

jeremy.dawkins@uts.edu.au

Endnotes

1. By 'right of everyone' I simply mean that to live an
urban life is a reasonable aspiration for all people
to achieve, without trying to invoke the more
complex (or fashionable) idea of Lefebvre's 'right
to the city' as a 'demand…[for] a transformed and
renewed access to urban life', or Harvey's (2008)
'right to the city' as 'a right to change ourselves
by changing the city', or – to cite one example
of how the term is being embraced –
San Francisco's 'right to the city' campaign on
behalf of tenants and the homeless.

2. Natural capital is a metaphor for the stock of
environmental goods and services and the
natural systems on which life – and human
development – depends (Hawken et al., 1999).

3. Established in 2007 by UNEP with financial support from the European Commission, Germany,
the United Kingdom, Netherlands, Norway,
Sweden and Japan, and led by banker Pavan
Suhkdev, the Economics of Ecosystems and
Biodiversity Study (TEEB) analysed the global
economic benefit of biological diversity, the costs
of the loss of biodiversity and the failure to take
protective measures versus the costs of effective conservation. The TEEB series of reports are
available at www.teebweb.org. In February 2011
TEEB launched the Bank of Natural Capital, a
website designed to communicate the TEEB
Study findings to citizens. Visit it here:
http://bankofnaturalcapital.com.

4. Coyle (1997) examines the trends in the use of
fewer resources. She points out that, despite
real incomes in most industrialised countries
increasing twenty times from the beginning of the
twentieth century, such was the reduction in the
use of materials that the weight of all that was
produced was much the same at the end of the
century as it was at the beginning. On the other
hand, this greater efficiency may be overwhelmed
by increases in consumption. Take the single example of the metal copper. 'We need more copper
in the next 20 years [600 million tons] than was
mined in the last 110 years [585 million tons],'
Ivanhoe Mines Ltd Chairman Robert Friedland
said today at the Diggers and Dealers conference
in Kalgoorlie, Western Australia (quoted from
www.bloomberg. com/news/2010-08-04; see also
www.businessday.com.au). And that is not count-
ing the demand for copper to make electric cars.
'Cars are going to be electric,' said Mr Friedland,
'and 80% of the weight of a lithium battery is copper – 200-300 kg per car, wanted by half a billion
people in the next decade or two.'

5. Many planners anticipate – apparently with some
pleasure – that sustainability entails deprivation, and specifically a return to human-powered
transport supplemented by pre-car forms of public transport. Sustainability does mean the end
of the fossil-fueled car and the end of the private
vehicle as the main mode for the journey to work,
but for most, an urban life will offer increased
physical mobility, not less.

References

Buijs, Steef et al. (editors) (2010) *Megacities: Exploring a sustainable future*, Rotterdam: 010 Publishers.

Coyle, Diane (1997) *The weightless world*. Oxford: Capstone.

Harvey, David (2008) "The right to the city", *New Left Review 53, pages 23-40*.

ISOCARP (2010) *Liveable cities in a rapidly urbanizing world*, available at http://www.isocarp.org/fileadmin/user_upload/network/ISOCARP_UPAT_final_20110114.pdf.

Mars, Neville and Adrian Hornsby with the Dynamic City Foundation (Beijing) (2008) *The Chinese dream: a society under construction*. Rotterdam: 010 Publishers.

Hawken, Paul, Amory Lovins and Hunter Lovins (1999) *Natural capitalism: Creating the next industrial revolution*, Boston: Little Brown.

The Economics of Ecosystems and Biodiversity Study (TEEB) (2009) (2010) (2011) www.teebweb.org. Reports include *TEEB for business, TEEB for citizens, TEEB climate issues update, TEEB for local and regional policy* and *TEEB for policy*. In February 2011 TEEB launched the Bank of Natural Capital, a website designed to communicate the TEEB Study findings to citizens: http://bankofnaturalcapital.com.

Webster, Douglas (2004) "Bangkok: evolution and adaptation under stress" in Josef Gugler (ed), *World cities beyond the west: globalization, development and inequality*, Cambridge University Press.

Wilkinson, Richard and Kate Pickett (2010) *The spirit level. Why equality is better for everyone*. Penguin Books.

Towards a Liveable Urban Climate: Lessons from Stuttgart

Michael Hebbert

Brian Webb

Introduction

It has been known for centuries that the physical design of a city affects climatic variables - temperature, wind patterns, humidity, precipitation, air quality – which in turn have direct consequences for liveability. This paper considers how the climatic impacts of urban form can enhance or reduce the quality of urban life, drawing valuable lessons from the experience of a city that deliberately studied the behaviour of its local weather systems and learned how to manage them through physical planning.

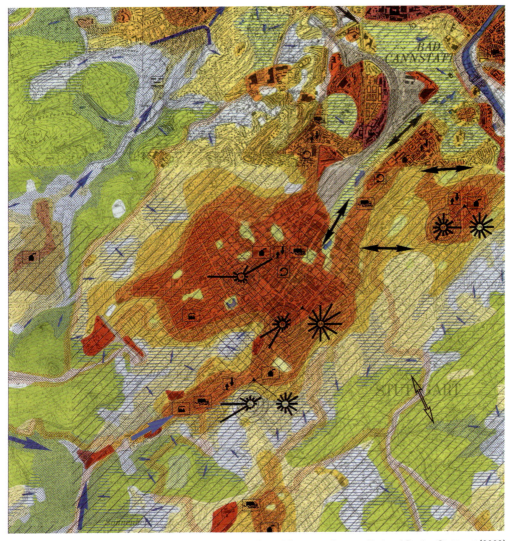

Figure 1: Climate Analysis Map of the City of Stuttgart. Source: Verband Region Stuttgart (2008)

Urban Climatology and its Application

The history of design for a liveable urban climate has solid roots in practical precedents of traditional vernacular building typology, and a more elusive basis in abstract systems such as Chinese geomantic *feng shue* or Greco-Roman wind theory. Some enigmatic principles of healthy ventilation set out more than two thousand years ago for the Emperor Augustus by the engineer Vitruvius in Book One of his treatise *De Architectura* continued to be invoked by nineteenth and early twentieth century planners, slim though their scientific basis was. After the First World War the Modern Movement put 'light and air', *Licht und Luft*, at the centre of their rational design philosophy, orienting buildings towards the sun and arranging functional uses in accordance with 'prevailing wind'. Unfortunately the evidence basis remained sketchy, since designers had little empirical understanding of the complex nature of urban microclimates, and particularly of the impact of tall free-standing buildings on air turbulence and outdoor temperature.

Urban climatology was placed on a more solid scientific footing around the mid twentieth century, the seminal text being Albert Kratzer's *Stadtklima* published in 1937 and revised in 1956. Developing rapidly across the disciplines of applied meteorology and physical geography, the science appeared to hold great promise for climatically-informed town planning. Data-gathering was enhanced by new techniques such as vehicle-mounted ob-

Figure 2: above: Street canyon in Chicago. Source: Authors
Figure 3: right: A dense high-rise city block is not conducive to wind flow at street level. Source: Authors

servation points, high density weather stations on public buildings, balloon mounted sensors for monitoring city air-flow, radar, aerial photography and remote sensing of atmospheric conditions. The state of the art shifted from descriptive research to process analysis of energy exchanges and air circulation within the complex three-dimensional geometry of urban landscapes, using physical and then numerical models (Oke 1976).

Urban climatologists addressed anthropogenic variables that are perfectly familiar to town planners: street orientation, street width-to-height ratios, building height and spacing, architectural detail of street frontages, heat-reflectiveness (albedo) of building form and materials, the placing of street trees, parks and water-spaces, and the effects of vehicle movement (Givoni 1998; Erell 2011). The street canyon became an especially interesting point of intersection between climatology and design: this quintessential urban space can be represented as a rectangular trough with height and width dimensions composed of surface materials orientated at a particular angle, framing a sky view whose geometry determines sun access by day and loss of energy by night. Detailed studies have been done on its energy balances and air movement patterns and the optimal geometry of height, width and orientation (Oke, 1988). Digital modelling has brought a further level of sophistication, integrating design factors and climatic effects with biometeorological variables so human comfort levels can be estimated under different climate scenarios and design settings (Matzarakis et al. 1999). Urban climatology has come of age in recent years as a distinct scientific specialism with its own global network, the International Association for Urban Climate (IAUC)[1].

Alas, whilst the science of urban climatology has progressed its practical application has not. Perhaps because of the rise of air-conditioning and motorisation, perhaps because of the decline in pedestrianism or visible carbon pollution, city planning became less climate-aware in the decades after 1950. Planners addressed a dauntingly long and growing list of factors, but 'weather' was not generally one of them. With the honourable exceptions of German (and German-speaking) cities to which we return later in this chapter, wind-roses and rainfall distribution maps tended to disappear from planning documents. Climatic factors became little understood and weakly regulated. In the name of traffic flow streets were often widened and sidewalks narrowed to the detriment of outdoor air quality. Small city blocks were consolidated to allow the construction of large-scale climate controlled buildings, blocking air circulation or creating man-made wind tunnels. The higher heat absorption capacity of man-made materials, such as asphalt and cement, boosted urban heat island effects. The impervious surfaces of buildings, roads and parking lots accelerated storm-water run-off and flood risk. Tree removal deprived streets of pollution filters and exacerbated outdoor temperature extremes. Development pressure and architectural desire for visual impact combined in vertical building booms that too often turned daylight into shadow. Urban environmental management, where it occurred, was seen less as an urban design issue than a topic for microlevel building performance modification by architects, engineers and building services technicians (Bosselmann 1998; Doucet 2007; Schiller et al. 2006).

Scientists specialising in city weather patterns - urban climatologists - were well aware of adverse trends affecting outdoor liveability, as the writings of Tony Chandler (1976), Helmut Landsberg (1981), Arieh Bitan (1984) and Baruch Givoni (1998) bear witness. Using the institutional networks of the World Meteorological Organisation, the United Nations Environment Programme, the International Society for Biometeorology, the International Federation for Housing and Planning and the

Confédération Internationale du Bâtiment the science community made persistent efforts in postwar decades to alert urban planners to anthropogenic climate change at the urban scale. Their climate awareness campaign met with little success (Hebbert & MacKillop 2011).

It is interesting to compare the disappointing record of knowledge transfer in urban-scale climatology with the impact of anthropogenic climate change at *the* global scale. The IPCC process and the UN Framework Convention on Climate Change have at last galvanised urban decision-makers. Climate change is the vogue topic in urban affairs. Most of the world's leading cities have adopted some form of action plan, and their example is energetically communicated through the policy networks of ICLEI's Cities for Climate Protection programme, the Climate Alliance, the Energies-Cités movement or the C40 group. Hardly a month goes by without a fresh urban initiative on carbon mitigation or adaptation to global warming, such as - at the moment of writing - UN-Habitat's Global Report for 2011 *Cities and Climate Change: Policy Directions* (UN-Habitat 2011) and 'ARC3', the First Assessment Report of the Urban Climate Change Research Network *Climate Change and Cities* (Rosenzweig et al. 2011).

The state-of-the art as summarised in these two substantial reports treats urban climate from a distinctive angle. The city is problematised as a factor in global emissions and as a site of vulnerability to climate change impacts. The time-frame extends up to ninety years in the future, an unusually remote horizon in urban planning. Climatic forecasts are downscaled from global circulation models via regional-scale models to a 'fine resolution' of pixels 12 kilometres square, an unusually coarse grain in urban planning. Attention is focussed on the catastrophic risks of inundation, drought, typhoons, or heat extremes, and the policy formulae are explicitly borrowed from the field of disaster preparedness planning.

Shagun Mehrotra and colleagues frame the entire issue in terms of an encounter between the two 'communities' of macro-scale climate modelling and disaster management (Rosenzweig 2011, p. 19). The knowledge community of urban climatology represented by the IAUC plays hardly any role.

Consequently the 'city climate' of the Urban Climate Change Research Network is a selective construct, focussed upon the exposure of cities to hazards that have a huge impact but a low frequency. It has little to say about the high-frequency and micro-scale climatic phenomena created within the anthropogenic environment of the city, such as the local circulations of regional winds, pollution and its dispersal on breezes, nocturnal cold air flows, variations in outdoor temperature and humidity, spatial patterns of sunshine and shade, shelter from wind and rain, and similar factors of significance for everyday liveability. These effects cannot be downscaled from a regional weather model, they are complex and require local observation and understanding. Patterns of urban wind circulation are typically diurnal, with breezes shifting direction between day and night, and intricate spatial distribution linked to topography, building form and landscape. Air ventilation and humidity directly affect human comfort and liveability within urban space. None of these factors are adequately considered in city climate analysis derived from model projections of extreme weather events.

So there is unfinished business here. While the challenge of global climate change has opened the door to city-level climatic awareness, city planners are still only beginning to factor in the full range of considerations that apply at the urban scale. The potential can be seen in the London Climate Change Mitigation and Adaptation Strategies (GLA 2010a, 2010b), which have benefited from the advisory role of the leading urban climatologist, and co-founder of IAUC, Professor Sue Grimmond

Table 1: Causes of urban warming and examples of mitigation strategies. Grimmond 2007, p. 84

Urban heat island causes	Mitigation strategy
Increased surface area Large vertical faces Reduced sky view factor - Increased absorption of shortwave (solar) radiation - Decreased longwave (terrestrial) radiation loss - Decreased total turbulent heat transport - Reduced wind speeds	High reflection building and road materials, high reflection paints for vehicles Spacing of buildings Variability of building heights
Surface materials *Thermal characteristics* - Higher heat capacities - Higher conductivities - Increased surface heat storage	Reduce surface temperatures (changing albedo and emissivity) Improved roof insulation
Moisture characteristics Urban areas have larger areas that are impervious - Shed water more rapidly – changes the hydrograph - Increased runoff with a more rapid peak - Decreased evapotranspiration (latent heat flux	Porous pavement Neighbourhood detention ponds and wetlands which collect stormwater Increase greenspace fraction Greenroofs, greenwalls
Additional supply of energy – *anthropogenic heat flux* Electricity and combustion of fossil fuels: heating and coolingsystems, machinery, vehicles. 3-D geometry of buildings – canyon geometry	Reduced solar loading internally, reduce need for active cooling (shades on windows, change materials) District heating and cooling systems Combined heat and power systems High reflection paint on vehicles to reduce temperature
Air pollution Human activities lead to ejection of pollutants and dust into the atmosphere - Increased longwave radiation from the sky - Greater absorption and re-emission ('greenhouse effect')	District heating and cooling systems Combined heat and power or cogeneration systems

(see Table 1). Even more significant exemplars are to be found in Germany. Here in the cradle of scientific urban climatology we find several cities which have maintained an active interest in atmospheric investigation for several decades and found means to factor it into design and regulation. The most important of these precedents is the city of Stuttgart.

The example of Stuttgart, Germany

Stuttgart, the state capital of Baden-Württemberg, has a population of about 600,000, in a metropolitan region of some 2.6 million inhabitants. It is an industrial city whose vigorous manufacturing sector includes the Daimler, Porsche and Bosch plants as well as Hewlett-Packard and IBM. The city is located in the steep valley of the Neckar, a landscape characterised by low wind speeds and weak air circulation. Consequently, air quality has been a long-standing concern. The city first established an Agency for Environmental Protection in 1938, including a municipal meteorologist to handle pollution-related aspects of its 1935 Urban Construction Bye-Law.

Climatically-aware design has an even longer history in the city. 'Unhindered access of light and air' was the chief design objective of the first workers suburb, *das Postdörfe* in 1868. The 1901 extension plan for the city included a technical appendix on the natural patterns of wind movement in the city valleys. During the Second World War the *Luftwaffe* exploited Stuttgart's topography, artificially generating fog to obstruct air bombers' view of target factories along the valley floor. A chance side-effect was to reveal longitudinal airflow conditions as the fog dissipated, resulting in the identification of cold air drainage areas

Figure 4: A topographical map of Stuttgart highlights the city's valley setting. Source: Landeshauptstadt Stuttgart

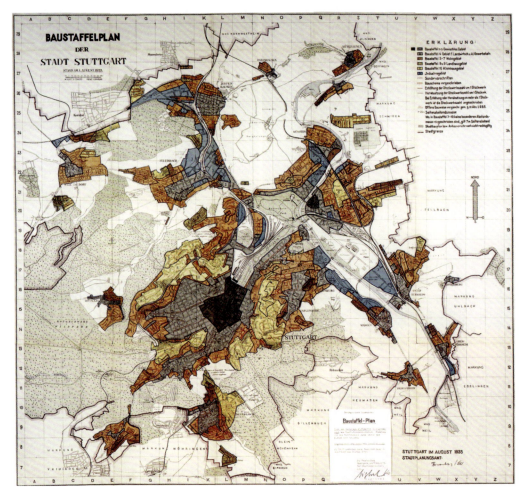

Figure 5: 1935 Urban Construction Bye-Law for the City of Stuttgart. Source: Landeshauptstadt Stuttgart

that came to be labelled as the city's fresh air swathes. The maintenance of these natural ventilators became a critical component of planning policy in Stuttgart, embodied in the city's post-war 1948 *General Binding Site Plan*. In 1953 the city adopted *Regulations for the Implementation of Functions in Climatology*, formalising the policy contribution of scientific evidence on meteorological and noise abatement issues.

With rising affluence and motorisation, air pollution remained prominent as a public health concern in the sixties, causing the city to initiate advanced monitoring systems for atmospheric carbon monoxide, sulphur dioxide, and dust precipitation. Stuttgart was a pioneer in streetside measurement of motor vehicle generated air pollution and thermographical measurement flights over the city. Its fine-grained urban heat island maps, *Data and Statements on Stuttgart's Urban Climate based* on *Infrared-Thermography* (1978) were highly advanced for their time, as was the importance given to environmental management by planners and elected officials within the city. It caused Stuttgart to be profiled in a celebrated documentary film shown by the West German government at the first UN-Habitat conference in Vancouver in 1976,[2] which led in turn to its being featured as an exemplar of Vitruvian understanding of climatic comfort in Anne Whiston Spirn's seminal text of urban environmental management *The Granite Garden* (1984).

Today, the City of Stuttgart's urban climatology and environmental pollution unit of ten scientists remains outstanding in Germany and so the world. Its influence on planning issues extends to the publication of a 'climate atlas' for the wider metropolitan region in which it sits (Ministry of Economy Baden-Württemburg 2008). The Klimaatlas offers a written description of the city climate supported by analysis maps at a 1:20,000 scale, a scale that corresponds to that of the city's land use maps. The analysis maps identify 'climatopes' defined by daily variation in thermal energy, vertical roughness of the land, topographical position, and type of land use. Stuttgart identifies eleven climatopes: water, open land, forest, greenbelt, garden city, city periphery, city, core city, commercial, industry, and railway land. Each has a climatic role with planning implications. The dense climatopes of the city require mitigation, the leafy canopy areas of the forest climatope require protection, and spatial planning can help these complementary zones work as a single climatic system.

The Klimaatlas is intended as a knowledge transfer mechanism, bridging the elusive gap between urban climatology and public policy. Climatope analysis provides the basis for spatial planning recommendations. With pixels of up to 100 metres, the planning maps are not detailed enough to apply to the individual lot level, but they provide neighbourhood-level

guidance, and a basis for localised micro-climatic appraisal where necessary. The thrust of the policy is to protect vegetation and green spaces for their positive influence on the micro-climate, especially larger, connected green spaces; discourage development on valley sites with potential to hinder regional winds or disrupt local air circulation during weak wind conditions; protect the cold and fresh-air transport function of hillsides near built-up areas; conserve saddle-like topographies on lee slopes that act as air induction corridors; employ linear greenspaces as ventilation passages and induction corridors to support air exchange; prevent long-term convergence of built-up neighbourhoods, ensuring that urban extensions include nearby landscapes for fresh and cold air production, and ventilation corridors for distribution; and the siting of industrial and commercial enterprises in relation to local wind patterns (Ministry of Economy Baden-Württemberg 2008, p. 5.6):

Taken together these principles aim to make the urban environment more comfortable and liveable for residents. To help identify sensitive zones the maps differentiate broadly between open sites and settled areas, showing climatic sensitivity in relation to development. Open sites are classified by level of climatic activity: significant (high climatic sensitivity to a change in land use), less significant (low climatic sensitivity to a change in land use), or low (relatively no climatic sensitivity to a change in land use). Settled areas are commonly divided into four categories: those with small functions of relevance to climate, functions of relevance to climate, significant function of relevance to climate, and areas disadvantaged and in need of renewal to improve the urban climate. The maps also highlight streets with a traffic count of more than 15,000 vehicles per day, for which pollution forecasts should be undertaken for adjacent developments.

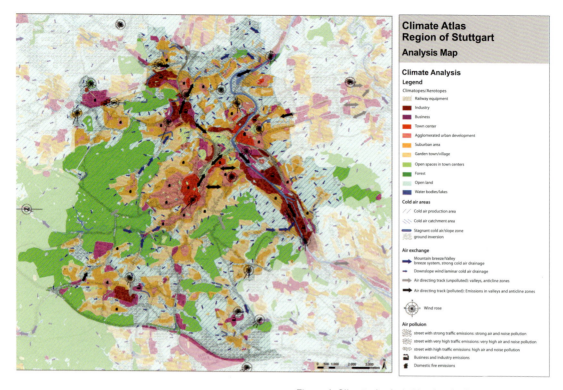

Figure 6: Climate Analysis Map for the Region of Stuttgart.
Source: Verband Region Stuttgart (Klimaatlas Region Stuttgart, Ed.: Verband Region Stuttgart 2008)

Alongside the *Klimaatlas* the city's *Climate Booklet for Urban Development* offers detailed analysis of the climatic system with management recommendations based on the following principles of climate sensitive planning (Ministry of Economy Baden-Württemberg 2008, p. 6.0):

• Improvement of living conditions relative to climate comfort / bioclimate
• Improvement in ventilation of developments
• Support of fresh-air provision through local wind systems
• Reducing the release of air pollutants and greenhouse gases
• Reporting and proper evaluation of current or expected pollution
• Proper reaction to pollution situations by adjusting land use concepts

To achieve these liveability goals the climate booklet provides planning advice on four key themes: preservation and acquisition of green space; securing the local air exchange; air pollution control; and the use of urban climate studies to inform decisions. (Ministry of Economy Baden-Württemberg 2008, pp. 6.1 – 6.4)

Practical application of these principles translates into regulatory requirements for façade greening of buildings (including suggested criteria for the selection of plants) and the role of green roofs for the preservation and acquisition of green space. Local air exchange is promoted by guidelines on the optimal arrangement of buildings including restraints upon excessive height, green corridors that

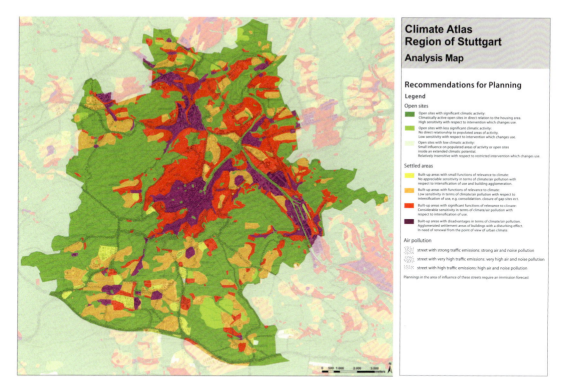

Figure 7: Planning Recommendation Map for the Region of Stuttgart.
Source: Verband Region Stuttgart (Klimaatlas Region Stuttgart, Ed.: Verband Region Stuttgart 2008)

act as ventilation zones, and the alignment of parks and streets to take advantage of airflows. Industrial and commercial development is tightly regulated to control air pollution and recommendations made for home heating systems. Measures to mitigate the harmful effects of highway pollution on residents include traffic calming schemes, the separation of intensive traffic uses from residential and recreation zones, noise protection barriers and dense plantings to mitigate exhaust pollution, and guidelines for street trees, broadly planted to allow for air flow (Ministry of Economy Baden-Württemberg 2008, pp. 6.1 – 6.4).

Stuttgart's long and consistent attention to climatic factors takes on a new relevance in the era of global climate change. Climate projections for the Baden-Württemberg region in 2050 show an increase in temperature of 2° Celsius in winter and 1.5 °C in summer, along with a 30% increase in the number of days with temperatures exceeding 25 °C and a doubling of days exceeding 30 °C. Further climate concerns related to precipitation are expected with reductions in rainfall by 10% in the summer and increases of up to 35% in winter. Thus long-standing efforts by the urban climatology and city planning departments to mitigate temperature extremes and manage climatic conditions will become all the more important in the future (Stuttgart 2010). The city already demonstrates the

Figure 8: A protected fresh air corridor in the City of Stuttgart. Source: Authors

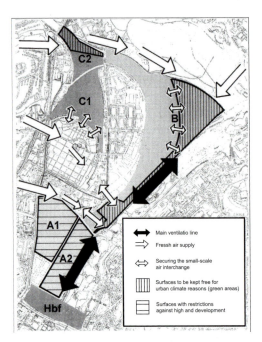

Figure 9: An example of the incorporation of climate conditions into detailed planning. Source: Amt für Umweltschutz der Landeshauptstadt Stuttgart

political will and ability to use its mechanisms of building control and green-space protection to maintain fresh air corridors, drainage lands and natural air filtration sources. It has the technical capacity to promote low carbon development through passive design, using building orientation, shading and sunlight. Its monitoring and regulatory systems are already up and running. Stuttgart has the institutional capacity other cities crave.

Learning from Stuttgart

The techniques developed in Stuttgart over decades have clear potential for application elsewhere. There is particular interest in the Klimaatlas or urban climatic map, as a means of making the connections between urban micro-climate, development and liveability. Already in 1993 the technique was adopted as a good-practice blueprint by the German Institute of Engineers under National Guideline VDI-3787 *Environmental Meteorology Climate and Air Pollution Maps for Cities and Regions*. A recent review by Ren, Ng, and Katzschner in the *International Journal of Climatology* finds worldwide applications, especially in European countries that suffered the effects of severe heat waves in 2003 and 2006, and Pacific Rim cities responding to the impact of the highly infectious SARS virus within dense, unventilated urban environments (Ren et al. 2010). The virtue of the technique is its combination of urban climatic analysis with planning recommendations. Ren, Ng and Katzschner show how the spatial medium of cartography supported by geographical information systems facilitates the integration of three broad categories of data: analytical maps of climatic elements such as air temperature, atmospheric humidity, wind velocity and direction, precipitation, fog and mist, and air pollution; geographic terrain information derived from topographic, slope/valley, and soil type maps; and a third layer of data on land use, landscape, and buildings, with associated planning parameters. This information is translated into the urban climatic analysis map where it can be interpreted into spatially specific recommen-dations - proactive, to improve and maintain desired micro-climates, and reactive, to deal with undesirable consequences of develop-ment. The methodology addresses precisely the urban-scale climatic issues that disaster managers and low energy designers tend to miss: how to reduce urban thermal loads; how to optimise existing urban ventilation paths and chart new air paths where needed; how to protect cold air production and drainage areas in the peri-urban landscape; and how to harness topography, land-sea breezes and the internal thermal circulation of the urban heat island. (Ren et al. 2010)

Equally, the *Klimaatlas* may provide a basis for distinguishing modes of planning response at the different spatial scales of building materials and surfaces; landscape and land use; building design and form; and zoning and urban morphology. Material and surface level interventions can be implemented through the use of building materials and pavements that are less energy absorbent, materials designed to cool roofs and building facades, porous pav-ing and the planting of greenery. At the land-scape/land use planning-level, interventions can be implemented through the creation of parks, open spaces, and green corridors that promote increased vegetation and cooler micro-climates and improved wind patterns, while street trees can be used to reduce air

Figure 10: Green roofs are a key component for mitigation of the urban heat island effect in city centres
Source: Authors

pollutants and reduce the temperature in the surrounding area. Building design-level interventions include stronger control over thermal exposure, better out-door provision for human shelter from sun and wind, and closer consideration of building heights in relation to street width. Urban planning/zoning-level interventions predominantly influence ventilation within the city through the provision of space for air paths, the proper division of land parcels, and the alignment of building lots and roads. Street orientation may also play an important role, depending on geographic location of the city in question.

The key benefit, and challenge, of urban climate mapping lies in the ability to translate complicated climate data into a spatial pattern that is comprehensible to non-experts and sufficiently robust to provide a basis for decision-making. It depends upon cross-disciplinary cooperation between urban climatologists and planners. Stuttgart was fortunate in having a well-established link between a municipal urban climatology unit and the municipal planning function. Few other cities have an in-house climatology team, or the support of a local public weather service; most rely on the more sporadic inputs of external partners, whether universities, research institutes or commercial consultants. Stuttgart and other German cities are also distinctive in the degree of public acceptance of restraint on private property for environmental purposes: the political culture recognizes the value of the urban climate as a public good, which is rare. Nevertheless, high-quality evidence can shift the boundaries of political possibility. For example, climate mapping has been successfully deployed by campaigners for public health and environmental justice in Hong Kong to demonstrate the harm caused to street-level ventilation by hyper-dense development. By linking three dimensional analysis of air movements, humidity and thermal loads to planning factors, the Hong Kong Urban Climatic Analysis Map has put outdoor micro-climates

onto the political agenda, causing planning codes to be revised and building volume to be restricted in areas of high climatic stress (Ng 2010; 2011). Despite the obvious differences between the two cities, Hong Kong has learned lessons from Stuttgart on why and how to make connections between urban climatology, planning and liveability.

Conclusions

The configuration of a city's built and natural environments is a significant factor for carbon mitigation as well as for local adaptation to global warming's weather consequences. Ultimately urban weather cannot be modelled without detailed understanding of the urban landscape, and cities cannot plan for climate change without knowledge of atmospheric hazards and potentials. The need to resolve particular environmental issues in Stuttgart resulted in systematic application of urban climatological principles to exploit feedback effects in the built form and urban landscape. Technical capacity was developed over a span of decades and science-into-action mechanisms developed by trial and error. The *Klimaatlas* proved its worth and this prototype urban climatic map has become widely imitated as cities around the world wake up to the importance of climate management in the 21st century context of global climate change.

The Stuttgart team make a very revealing comment in their 2010 report *Climate change - challenge facing urban climatology.* They observe that urban climatology and global climate adaptation/mitigation might seem like two sides of the same coin:

To the untrained observer, this combination of tasks might appear perfectly natural as a matter of course. However, in reality these two fields of activity involve completely different angles of approach which occasionally give rise to the need to draw attention to the differences between urban climatology and climate protection. It is the vast distinction in terms of scale - between regional and micro-climate on the one hand, and the global climate on the other - which clearly illustrates the difference between proactively protecting the climate along the lines of "think globally, act locally" and - as applied to urban climatology - making use of local climatic features to improve living conditions in the built-up urban landscape. (Stuttgart 2010, p. 13)

So we can take a double lesson from this case study. First it demonstrates the powerful contribution of micro-climatic observation and mapping, as in the *Klimaatlas*, towards urban strategy for carbon mitigation and climate change adaptation. And secondly it shows that climate-awareness is not just about GHG emissions and their disastrous consequences for the stratosphere. The scale of anthro-pogenic climate change which most affects liveability is closer to hand within the physical configuration of the built-up urban landscape, that is to say, the realm of city planning.

Acknowledgement

This chapter was researched at the University of Manchester UK, as an output of the ESRC Research Project *Climate Science and Urban Design - a Historical and Comparative Study* RES-062-23-2134. We gratefully acknowledge, with the usual disclaimers, the support of the Council and the help and guidance of Dr Ulrich Reuter, City of Stuttgart, the Amt für Umwelt-schutz der Landeshauptstadt Stuttgart, and Dr Vladimir Jankovic, Centre for the History of Science, Technology and Medicine, University of Manchester.

Endnotes

1. For more details on the IAUC, see www.urban-climate.org and http://urban-climate.com/wp3/newsletter for their quarterly Urban Climate News newsletter

2. The Stuttgart documentary film 'Urban Climate and Development' is available for viewing online at http://www.sed.manchester.ac.uk/architecture/research/csud/workshop/media

References

Bitan A ed (1984) *Applied Climatology and its Contribution to Planning and Building* Lausanne: Elsevier Sequoia

Bosselmann P (1998) *Representation of Places: reality and realism in city design* Berkeley: University

Chandler T J (1976) *Urban Climatology and its Relevance to Urban Design* WMO Technical Paper 149 Geneva: World Meteorological Organisation

Doucet C (2007) *Urban Meltdown: Cities Climate Change and Politics as Usual* Gabriola Island BC: New Society Publishers

Erell E, Pearlmutter D and Williamson T (2011) *Urban Microclimate: designing the spaces between buildings* London: Earthscan

Givoni B (1998) *Man Climate and Architecture* Amsterdam: Elsevier

GLA (2010a) *The Mayor's Climate Change Mitigation & Energy Strategy* London: Greater London Authority

GLA (2010b) *The Mayor's Climate Change Adaptation Strategy* London: Greater London Authority

Grimmond S (2007) "Urbanization and global environmental change: local effects of urban warming", *Geographical Journal,* 173, 83-88.

Hebbert M (2011) 'Vitruvian Revival Now !' *Urban Design* 117, 33-35

Hebbert M & MacKillop F (2011) 'Urban Climatology Applied to Urban Planning - a knowledge circulation failure' [pre-submission manuscript of contribution to *International Journal of Urban & Regional Research symposium* 'Planning Histories and Practices of Circulating Urban Knowledge', accessible at http://www.sed.manchester.ac.uk/architecture/research/csud/workingpapers/VJmodellingoct2010.pdf

Kratzer, A (1937, 1956) *Das Stadtklima* Braunschweig: Verlag Vieweg

Landsberg, H. (1981) *The Urban Climate,* New York and London: Academic Press

Matzarakis A, Mayer H, Iziomon M G (1999) 'Applications of a universal thermal index: physiological equivalent temperature' *International Journal of Biometeorology* 43,2,76-84

Ministry of Economy Baden-Württemburg (2008) *Climate Booklet for Urban Development Online* http://www.staedtebauliche-klimafibel.de/Climate_Booklet/index-1.htm

Ng E (2011) 'Application of Urban Climatic Map to Urban Planning of High Density Cities – An Experience from Hong Kong', accessible at http://www.sed.manchester.ac.uk/architecture/research/csud/workshop/programme/Ng_HongKongClimMaps.pdf

Ng, E. (2010) 'Towards a Planning and Practical Understanding for the Need of Meteorological and Climatic Information for the Design of High Density Cities – a case based study of Hong Kong' *International Journal of Climatology* DOI: 10.1002/joc.2292

Oke T (1976) "The distinction between canopy and urban boundary-layer heat islands", *Atmosphere*, 14, 268-277.

Oke T (1988) "Street design and urban layer climate", *Energy and Buildings*, 11, pp. 103–113.

Ren C, Ng E, and Katzschner L. (2010) "Urban climatic map studies: a review" *International Journal of Climatology*, 31, doi: 10.1002/joc.2237

Rosenzweig C, Solecki W D, Hammer S A, Mehrotra S eds (2011) *Climate Change and Cities* (First Assessment Report of the Urban Climate Change Research Network) Cambridge: Cambridge University Press

Schiller S de, et al. (2006) 'Sustainable Urban Form: Environment and Climate Responsive Design' ch 10 pp. 163-178 in Zetter R, and Butina Watson G eds *Designing Sustainable Cities in the Developing World* Aldershot: Ashgate

Stuttgart (2010) *Climate Change - challenge facing urban climatology* (Schriftenreihe des Amtes für Umweltschutz - Heft 3/2010) "http://www.stadtklima-stuttgart.de/index.php?klima_klimawandel_heft-3-2010" www.stadtklima-stuttgart.de/index.php?klima_klimawandel_heft-3-2010 Stuttgart: Landeshaupstadt Stuttgart, Referat Städtebau und Umwelt

UN-Habitat (2011) *Cities and Climate Change* (United Nations Human Settlements Programme Global Report on Human Settlements 2011) London: Earthscan

Verband Region Stuttgart (2008) *Klimaatlas Region Stuttgart Stuttgart:* Verband Region Stuttgart

Bernd Scholl

Strategies for Integrated Spatial Development along the European North-South Railway Link

Bernd Scholl

Bernd Scholl

On Spatial Strategies – Preliminary Remarks

Realising a national and continental high-quality transport infrastructure needs a clear strategy. Spatial and transport development are two sides of the same coin. This holds even more for rail transport, which fits extraordinarily well with the basic spatial planning strategy of 'redevelopment before new development' and includes brownfield development before greenfield development. An attractive, well-connected public rail transport system is the backbone of any settlement development in which the development and transformation of the building stock has priority over the further consumption of valuable cultural landscapes.

This will also help to achieve more liveable cities. Well-developed public transport on all levels is a fundamental precondition for this. The integrated development of public transport, the transformation of the building stock and the development of existing reserves are challenging tasks that cannot be solved with the usual instruments and processes of simply expanding settlement areas. This is where strategies come into play.

Strategies are guidelines for the implementation of an integrated spatial solution that, once approved, may take many years or even decades to realise. An overview and focal points are necessary elements of a nascent strategy, and problems, understood here as difficult unsolved tasks, are the central starting point. Difficult situations can be identified by the fact that the unforeseeable must be part of the calculations.

Policies are concerned with the details of an operation, while strategies bring more flexibility into constantly changing situations and take existing uncertainties into consideration.

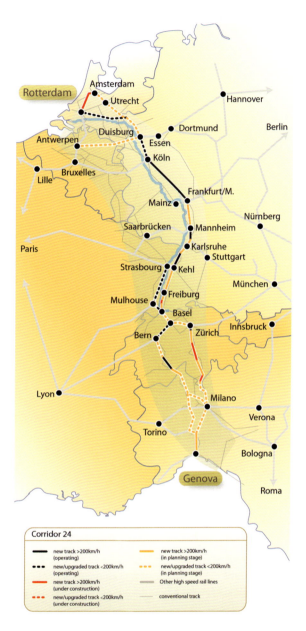

Figure 1: The North-South Railway Link

The approach to limited means and resources, along with risks and surprises, plays a central role. Strategies always contain deliberations on the use of restricted resources: time, financing and qualified specialists. The use of strategies recognises that even with the best planning, reality can never be completely controlled. Thus, the availability of reserves is a central precondition for being able to solve difficult tasks.

In order to be able to develop strategies at all, clear periodic evaluations of the situation are needed. These call for the creation and evaluation of important overviews, a clear appreciation of the central tasks, examination of the results and, finally, concentration on the essentials needed for the next period. Site evaluations lead to decisions on the use of resources and limited resources force a concentration on the essentials. A strategy helps to differentiate the essential from the unessential. Strategic thinking is not a new planning theory; it is an expansion of the approaches already available.

Such strategies are missing in important national and European plans for spatial and infrastructure development. Therefore, the necessary and systematic approach to risks does not take place, even less than the necessary concentration on spatial and resource figures. It is obvious that this increases the danger of getting bogged down and promotes the tendency to 'muddle through' (Lindblom, 1959). This is the antithesis of sustainable spatial and transport development and ultimately weakens those affected by the economically advantaged countries of Europe and creates undesirable effects for spatial and transport development.

In a report (Hesse et al., 2010) on the development of large-scale transport infrastructure initiated by the German Academy for Spatial Research and Planning, it is stated:

> "The Working Committee has... established that in the area of large-scale transport development such a strategy is missing or the strategies available show considerable

deficits. Achieving planning security as a result of a successful strategy is something that cannot be too highly valued by the acting and decision-making actors. A strategy for large-scale transport must also consider that investments in transport are spatially relevant and, in the sense of a sustainable solution for space and environment, thus must be integrated solutions for the entire living space. On the one hand, this certainly increases the effort needed for coordination, cooperation and communication in the run-up to physical and operational measures, while on the other hand, it provides the opportunity for a uniform, implementable solution through related endeavours".

The Working Committee strongly advocated taking an integrated approach to future spatial and transport development, one that is based on the large-scale spatial and transport strategies that have been developed and, of course, based on the decisions taken on the use of the resources of space, time and investment.

Using the example of the North-South Link Rotterdam–Genoa, the main artery of the European railway network, questions concerning the lack of a strategy will be pursued. The starting hypothesis is that at the national and European levels there are no strategies for the realisation of this large project. Fundamental questions of sustainable development for the most important European North-South Railway Link, with a catchment area of 70 million people, are focused upon this corridor. If we can't manage to provide a high-quality transport infrastructure at the right time, the competitiveness of the participating countries and of Europe will suffer and this will create undesirable, partially irreversible effects in the area of spatial and transport development.

Bernd Scholl

The European North-South Railway Link – Main Artery of the Railway Network

The European North-South Railway Link from Rotterdam to Genoa is one of the most important railway connections in Europe.

The 1200 km transport route has grown up over centuries and today connects the largest North Sea ports of the Netherlands and Belgium with Germany, Switzerland, northern Italy and the Mediterranean. The main goal of the Railway Link is to attract cross-border railway transport and to transfer trans-alpine goods traffic from road to rail. The core of this system is the level railway links through the Alpine Base Tunnels, which will increase train speed and volume.

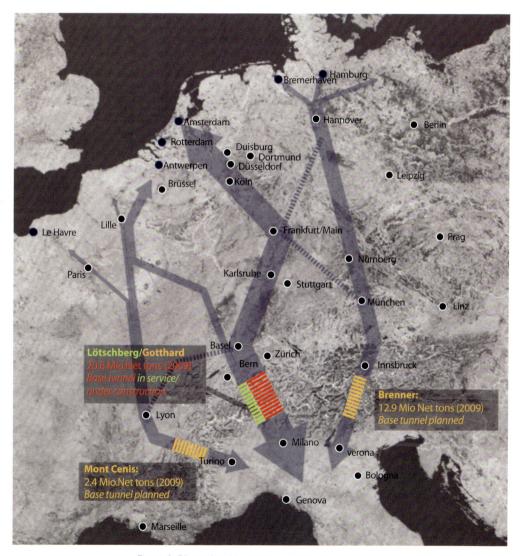

Figure 2: Planned and in-progress Alpine Base Tunnels. Source: IRL, ETH Zurich 2006

Major investments in railway-related infrastructures of more than 40 billion euros will be undertaken along this axis. In Switzerland alone, the construction of two new tunnel routes will require investments of about 15 billion euros (including noise protection).

The opening of the first Alpine Base Tunnel, Lötschberg, in 2007 and the planned opening of the Gotthard in 2016/17 constitutes a quantum leap in railway development, and not only in the alpine area. Tunnel construction, including its approach routes, should bring with it favourable connections for cross-border goods and passenger transport in the central European North-South Corridor.[1]

Two additional tunnels in the alpine EU area, namely, the Brenner Base Tunnel and the Mont Cenis Base Tunnel in France, are also planned as a component of the Trans-European Transport Network (TEN). The Mont Cenis Tunnel between Lyon and Turin is still in the planning stages and construction of the approximately 50 km Brenner Base Tunnel started in early 2011, according to the plans of the Brenner Construction Consortium[2] (see Figure 2).

Figure 3: Breakthrough in the Gotthard
Tunnel on 15th October 2010
The longest tunnel in the world
Source: Alptransit

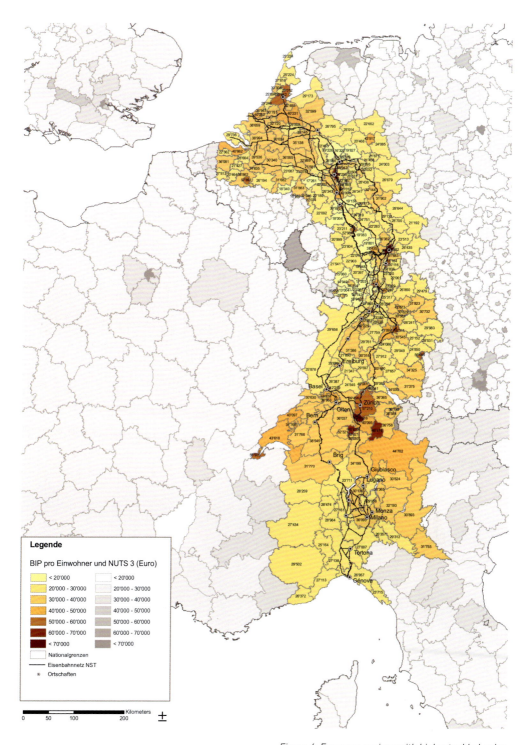

Figure 4: European regions with highest added-value

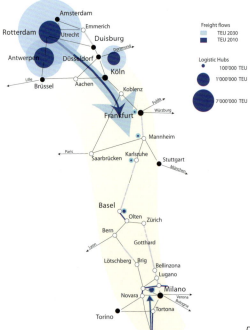

Figure 5: Port development to 2030

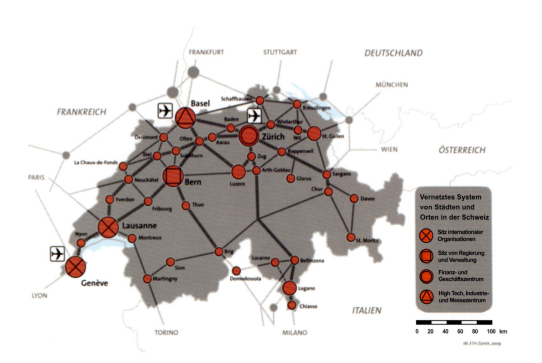

Figure 6: Swiss network of cities and locations.

The North-South Link runs through European regions with a high added-value rate, a strong transport tax revenue on a major rail and road network and a high settlement density (see Figure 4). Nearly 70 million people, approximately one fifth of the expanded EU of 2004, live within its catchment area and annually 700 million tons of freight move from the northern ports to its hinterlands and south through the Alps, which is over 50% of the total freight travelling north-south across Europe.

A further increase in the demand for transport over the North-South Link is expected by 2030. However, since the ports in northern Europe, mainly Rotterdam, are investing massively in the construction of infrastructure, it will be increasingly difficult to transfer traffic to the hinterlands. Traffic congestion in the areas around the ports and their surroundings is already a daily matter. It's now a necessity to transfer a portion of the hinterlands transport onto water routes (Rhine) and, in particular, to upgrade the railway system (see Figure 5).

As mentioned, the investment for the railway-related infrastructure of the entire North-South Link requires major resources, the approximately 40 billion euros mentioned above. These resources are not available in the individual countries or in the EU budget. It is becoming apparent that countless bottlenecks will exist because not enough capacity will be available for all the desired rail transport. There is a risk that regional transport, important for public transportation, will be displaced through increasing goods transport. Without an attractive public passenger service, the desired goal of settlement development as redevelopment will be endangered.

Switzerland is a good example of the use of a strategy in its network of cities and places (see Figure 6). The decentralised pattern of settlement in the country, a reflection of its

federal structure, demands an efficient public transport system, mainly in the area of rail transport. This is the strategic backbone of its spatial development, because through its secure, efficient and well-conducted operation, mobility is ensured for the highly specialised workplaces in Switzerland and bordering countries now and in future. Prosperity and competitiveness are closely related to this transportation system, even when its contribution to the total transport performance is "only" about 20% of total passenger km travelled. Scope for mobility on the rails is a contribution to the social stability of the nation[3] (Scholl, 2007) and its historic spatial paradigm. Thus, social networks can be maintained even with a change of workplace. Problems of excessive concentration of population in less densely settled centres could also be avoided, as with the problem of the depopulation of peripheral areas.

The further development of the railway network is not about the construction of new lines, but more about sufficient and reliable capacities of the main routes. For this reason, Switzerland has invested heavily in this infrastructure. At present, this is about two billion CHF per year, almost as much as Germany, which is ten times larger, has invested in the total railway sector. Switzerland is also facing diminishing resources, which is why clear priorities must be set. Securing the quality of the stock and its robustness as well as a measured increase in service capability must therefore have priority over an increase in speed (i.e. building new routes).

Strategies for Integrated Spatial Development
The CODE 24 Initiative

The example of the North-South Railway Link clearly illustrates that there are many questions still unresolved about the realisation of this strategic trans-European connection. If this railway connection cannot be realised and sufficient capacity does not become available, there is the danger that the quality of the development in some of the most intensive wealth-creating areas of Europe will deteriorate significantly. Increasing upheaval in operations and exceeding capacity in some systems are to be expected, which could cause increased delays and operational breakdowns, especially of the regional and long-distance public transport system. A shift of the traffic load to the road system would be the result, along with increasing traffic congestion because it would not be possible to create sufficient capacity within an appropriate timeframe. As a result, the additional costs would have negative consequences for the economic areas affected, which in turn could lead to a reduction in financial resources for the less prosperous areas of Europe, not to mention the ecological effects and consequences. Moreover, capacity bottlenecks and pressure from the regional commuter network serving the major cities could work against the brownfield areas intended for mixed-use redevelopment, mainly in the catchment area for public transport.

The following hypotheses sum up the starting position:

• Europe must invest heavily, mainly in rail infrastructure and multi-modal transfer facilities if the continent wants to remain globally competitive.
• There are not sufficient resources available over the next three decades to finance all the desired projects.
• For an economical approach to the use of land and an efficient approach to mobility, settlement development needs to be oriented towards the catchment areas of the infrastructure of the public transport system.

Figure 7: Web site of CODE24

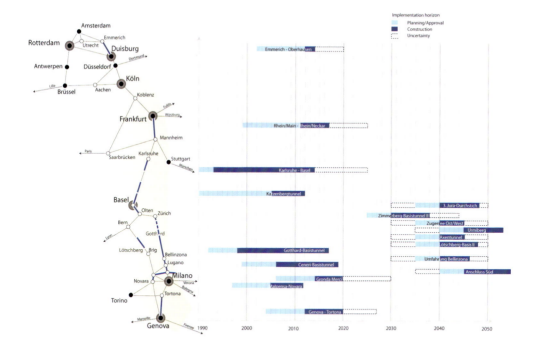

Figure 8: Overview of bottlenecks on the North-South Railway Link as of May 2011
Source: ETH Zurich, IRL 2011

- Goods transport must be transacted in an efficient and environmentally friendly manner. As much as possible, it should be transferred to the rail system.
- There is consensus among experts about the need for development and its broad application. However, the politicians and the population, especially in the catchment areas of the corridor, must be much more keenly aware of the conflicts and unresolved questions related to the different projects.

Without a special initiative, a final danger exists that liveability in the cities in the approach area to the North-South Link will deteriorate.

This situation brought about the idea of increasing national and international

awareness, especially on the political level, through an EU project. After several years of preparation, a EU Interreg Project was launched. It received the name CODE24[4] (corridor development of Route 24) after the corridor of the trans-European network. The EU office that approved the plan recognised its significance and designated the project as strategically important.

Over twenty partners are involved in the initiative. Some of these are the planning regions and chambers of commerce of the participating countries, the ports of Rotterdam and Genoa and numerous universities. Switzerland was represented by the ETH Zurich Chair for Spatial Development and is supported by the Federal Office of Spatial Development and the cantons adjacent to the

Gotthard tunnel axis, the so-called Gotthard Committee. The German Rhein-Neckar Regional Association is at the forefront.

The challenges of the North-South Link should be approached under four project headings, namely, spatial and infrastructure development, environment and noise, increasing regional economic benefits and communication.

The project was begun in early 2010 and should be completed by the end of 2013. For the first time, a planning information system for the entire corridor will be established. A comprehensive overview of important information on the individual plans, the status of the work and important open questions that comprise general public concerns will be produced. The participating actors should be able to update the overview locally.

The first overviews put together from multiple regional workshops show that numerous bottlenecks are likely to exist along the North link in the next ten to twenty years (and after the opening of the Gotthard Base Tunnel). The task, done as part of CODE24, will be to show selected hot spots as well as what integrated solutions for the spatial development of these bottlenecks might look like. Of course, a delay is possible, but a rapid implementation is also conceivable.

Integrated Spatial and Railway Development: Three Case Studies

Some of the hot spots have potential for the development of integrated solutions for spatial and transport development. Hot spots are designated areas in the corridor where problems are already visible and where

comprehensive solutions for the functioning of the North-South Link are needed. Three hot spots are discussed here: the Canton of Uri, the Canton of Schwyz and the European Quarter of Frankfurt am Main. The case studies used the test planning method, which will be explained later on in this article, and demonstrate how it can be applied to resolve difficult problems and tasks.

Canton Uri: test planning process for the Lower Reuss Valley

The North-South Link runs through the main residential area of the Canton of Uri, which has nearly forty thousand residents. One of the central questions is the future location of the routes for the North-South Railway Link in the Lower Reuss section, which is also the site of the tunnel entrance to the Gotthard Base Tunnel.

One of the consequences of the extensive planning time needed for the NEAT (Neue Eisenbahn-Alpentransversale), as the Swiss part of the North-South Link is called, was that the dispute brought a great deal of uncertainty, which then blocked many other necessary planning processes.

The clarification of the NEAT routes and of the wider advantages that they offered cleared the way for other problems concerning the valley (flood protection, avoiding sprawl, optimising roads for through-traffic) to be addressed. The knowledge of a possible counterpoint to the usual Swiss stagnating economy, unfavourable population development, increases in the tax burden and other problems, slowly penetrated the local awareness. This produced a rethink, acknowledging that other problems were also pending and needed a rapid integrated solution and that the canton did not want to continue to fall behind. The flooding of August 2005 brought home the realisation that everyone was in the same situation,

Figure 9: Area of the test planning procedure: spatial development for the Lower Reuss Valley, viewed from North

Figure 10: Area for the test planning procedure: spatial development for the Lower Reuss Valley, viewed from the South

the population as well as the communities, and that the problems could only be solved together.

The Lower Reuss Valley is the lifeblood of the canton. Over 80% of the population live and work in this area. In this narrow valley, various infrastructures of European, national and regional importance are also concentrated. These infrastructure systems are a boon, but, as with emissions, they are also a burden.

At the beginning of 2006, the cantonal government initiated a test planning process for the Lower Reuss Valley. The test planning process envisaged the role of the Reuss Valley as part of the North-South Link and considered solutions that allowed integration with more local issues, such as the future settlement development of each city and village.

Together with natural processes, such as the flooding of the Reuss and Schächen rivers, this narrow alpine valley space yielded some especially demanding tasks for spatial development.

The central task of the process was to investigate, without bias, the short-, middle- and long-term perspectives of spatial development for the Lower Reuss Valley, identify the scope for development opportunities, namely, areas of settlement, landscape and infrastructure, and develop suggestions for their protection within the framework of the regional Planning Guide.

Important recommendations of the evaluation committee concerned, for example:

- The decision for the site of the cantonal train station in Altdorf
- Cross-border clarifications in connection with the renovation of the existing axis tunnel

- The development of an overall concept for the road network
- Landscape development for the valley floor
- Community cross-border settlement development and the resulting consequences for cooperation.

The results were published in 2007[5] and discussed with the representatives of the Community Council of the Lower Reuss Valley. In a closing consolidation phase, particularly difficult questions were more closely examined and presented in an integrated report.

In the follow-up, the cantonal government took up the recommendations and in 2008 set the specifications for updating the cantonal guidelines. This allowed, for example, the development of focal points in the towns of Flüelen and Altdorf to be established. These also form the basis for the continuing processes and projects.

Canton of Schwyz: test planning process in the Felderboden/Urmiberg axis

The development of the Urmiberg axis is of strategic importance for the settlement and economic development of the Rigi-Mythen region and the Canton of Schwyz as a whole. Infrastructures of national and European importance run through this main alpine settlement area. In a test planning process in 2002/03, the canton reorganised the transport infrastructure. In particular, a solution was found for the approach to the new axis tunnel: a junction from the main trunk line that can be implemented gradually, and combined with future changes to the railway and automobile network to save space. These are now basic conditions for any further ideas for the development of this area.

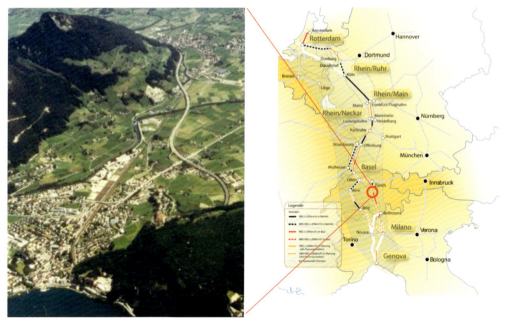

Figure 11: Felderboden/Urmiberg axis,
Canton Schwyz

Figure 12: Coordinated infrastructure development Felderboden,
Canton Schwyz

Among the development areas of the Urmiberg axis is a large contiguous plot of land with above average individual plot sizes. The development of this area can be pursued within the spatial planning principle of redevelopment before new development because the area lies close to the centre and already has a relatively favourable position to the local public infrastructure system. An area of ca. 25 hectares is available within the perimeter of the contiguous premises that would allow the step-by-step realisation of ca. 100,000–150,000 m² cross-floor area in the Brunnen Nord area alone. An important consideration is that in the surroundings of the Urmiberg axis, and dependent on it, investment in the order of more than 2.5 billion euros (at June 2011) will be transacted in the next ten to twenty years. Parts of this will be the realisation of the Morschacher Tunnel, the renovation of the existing highway network and the gradual implementation of the NEAT.

The area lies on the main artery of the north-south transport routes, which provide easy access and will give impetus to the marketing of the area. Good transport connections are an indispensable precondition and help develop liveable alpine communities in the area. The realisation of the NEAT approach routes in the Canton of Schwyz with a connecting junction in Felderboden opens the way to relieving the SBB main lines of goods transport. The test plan results recommended pursuing this plan in order to achieve the earliest possible realisation. This must be considered in the context that a high-capacity connection in the direct approach to the Gotthard Base Tunnel is of extraordinary importance for a robust and secure operation of the entire north-south rail connection. It should be noted that work begins at the earliest in 2016, but might only start after 2030.

The evaluation committee recommended concentrating future settlement development around the two poles of the Urmiberg axis, Seewen in the north and Brunnen in the south, to create a green space in the middle, free from further construction and outside of the already zoned and built areas.. Keeping landscape space away from construction also puts the settlement poles in a better marketing position. The basic thinking behind the concentration of future settlement development corresponds to the general principle of 'redevelopment before new development'.

European Quarter of Frankfurt am Main – Consilium

The focus now moves to an urban area in Germany. Here a disused interchange/terminus station in the heart of the Rhine-Main region presented a special opportunity for the urban development of the city of Frankfurt, an economic motor of the region. This case study of a large German city illustrates the interconnections between the railway and settlement development in the direction of a more liveable city.

Frankfurt is a central node in the national and European railway networks and lies on the North-South Railway Link. Alongside a reliable regional public transport system to connect the cities of the metropolitan areas of the Rhine-Main region, a functioning long-distance public transport system, as part of the German city network, is essential for a liveable future city development. This section shows that Frankfurt-Mannheim is a strategically important bottleneck that can be a problem for rail transport moving in the direction Basel-Gotthard, as well as Munich/Brenner. Limitations in the development especially of the regional public transport could be the result. At the same time, there is great potential for redevelopment in the land area that still exists in the Rhine-Main area. These are of great importance for future development because few greenfields are available for settlement in this area. The inner city reserves of building stock have strategic importance for the city's development and the European Quarter is a model example. Its development began in the early 1990s. After more than 10 years of planning with many ups and downs, the breakthrough began with the formation of the so-called Consilium in 2001.

Following an initiative by the landowners of the 'Europaviertel[6]' (Vivico Real Estate and Aurelis), a so-called Consilium was founded. Members of this Consilium were private companies, the landowners and representatives of city, regional and state administrations. The Consilium was designed as a special ad hoc organisation based on the principles of action planning. Important preparations were made by a private planning office, which was also responsible for the preparation, organisational execution and realisation of the recommendations of the Consilium and support for planning teams. The Consilium met regularly every three months to discuss all the important issues in direct dialogue. At first, the process was planned for one year. It was then extended for a second year at the request of the members in order to achieve a breakthrough in resolving the problems which loomed at strategic points.

As a result of these preparations, the decision-makers in the private companies and the city administration formed a task force that focused on the infrastructure that needed private investors. In 2004, an agreement was reached. In this phase of the process, the organisational structure and the integration of the top decision-makers was still very difficult but, in the meantime, essential. In tandem with the task force, the decision-makers also met every three months to prepare and comply with the necessary agreements.

Figure 13: Frankfurt redevelopment of the old railway freight terminal (ca. 100 ha)

Figure 14: View of the European Quarter of Frankfurt

Figure 15: Hall No. 11 and entrance building of the Frankfurt Fair. Source: Author 2010

and buildings by 2020. The entrance building with Hall No. 11 was completed in 2010. The grounds to the west of the Fair give a completely new and impressive face to urban design.

The overall estimated investment for the project ranges from 4 to 5 billion euros. This makes the European Quarter one of the most important urban development projects in Germany.

Meanwhile, the first part of the railway tracks west of the Emser Bridge were removed and the Fair was able to buy 10 hectares of the area for an extension. The first elements of the traffic infrastructure were constructed. At the same time, the formal planning was done. At the end of 2004, the chief mayor of Frankfurt assigned a project team within the city administration to the realisation process. It works comprehensively with all departments.

The development of this area also follows the strategy of 'redevelopment before new development', which includes the principle of the sustainable use of land resources. Redevelopment of cities improves the quality of existing infrastructures and creates an appropriate living environment. The renaissance of cities for urban living is one of the key tasks for the coming generations (Scholl, 2005).

Over the next ten years, an inner-city district of approximately 100 hectares will be developed in Frankfurt on the old freight depot and marshalling yard of the Deutsche Bahn. The new district will include different functions, such as housing, offices and recreational and cultural facilities for 30,000 to 50,000 inhabitants on a floor-space of approximately two million m².

The Frankfurt Exhibition Center is located directly in the European Quarter. The exhibition center has always been closely linked to the economic development of the city and the region around Frankfurt. To maintain the competitiveness of the Fair, it is planned to extend and modernise its infrastructure

For points of strategic importance for the entire development, more detailed solutions will be prepared, e.g., urban design, including the design of technical infrastructures and the design of public space by means of test planning and subsequently an urban design competition. A test planning process to explore the range of possible solutions and basic guidelines for further steps in planning and realisation is particularly important. It's always true that: "The criteria are as unknown as the solution, which should be used to prove that the solution is the right one. It is not wrong to say that both should be investigated simultaneously" (Gerettsegger; Peintner 1986).

For the future development of the area west of the Emser Bridge, it was very important to have clarity about the future situation of the street tunnel and the planned underground train in the planned central park, the Europa Garden, as they are part of the same system.

Figure 16: Europa Garden development plan 2009 (top) and reality 2011(bottom)
Sources: Aurelis 2009 and author

Therefore, the suggestion was accepted to accelerate the coordination of this important transport infrastructure through the announcement of a landscape planning competition. In addition, the quick realisation of the 'green heart' would improve the quality of the location and thus its marketing chances as well. The competition was conducted and judged in 2008 and its realisation began in 2009. Three-quarters of the ground plots had already been sold to investors by spring 2011, well before the planned deadline.

Today, the European Quarter is a large construction site. The construction of the street tunnel and the underground train will begin in 2012 and will in all probability be completed by 2020.

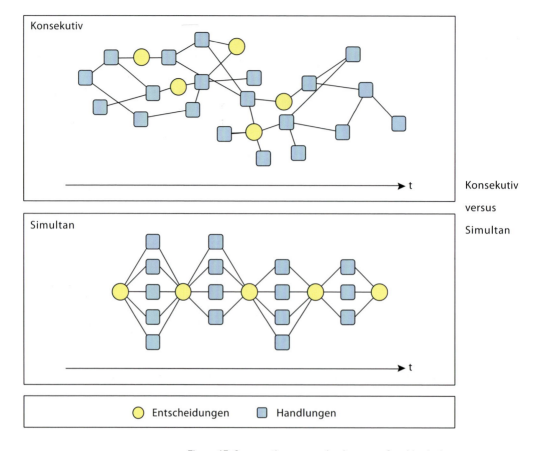

Figure 17: Consecutive versus simultaneous. Graphic: Author

The case study of the Europaviertel in Frankfurt clearly shows that great potential exists for redevelopment in the area of the North-South Railway Link. In particular, office buildings in the metropolitan region offering thousands of workplaces are a great magnet for commuters who are dependent on a reliable regional public transport. Their best possible use, however, can only be taken advantage of when the bottlenecks, especially in the area of the most important European railway nodes, are eliminated.

The task of Interreg CODE24 will be to investigate all the relevant redevelopment potential in the catchment area of the North-South Railway Link.

Learning by doing – the test planning method

The examples demonstrate that integrated solutions for difficult tasks can be developed within a manageable time frame. Each example applied the same method of test planning. This method, tested on many different kinds of difficult tasks, can lead to integrated solutions and breakthroughs. The core of the test planning process is based on certain principles and enables the pros and cons of solutions to be discussed directly and immediately. The testing of such ideas in the interplay of suggestions and critique allows basic solution approaches to crystallise within a time period of about nine months.

In order to achieve this, test planning requires clear role differentiation. In addition, the central elements are: cooperation among the teams that are seeking solutions, a committee of experts who lead, accompany and evaluate the process, and executive representatives who distribute the tasks for conducting the test planning and who regularly communicate with the expert committee about the progress of the work, interim results and final report. Important for the course of the test planning is the introduction of a binding overall programme of events. There must be sufficient time between those events to allow for preparation and work time for the individual tasks. A total of about one year is needed for the entire process to unfold. In some situations, a consolidation phase is necessary.

Space does not allow a detailed description of the entire test planning process. Full descriptions can be found in numerous other publications (Scholl, 2010; 2011).

Conclusions

In Europe, liveable cities demand a well-developed public transport system on all levels. The article illustrates important connections between railway and settlement development on the most import European North-South Railway Link. The case studies show that coordination, cooperation and communication between the relevant actors and stakeholders must be greatly improved, especially in cross-border areas. Integrated spatial and railway development will remain

one of the most challenging and strategically significant tasks in Europe in the coming years and decades. From the point of view of spatial planning, further enhancements and developments of the existing railway system are imminent, as they will strengthen public transport and relieve the already over-utilised road systems. The development of the railway system can thus be seen as a preventative measure.

Having a railway transport system people want to use can be a breakthrough towards the primacy of settlement redevelopment in order to also strengthen the liveability of cities. Today, solutions have to be found in highly populated areas, in contrast to past decades. In democratic societies, this cannot be done without the consent of the population. In Switzerland, with its system of direct democracy, the final word is with the people. As voting for projects is always connected to their financing, one result is that the planning safeguards so vital for large projects are secured. This also allows the long-term planning of thousands of individual actions and decisions.

Challenges in the areas of cooperation, coordination and communication are on the increase. The number of conflicts arising as a result cannot be resolved by the standard procedures. Informal additions are necessary, as suggested in action-oriented planning (Scholl 1995). Border regions offer special opportunities in this case, as it is the national borders where different formal planning systems and cultures meet. No country can force their system onto another. The solution is to address concrete problems. This has proved successful in some important European cases, notably, securing Lake Constance as a reservoir and the integrated flood control of the Rhine.

The integrated development of the North-South Link is also a project of European significance and in the interests of the entire European community. Its contribution to mobility in and between regions provides a high level of value-added importance and it plays a vital role too in the protection of the environment. Just as significant is its contribution to redevelopment-oriented settlement. This demands an efficient adjustment in the balance of goods and passenger transport and relevant business concepts as a basis for structural developments. It would be ill advised to focus these efforts solely on high-speed traffic. Cities and regions definitely need excellent national and international connections, but efficient regional traffic that is well connected to metropolitan and national traffic is at least as important.

The related responsibilities are complex and demand special, and increasingly, international provisions for cooperation, coordination and communication. The

strategically designated EU Interreg Project CODE 24 will contribute to that. By 2013, the overview of all the central difficulties and conflicts of the project is expected to be complete, regular assessments implemented and solutions found for those until now unresolved, complex problems, and passed on to the responsible political representatives of the participating countries and the EU.

After 2013, it is conceivable that a follow-up organisation will be set up in order to help the integrated railway and spatial development in the all-important North-South Corridor of Europe. If this comes about, it would be a sign that highly developed, democratic civil societies can master challenging tasks that lie in their mutual interests.

Endnotes

1. www.alptransit.ch

2. www.bbt-se.com

3. Scholl, B (editor): *Perspectives on Spatial Planning and Development in Switzerland. Report of the International Group of Experts.* pp. 7-8 Bern 2007.

4. www.code24.eu

5. irl.ethz.ch/re/cooperation/closed/index_EN

6. http://www.europaviertel.de

References

Geretsegger, Heinz; Peintner, Max (1986) "Otto Wagner". Unbegrenzte Großstadt. p. 50 Wien

Hesse, Markus; Beckmann, Klaus; Heinrichs; Bernhard; Scholl, Bernd et al. (2010)
Neue Rahmenbedingungen, Herausforderungen und Strategien für die grossräumige Verkehrsabwicklung
(New spatial requirements, challenges and strategies for large-scale traffic development). Forschungs-
und Sitzungsbericht der ARL, Hannover

Lindblom, Charles E. (1959) "Public Administration Review", Vol. 19, No. 2. (Spring, 1959), pp. 79 -88.

Scholl, Bernd (1995) Aktionsplanung. Zur Behandlung komplexer Schwerpunktaufgaben in der
Raumplanung, vdf Verlag. Zurich, 1995

Scholl, Bernd (2005): "The European Quarter Project. Making Spaces for the Creative Economy", p. 220,
ISOCARP Review. The Hague, 2005

Scholl, Bernd (2010) "Testplanungen als neue Methode" (Test planning as a new method). In: TEC21.
Nr. 29-30 / 2010. Fachzeitschrift für Architektur, Ingenieurwesen und Umwelt, Zurich 2010

Scholl, Bernd (2011) "Die Methode der Testplanung. Exemplarische Veranschaulichung für die Auswahl und
den Einsatz von Methoden in Klärungsprozessen" (Methods of test planning. Exemplary illustrations for the
selection and use of methods in clarification processes). In: Grundriss der Raumentwicklung. Akademie für
Raumforschung und Landesplanung, Hannover 2011

Scholl, Bernd (editor) (2007) Perspectives on Spatial Planning and Development in Switzerland. Report of
the International Group of Experts. Commissioned by the Swiss Federal Office of Spatial Planning (ARE).
Bern, 2007. Also available in German, French and Italian

The Contribution of Mobility to Liveable Cities

Pierre Laconte

Introduction

Achieving sustainable cities includes social and economic as well as environmental factors that make cities attractive and liveable. What sorts of transport systems are appropriate for a sustainable city, seen from each of these points of view?

Achieving an integrated sustainable urban mobility concept could include some of the following components:

- Decoupling income progression from increase in energy use by citizens of a city and its region.
- Encouraging life styles favouring non motorised transport clusters all over the urban region, and reducing subsidies for fossil fuel, increasing the population density.

- Optimising the use of each transport mode and interconnecting transport modes. That means ensuring effective rail networks, networks of tram/bus rights-of-ways, convenient intermodal hubs, easy use of bicycles and availability of rented bicycles and of taxis.
- Assessing the health effects of a switch from motorised transport to non-motorised transport (walking and cycling).
- Implementing synergy between the supply of public transport and restraint on the use of the car in the city.

The paper includes examples of integrated sustainable mobility.

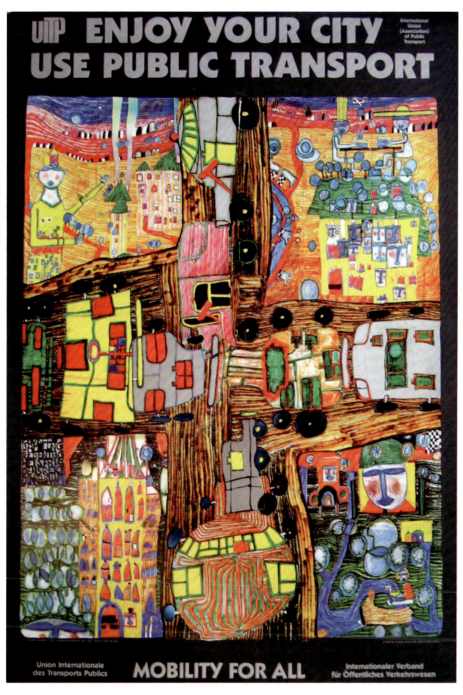

Mobility and Liveable Cities - Enjoyment as a Key to Liveability. Poster by Friedensreich Hundertwasser for UITP (1995)

Figure 1: View of Chicago in the 1930s, showing the street full of cars while the streetcars (trams) could no longer move, as they had no right of way even though they paid entirely for their infrastructure and its maintenance. Streetcar companies went bankrupt one after the other and public transport gradually left the realm of urban business services to enter the realm of public social services.

Transport and Mobility Planning - Post-War Trends and Consequences for Cities and Urban Dwellers

Trends

The post war era witnessed a shift in citizens' attitudes towards society in general and urban life in particular. French political scientist Marcel Gauchet has referred to this phenomenon as "mass individualism" (Gauchet, 1985).

Mass individualism is characterized by the increased consumption of positional goods – goods that position individuals in relation to others – notably freestanding, single-family houses and private cars.

This shift in consumer preferences found its origin in the United States. It was largely shaped through the common interests of three industrial sectors: the nascent automobile sector (which was championed by Henry Ford); the oil sector (whose market had practically disappeared following the replacement of petroleum lamps by electric lighting but was revived by the oil consuming automobile); and the various industries associated with highway construction and suburban development.

Together, these sectors became incomparably stronger – in political and economic terms –

than the large railway companies, which had been all-powerful in the late 19th century and the beginning of the 20th century. While the railways and tramway companies still had to finance their infrastructure, from that period, road infrastructure and maintenance were financed by the public sector and no longer by tolls or user charges as had been the case throughout history.

Therefore personal investment in cars was encouraged, not only by the lifestyle change resulting from increased household income, but also by strong public policies and market distortions. The effect of those one-sided factors is starkly illustrated by the case of Chicago where the street car (tram) was quickly displaced through the advance of the automobile (see Figure 1).

Cities

The success story of the automobile may be seen as the main cause of urban SPRAWL and its consequences for people, their health and their quality of life (air quality, dilution of urban and neighbourhood fabric, distances travelled), and for nature (landscapes, open space, agriculture and bio-diversity). An extreme example is the endless suburban expansion in the USA (see Figure 2). The phenomenon of urban sprawl has been analysed by, among others, the European Environment Agency (EEA, 2006) (see Figure 3).

In terms of mobility, the use of the car as the dominant mode ("auto-mobility") has entailed dramatic changes in both land use and individuals' behaviour.

In URBAN LAND USE, lower density and longer distances for urban trips have occurred, as an effect of motorisation. The car takes about 18 times more space than a pedestrian, as it moves, but it requires parking every time it does not move, i.e. most of its life cycle (see Figure 4). The 'land spread'

Figure 2: Urban sprawl is well illustrated by this suburb near Phoenix, Arizona. Homes are exclusively reached by road

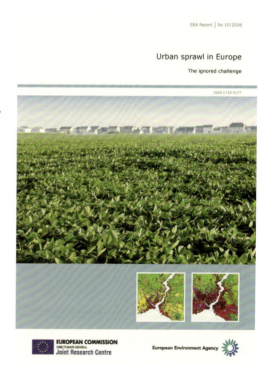

Figure 3: Urban sprawl was analysed, among others, by the European Environment Agency in its 2006 Report "Urban Sprawl in Europe"

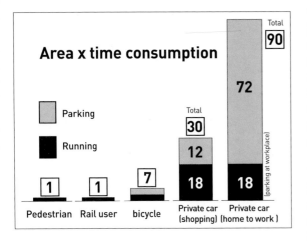

Area x time consumption

Parking

Running

Pedestrian	Rail user	bicycle	Private car (shopping)	Private car (home to work)

Figure 4: If one takes the land consumption by a pedestrian as the benchmark, the car takes up about 18 times more space than a pedestrian, as it moves, but it requires parking for the time it does not move, i.e. for some 90 % of its life cycle. Land consumption therefore has an area x time dimension Source: Louis Marchand, RATP for UITP

effect is thus enhanced by this difference in scale of automobile use, up to one to ninety, as compared to the pedestrian/tramway city. This meant that short trips to proximity services that were once done by walking or cycling, became longer, even more so because the shortest way for the walker or cyclist is not generally the one used by the driver, as the road network is scaled for the automobile. As an example, a one way street system increases by half the average length of trips and the amount of fuel used.

Similarly, spaces used for recreation and amenity are in conflict with the ever increasing demand for parking space.

People

As to the urban dweller's HEALTH, the main effect has been the decline in walking as a means of transport, as muscle power gave way to fossil-fed horsepower.

This had effects not only on personal mobility (increase in vehicle km travelled) but also on environmental health (road accidents, pollution-related respiratory diseases and obesity). Among the related studies, the relationship between car use, obesity and carbon dioxide emissions has been the subject of a 2007 report by the Institute for European Environmental Policy and Adrian Davis (Davis, 2007).

The effects of urban environments on health (both physical and mental) were the subject of a 2008 Conference held by the UK-Man and Biosphere Urban Forum at UCL London. Proceedings were published under the title "Statins and Greenspaces" (Dawe, 2008). The contribution by William Bird and Huw Davies includes data from the UK National Centre for Chronic Disease Prevention which addresses the cost of additional healthcare due to inactivity, by age group (see Figure 5 and 6).

The data on ROAD ACCIDENTS collected by the former European Council of Ministers of Transport (now The International Transport Forum) reveal that 'road crashes account for 180,000 deaths every year in OECD and the ITF countries (....) while worldwide the WHO estimates the annual road deaths toll at 1.2 million people' (ITF, 2008)

Indicators of Sustainable Mobility – Findings and Comments

Indicators of mobility and land use were analyzed by the International Association of Public Transport (UITP) in its "Millennium Cities Database for Sustainable Mobility" (UITP, 2001). The data covered, among others, demography, urban economy, urban structure, number of

Figure 5: A dramatic rise in diseases linked to obesity is expected by 2023

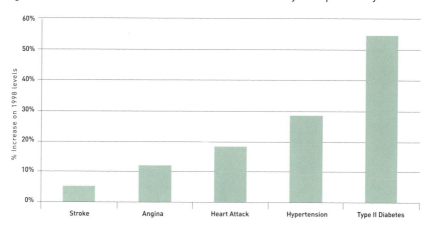

Figure 5: According to the UK Department of Health, the rampant increase in obesity will result in a strong increase in related diseases. Source: 2008 Conference held by the UK-Man and Biosphere Urban Forum at UCL London. Proceedings were published under the title "Statins and Greenspaces" (Gerald Dawe and Alison Millward, Eds)

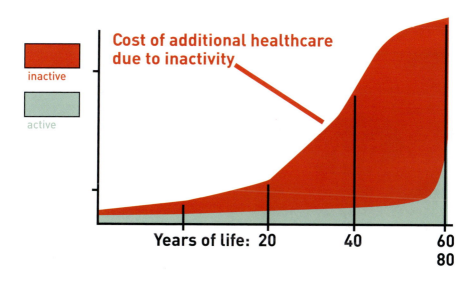

Figure 6: This graph shows the cost of additional health care entailed by inactivity as estimated by the UK National Centre for Chronic Disease Prevention Source: Dawe, G., 2007

Figure 8: Bordeaux opted for a light rail network
instead of a metro line and connecting buses.
A notable feature is the absence of catenaries
(overhead and supporting poles) in the historic part of
the city, for aesthetic reasons
Source: City of Bordeaux

Figure 7: Nantes has been a pioneer of the tramways revival
since 1982, complemented today by a bicycle rental scheme.
Tramways are not only a tool for sustainable mobility. They are
an opportunity for enhancing the street network and creating
pedestrian-friendly environments. As initiated in Karlsruhe,
Germany in 1992, some tram networks are using existing
railway tracks, and complementing them with new tramway
routes, thus allowing seamless travel
Source: City of Nantes

private motor vehicles, taxis, road and public
transport network, modal choice, transport
costs as percentage of metropolitan GDP,
energy consumption, pollution and number of
accidents, but not health as such.

The general findings, analysed by J. Vivier,
could be summarized and commented on as
follows:

- Public transport consumes on average four
  times less energy per passenger-kilometre
  than the single-occupancy automobile.
  This includes both rail and road transport
  vehicles and is subject to strong variations
  according the density of land use and the
  level of operating subsidies.
- The dense cities of Europe, well served by
  public transport and non motorised transport modes, are spending much less for
  their mobility than the spread-out cities

As an example of practical differences, the comparison between Bangkok and Copenhagen indicates the following:

- Bangkok is characterised by a high level of motorized mobility, entailing very long and costly travel times, and poor accessibility. Road investment, recommended by the World Bank, has been proven to be ill-suited to the dense urban structure of the conurbation, while public transport investment was deferred. In addition, the covering over of many canals by roads has markedly increased urban temperatures.
- In an outstanding contrast, Copenhagen spends only 4.1% of its GDP on transport, due to a combination of restrictions on individual automobile use and high use of the bicycle, notwithstanding the Nordic climate. Munich, Frankfurt, Vienna, Milan, Paris and London all spend less than 7% of their GDPs on transport.

Modal comments

In any intermodal comparative exercise a difficulty arises at the INTERFACE between transport modes. Complex daily trips (trips which are not only home to work) make up a growing proportion of the total. Calculations of cost and time are therefore increasingly difficult to make. A complex example is the place taken by trips to school in the total number of trips. Parents' safety concerns combine with status exposure to increase this type of trips.

RAIL mass transit is usually recognised as the best way to ensure citizen's mobility in large conurbations. The emergence of an efficient guided mode of transport serving a specific route usually entails a reallocation of trips to make use of this new mode where it is available. A case in point is the tram network of Nantes. The central city tram network has been planned for use as the only motorised mode for a trip, complemented by walking or cycling rather than by feeder buses or park

of America, both in monetary terms and in terms of accidents. Sustainable urban mobility requires an integrated supply of built space, public transport, parking and amenities. The higher the density, the higher the patronage. Notable exceptions exist in America, as illustrated by New York or Portland, Oregon.

- Growth in income does not necessarily imply an urban development model based on the automobile and urban sprawl. There is a clear relationship between public transport use and the supply of parking.
- Sustainable mobility calls for an integrated transport policy combining urban planning, parking controls and a significant role for public transport, so that this again becomes the mode of choice for all, as it once was, and not just of the elderly and the poor. In the tramway age, public transport was part of the mainstream urban economy, and not a social service. Public transport being part of the mainstream economy is not at all incompatible with subsidies to some groups of users. An early example was the cheap workers' commuter train pass system introduced in Belgium in 1869. This system allowed workers to continue living in their rural environment instead of agglomerating in suburban slums, as in France.

Figure 9: The Bogota TransMilenio is derived from the pioneering Curitiba Bus Rapid Transit (BRT) network that started in 1976 which has proven its mass transit capacity while providing for enhanced safety and security through its staffed stations. BRT achieves very high commercial speeds, as it is given a total right-of-way and all ticketing takes place at stations. Note the possibility of express buses to pass all-stops buses. In narrower roads and urban streets, space can be saved by using guided buses (e.g. through an optical guidance system)
Source: Transmilenio

and ride (see Figure 7). Bordeaux has a comparable philosophy (see Figure 8).

'Park-and-Ride' may feed a rail system but the differential of land use requirement by pedestrians and cars cannot be forgotten. It means that "Park and Ride" consumes a huge amount of urban land that could be used more efficiently. "Kiss and Ride" and feeder buses can save the space used for day-long commuter parking.

The same is true for electric car/plug in vehicles. They certainly reduce direct pollution (indirect, greenhouse gas pollution depends on the source of the electricity supply) but they do not reduce the urban space consumed by the car, whatever its fuel.

Bus Rapid Transit (BRT) networks, with full right of way and off-vehicle ticketing are a valid and affordable alternative to mass rail transit. They are, however, more space-consuming, unless the bus is guided, for example

Figure 10: A glimpse into the future. For the occasion of the World Cup 2014, Porto Alegre (Brazil) intends to introduce the Coester AEROMOVEL, a pioneering, low-energy compressed air automated people mover (design e Arquitetura: Ado Azevedo). This system was first developed in Porto Alegre (inspired by a 19th century project by the British engineer Isambard Brunel), but, until now, only a short line operates in Jakarta, Indonesia. Other pioneering projects under implementation include the London Heathrow ASTRA Personal Rapid Transit system linking car parks to the Airport's Terminal 5

through an optical guidance system (Rouen). The pioneering BRT city was Curitiba, starting in 1976 and still expanding (Linha Verde). Its concept was successfully adopted by Bogota (see Figure 9). BRT has now been implemented all over world, in China (Kunming), India (Delhi), Australia (Brisbane) and Turkey (Istanbul).

Automated people movers (APM) have proven a mode well adapted to short distances (Trans.21, 2010), sometimes cable - propelled

An original very light APM is the Brazilian AEROMOVEL This compressed air propulsion system, was developed in Brazil by Oskar Coester and is due to open for regular traffic in 2014. The vehicle is driven by a pneumatic system which converts electrical power into compressed air and transmits thrust directly to the vehicle without gears or intervening electric circuits. Stationary electrical blowers, located close to the passenger stations produce the pressurized air needed to propel the vehicles (see Figure 10).

Figure 11: Copenhagen's high-density low-rise urban planning, its pedestrianised streets (introduced from 1962), its bicycle network (36% of commuters use bicycles, notwithstanding the Scandinavian climate), and its expanding driverless urban metro network have enhanced liveability. The Copenhagen metro lines also reinforce the "finger-plan", which concentrates development along public transport radial corridors
Source: City of Copenhagen

Finally, one should mention public transport making use of individual vehicles, such as shared TAXIS, or taxis accepting several passengers, e.g. taxis equipped with a meter allowing fare reduction for each existing passenger if a new passenger steps in. They are well adapted to linear urban configurations, such as coastal cities (for example, Thessaloniki). Special mention must be made of car-sharing (or car clubs). While not an alternative to individual car use, it allows more efficient use of existing fleets (although less than shared taxis). Car sharing/car clubs recently started to attract car rental business (membership-based car-on-demand hourly rental schemes).

The availability of hand-held GPS path finding devices specially designed for pedestrians should also encourage walking without having to consult a city map. Signage giving distances or walking time to key destinations has proven to encourage walking (for example in Geneva).

Policies and Measures for a Sustainable Mobility – Some Practices

Achieving an integrated urban planning and mobility concept could include some of the following components:

Encouraging LIFE STYLES favouring non motorised transport clusters throughout the urban region, and reducing subsidies for fossil fuel.

Copenhagen is a notable example through its high-density, low-rise urban planning, its pedestrianised streets (introduced from 1962), its bicycle network (36% of commut-

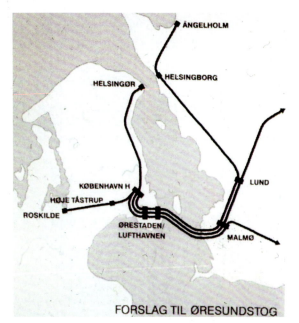

Figure 12: In addition to the intra urban metro, the commuter line linking Copenhagen, Kastrup airport and Malmo has created an integrated, trans-border urban agglomeration
Source: City of Copenhagen

Figure 13: Singapore Area Licensing Scheme 1975-2000

Through its pioneering restraint of car ownership (a monthly auction of new licensing plates, with a maximum yearly increase in car ownership of 2.5 %), its congestion pricing, its network of driverless subway trains linked with pedestrian malls and its highly convenient intermodal multi-use Easylink card, Singapore is considered a best practice in sustainable transport. Its "area licensing scheme" was launched in 1975, requiring drivers entering the city to pay a fee or accept three passengers. It confirms that oblique approaches are politically the most successful, especially in a difficult context (nobody could protest against such a scheme)

Source: author

Figure 14: In 2000 in Singapore the fee to enter the city was replaced by Electronic Road Pricing. The new system was applied to all drivers but the fee level varied according to the type of traffic congestion (the fee increases at peak times as a way to reduce congestion). This was also a signal to the user that the fee was in effect a congestion charge, not an additional tax on automobile use

Source: author

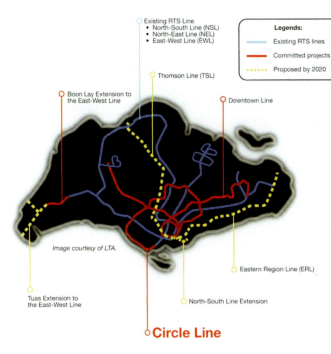

Existing RTS Line
- North-South Line (NSL)
- North-East Line (NEL)
- East-West Line (EWL)

Legends:

Existing RTS lines

Committed projects

Proposed by 2020

Thomson Line (TSL)

Boon Lay Extension to
the East-West Line

Downtown Line

Image courtesy of LTA.

Eastern Region Line (ERL)

Tuas Extension to
the East-West Line

North-South Line Extension

Circle Line

Figure 15: Singapore has been the pioneer of driverless high-capacity metro networks (starting with the North-East Line in 2003) Absence of drivers means shorter intervals between trains, higher capacity and higher safety levels. Most of the staff interfaces with passengers, rather than just sitting in a tunnel. This network has set the standard for future metros around the world. Nuremberg, Brussels and other cities are retrofitting existing lines to make them driverless and increase their capacity
Source: Land Transport Authority, Singapore

ers using bikes), and its expanding driverless metro network. The Copenhagen metro lines reinforce the "finger-plan" (see Figure 11), while the commuter rail line linking Copenhagen, Kastrup airport and Malmö has created an integrated trans-border urban agglomeration (see Figure 12). With changing urban life styles, more account is being taken of water in and around the city, not only as resource and tool for urban climate change adaptation but also as mobility tool. Copenhagen is a pioneer in this respect too, providing a year-round scheduled boat system, accessible with the same tickets as the metro and buses. A multidisciplinary approach to water in the city would lead towards water-centric communities (Novotny et al., 2010).

DECOUPLING income progression from increase in energy use by citizens of a city and its region.

The most obvious case of decoupling is affluent Singapore, through among others its pioneering car ownership restraint (monthly

auction of new licence plates), its congestion pricing, its network of driverless subway trains linked with pedestrian malls, and its convenient intermodal and multi-use Easylink card (Mah, 2009). Singapore is considered a good example of integrated sustainable transport (see Figures 13-15). Protection of pedestrian walking in the streets in equatorial conditions could still be improved by trees providing shade and by canopies. In the case of multi-use cards, London's Oyster Card and Hong Kong's Octopus are also regarded as best practices.

Among smaller cities, Freiburg (Germany) is a notable example, thanks to its urban development clusters and its synergy between low energy buildings and low energy mobility. The university city of Heidelberg is also highly ranked. Even in lower density areas, such as rural cantons of Switzerland, public transport has a chance, if it is reliable (Mees, 2009).

The university town of Louvain-la-Neuve (New Louvain), 27 km south of central Brussels is

Figure 16: The university town of Louvain-la-Neuve (New Louvain) is a prime example of a sustainable, liveable development. It is centred on a new railway station and is entirely pedestrian, parking space being provided outside the town or underground. It has many ecological features and has a present population of 40.000. All storm water is led to a reservoir landscaped as an artificial lake, with a stable water level
Source: Wilhelm & Co.

an early example of transit oriented development (TOD) (Laconte 2009). Begun in 1969, it has become a regional growth magnet. This high density-low rise development, modelled after the historic university town of Leuven, is centred on a new railway station and is entirely pedestrian, parking space being provided outside or underground. The new town also displays many ecological features (see Figures 16-18).

Figure 17: View of the entrance to the railway station which is below this pedestrian street combining university buildings, shopping and residences
Source: author

Figure 18: View of one the numerous small piazzas on the pedestrian streets network. Cars are parked underneath
Source: author

Contributing to integrated mobility through effective tram/bus rights-of-ways and innovative use of rented bicycles for short trips.

Paris is a case in point. The extensive use of bus rights of way (more recently also for trams), protected by "banquettes" and passenger information about waiting times has triggered a strong revival of surface transport. The Paris bicycle rental "Velib" scheme, which provides close to 20.000 bikes dispersed around the city, is reported as having substantially modified life-styles in favor of non-motorized transport, as well as having been politically rewarding. Some 30 million rentals were recorded in the first full year of operation (2008), together with a 94% rate of user satisfaction. The scheme was pioneered in Lyons and is now replicated all over Europe, lately in

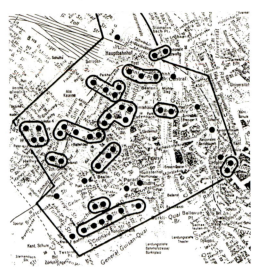

Figure 20: Zurich's automobile traffic calming through traffic light cycle control:Traffic-calming is ensured by adapting the traffic lights system (a much shorter cycle favouring pedestrians, cyclists and public transport)
Source: City of Zurich Police Department

Figure 19: Excellence in public transport –
the City of Zurich, Switzerland
In Zurich, trams and buses enjoy absolute priority on street. When approaching a traffic light the sensor shown on the lower left ensures they have a green light at any time of the day. The City's modal split is around 80% in favour of public transport
Source: City of Zurich Police Department

London (see also Figure 7). The private investors and operators of the Paris scheme were among the 2008 Time magazine's "Heroes of the Environment". Extension of the system to the periphery and a network of bicycle lanes remain to be implemented (Guet, 2009).

London has also introduced a congestion charging scheme in its central area that has improved surface transport.

For very large world conurbations, the traditional underground rail system remains unequalled in terms of capacity and speed. While China - in particular Shanghai - has been the champion of fast construction of metropolitan railways (after years of absolute priority to road investments), followed by New Delhi, the state of the art system remains that in Singapore, with its high-capacity driverless trains (see Figure 15).

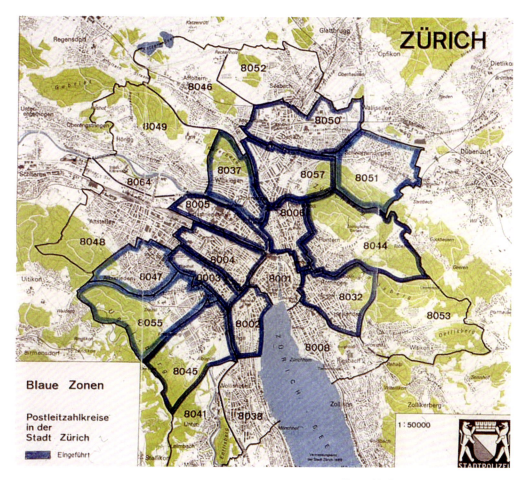

Figure 21: Zurich parking management
Unrestricted on-street parking is exclusively reserved for Zurich-registered residents, while automobile commuters entering the city from other municipalities are subject to limits on their parking time. Conversely, rail commuters have benefited from an increased service. The parking measure has brought a return of inhabitants to the city (who are able to park), and has been politically rewarding for the city fathers, while suburban rail travel has been made easierSource: City of Zurich Police Department

Figure 22: Mobility and Liveable Cities – the Transport Network Irrigating the City
Poster by Friedensreich Hundertwasser (1928-2000) for UITP (1991)

Assessing the health effects of the switch from motorized transport to non-motorized bicycle transport.

There may be a case for stronger collaboration between mobility and health services. As an example, the findings of Professor Richard Davison, of Napier University in Edinburgh (and Chair of the British Association of Sport and Exercise Sciences), quantify the benefits of cycling according to gradient levels. They confirm that hilly cities are not at all deterring cyclists: this is also shown by the Paris Velib' success, notwithstanding the hills. Effects of obesity and physical inactivity on health have been discussed above.

Implementing synergy between the supply of regional public transport and restraint on the use of the car in the city.

A case in point is the city of Zurich and its region. Trams and buses enjoy absolute on-street priority. Traffic calming is ensured by shortening the traffic lights cycle. On-street parking without a time limit is reserved for Zurich-registered residents with a sticker, while car commuters entering the city from other municipalities are subject to a limitation on their parking time. Conversely rail commuters have benefited from an increased service supply and easier rail travel. These parking measures have brought a return of inhabitants to the city (to be able to park) and have been politically rewarding to the city fathers, while suburban rail travel was easier for commuters. It also suggests that oblique approaches are the most successful, especially in a difficult political context (see Figures 19 -21).

Governance and continuity

Implementation of any policies and measures in favour of sustainable cities requires not only a tool kit but also appropriate governance and timing (Rydin, 2010). An outstanding example

of governance and continuity is provided by the city of Bilbao, which was led by the same team since 1989 (Vegara, 2005). Bilbao was the winner of the Singapore World-Cities Award 2010.

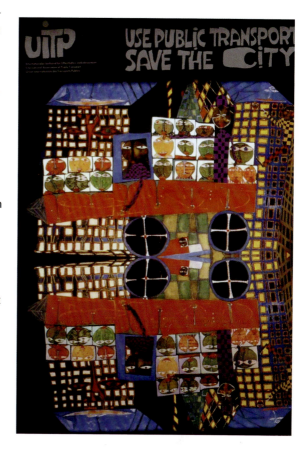

Figure 23: Mobility and Liveable Cities - the Compact City Poster by Friedensreich Hundertwasser for UITP (1993)

Conclusion

The examples described in this paper suggest that the best contribution of mobility to sustainable cities is optimising the use of each transport mode and interconnecting transport modes, whatever the size of the city. That means namely:

- Encouraging non motorised modes of transport though pleasant walkways (including signs indicating distances by foot) and a bicycle paths system, with places to park the bicycles, and easy to use rental bicycles. Easy availability of taxis in the streets and of shared taxis (club taxis) are adding to sustainable mobility.
- Ensuring effective public transport: regional networks, networks of tram/bus benefitting from right-of-ways, and convenient inter-modal hubs.
- Giving the car its proper place, preventing it from dominating the city and effectively limiting its speed.

Let us end by referring to the Austrian painter Friedensreich Hundertwasser (1928-2000) who summarized the contribution of mobility to the liveable city through three posters illustrating the notions of transport networks irrigating the city, the compact city as a prerequisite for sustainable mobility by favouring shorter trips, and citizen enjoyment as key to liveability (see Figures 22-23).

Acknowledgement

The author acknowledges the kind help of Chris Gossop, John Cartledge and Sir Peter Hall in finalising the manuscript.

References

Davis, A. (2007) Report by the Institute for European Environmental Policy and Adrian Davis, London: IEEP 2007

Dawe, G., Millward, A., Eds (2008) "Statins and Greenspaces", Proceedings of Conference held by the UK-Man and Biosphere Urban Forum at UCL, London: UCL 2008

EEA, (2006) European Environment Agency Report "Urban Sprawl in Europe", Copenhagen: EEA 2006 (www.eea.europa.eu)

Gauchet, M. (1985) Le désenchantement du monde, Paris: Gallimard 1985

Guet, J.F. (2009), Mobility and the compact city: The bike is back, ISOCARP Review 04, 2009
ITF (2008) Eliminating death and serious injuries in road transport Paris: Press release, 3 October 2008

Laconte, P. (2007) "Policy advice on urban planning, environment and health", Paper presented at the World Health Organisation Expert Meeting, Bonn, Germany, 24-25 November 2008

Laconte, P. (2009) "La recherche de la qualité environnementale et urbaine: Le cas de Louvain-la-Neuve (Belgique), Lyons; Editions du Certu 2009

Mah, B.T. (2009) Building Sustainable Cities: The Singapore Experience Keynote address delivered by Minister Mah Bow Tan at the 45th ISOCARP Congress

Mees, P. (2009) "Transport for Suburbia: Beyond the Automobile Age", Earthscan 2009

Novotny, V., Ahern, J., Brown, P. (2010) "Water Centric Sustainable Communities: planning, retrofitting, and building the next urban environment", New York: Wiley 2010

Rydin, Y (2010) "Governing for Sustainable Urban Development", London: Earthscan / James & James 2010

Trans.21 (2010), "Building a Sustainable Tomorrow with Smart Urban Mobility", Trans.21 2010.

UITP (2001) International Association of Public Transport "Millennium Cities Database for Sustainable Mobility", Brussels: UITP 2001.

Vegara, A. (2005) General Assembly Address at the 41st ISOCARP Congress, Bilbao:
The Hague: ISOCARP 2005.

Linking People, Linking Nature: The Park Connector Network of Singapore

Lena Chan

Cheng Hai Sim

Meng Tong Yeo

Kartini Omar-Hor

Background

Singapore is a city state with a population of 5.08 million people residing in 712 square kilometres (Singapore Statistics Department, 2010). Despite having a population density of over 7,000 persons per square kilometre, Singapore harbours rich biodiversity by virtue of its geographical location in the Malesian region[1] (see Figure 1). The island has more than 2,000 native vascular plant species, 57 species of mammal, more than 355 bird species, 98 reptile species, 26 amphibian species, over 280 butterfly species and around 124 species of dragonflies (National Parks Board, 2009). Its marine biodiversity is equally rich but this paper will focus only on its terrestrial habitats.

There is a growing awareness of the role of biodiversity in improving the quality of life in cities. Given Singapore's small land area and the need for economic growth, we have by necessity adopted a pragmatic approach to development with biodiversity conservation. In our quest for positive solutions, we have created a unique biodiversity conservation model that champions environmental sustainability in a small urban setting with well-endowed natural heritage.

Singapore has four Nature Reserves, i.e. Bukit Timah Nature Reserve which consists of mainly lowland dipterocarp forest,[2] Central Catchment Nature Reserve that comprises lowland dipterocarp forests and freshwater swamp forests, Sungei Buloh Wetland Reserve that harbours mangroves, freshwater habitats and grasslands, and Labrador Nature Reserve that has coastal hill forests and rocky shores. The Nature Reserves are legally protected under the Parks and Trees Act, administered by the National Parks Board[3] (NParks) of Singapore. Complementing these gazetted areas are Nature Areas that have rich biodiversity (see Figure 2) and

these are captured administratively under the Special and Detailed Controls Plan of the Urban Redevelopment Authority[4] (URA) Masterplan. NParks is also responsible for the management of over 300 parks and the streetscape (or roadside greenery). There is a hierarchy and diversity of parks, ranging from large regional parks to neighbourhood parks and playgrounds, where a spectrum of natural ecosystems co-exists with horticultural gardens. In this whole scheme, the Park Connector Network (PCN), as its name suggests, serves as the network that connects all these green assets together (see Figure 3).

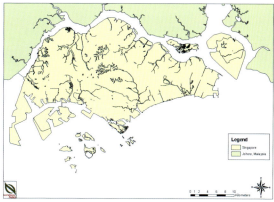

Figure 1: Map of Singapore
Source: NParks

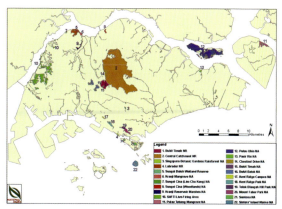

Figure 2: Map of the 4 Nature Reserves (NR) and 18 Nature Areas (NA) in Singapore
Source: NParks

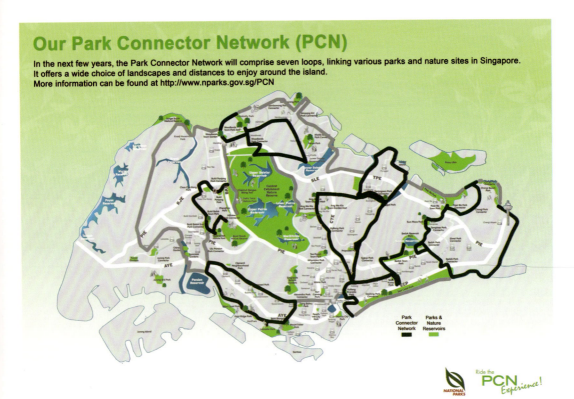

Our Park Connector Network (PCN)

In the next few years, the Park Connector Network will comprise seven loops, linking various parks and nature sites in Singapore. It offers a wide choice of landscapes and distances to enjoy around the island. More information can be found at http://www.nparks.gov.sg/PCN

Figure 3: Map of the Park Connector Network
Source: NParks

The intricate tapestry of Nature Reserves, Nature Areas, parks, PCN and streetscape synergises with the Active, Beautiful, and Clean Waters (ABC Waters) Programme (see Figure 4) administered by PUB, Singapore's National Water Agency[5] (PUB). The pervasive greenery within development areas was the brainchild of Mr Lee Kuan Yew, the first Prime Minister of Singapore, whose vision it was to establish Singapore as a Garden City. These initiatives have since evolved into a City in A Garden, where the seamless blending of green and blue forms an extensive mantle that everyone experiences when they step out into the open environment.

History of the Park Connector Network (PCN) in Singapore

The concept of the park connectors took root in the early 1980s. Chris J Hails recommended, in his report for the improvement of the bird population of Singapore (Hails, 1985), that "Plans should be prepared for vegetated corridors for bird use and liaison made with the Drainage Department for their development. Planting should begin as soon as possible. The corridors must mature slightly ahead of the parks to achieve full benefit".

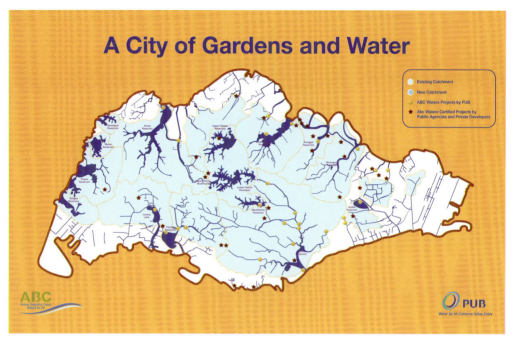

Figure 4: Map of the ABC Waters Programme
Source: PUB

The Garden City Action Committee (GCAC) approved the proposal to form a park connector network on 4 December 1991 (Tan, 2004). Around 360 kilometres of greenways were initially identified for development, phased over the next 20-30 years. The 1991 Concept Plan drawn up by URA included the PCN under its "Green & Blue Plan" (Urban Redevelopment Authority, 1991), ensuring that land for the PCN was safeguarded through the master planning process. The PCN continues to be reflected in the latest URA Parks and Waterbodies Plan (Urban Redevelopment Authority, 2008).

The Kallang Park Connector, completed in 1995, was the first park connector to be implemented. The nine kilometre park connector linked two regional parks, i.e.,

Bishan Park and Kallang Riverside Park. This was a first generation park connector using the Kallang River drainage reserves.

Another prototype project was the Ang Mo Kio Park Connector which tested the guidelines for park connectors that used road reserves. This pilot project which involved a one kilometre stretch linking Bishan Park to Ang Mo Kio Town Garden West was completed in August 2002. Many invaluable lessons were learnt from these two projects.

Functions of the PCN

The key rationale for the establishment of the PCN is for the enjoyment and well-being of people living in highly urbanised areas. By linking the Nature Reserves, Nature Areas, major parks, streetscape, and other open green and blue spaces through the PCN, recreational areas are made more accessible to the public. The PCN also offers a visual and psychological respite for people living in a highly urbanised landscape with extensive hardscapes, and in an island state where there is no large hinterland or rural areas to escape to during the weekends.

The park connectors have been specifically designed to cater to a diverse range of recreational uses, including walking, jogging cycling, inline skating , nature-watching, photography, and for both the young and the not so young (see Figures 5-10). The park connectors are also designed in such a way that they will serve as linear parks for residents in the vicinity. The health conscious modern generation partakes in more outdoor physical activities and hence, park connectors are increasingly being used by families and communities for their social bonding activities and expression of their healthy lifestyles.

Turning a constraint into an opportunity, the PCN optimises the use of linear pathways that are too narrow for any other use like road

Figure 5: People using the park connectors for cycling
Source: NParks

reserves, or it occupies land that is compatible such as drainage reserves. As park connectors link a diverse range of habitats, many of which are home to native biodiversity, they inevitably also serve as ecological corridors for small mammals, birds, reptiles, amphibians, butterflies, dragonflies, etc. In totality, the PCN now functions holistically to benefit the physical as well as the psychological and social well-being of the residents of Singapore while doubling as a haven and conduit for connecting biodiversity.

Planning for the PCN

Strategic planning is crucial for the success of the development of the PCN as it requires the cooperation of multiple agencies, optimises the usage of land, and serves multiple functions. Synchronising with the broader master planning process of Singapore, the PCN has been incorporated into URA's Parks and Waterbodies Plan. Through two decades of planning, implementing and managing the PCN, park connectors have evolved from being a connecting network to be key recreational destinations on their own merit. This is through careful planning so that they offer unique long-distance travel recreational experiences by opening up previously inaccessible areas along the way, as well as closely integrating with surrounding land uses, hence creating new urban experiences.

The network is strategically prioritised into regional loops of between 20 to 40 kilometre lengths that serve to increase park accessibility. Currently, a total of seven loops covering the eastern, northern, western, north-eastern, central, southern and south-eastern parts of Singapore have been planned. Each regional loop takes on the character of the neighbourhoods and parks it passes through, such as the Eastern Coastal PCN, Northern Explorer PCN and Western Adventure PCN. These regional loops are then linked together to create an island-wide green matrix of linear park space. Although 360km of PCN were originally estimated, after careful feasibility studies and detailed planning were carried out, the total length of the PCN would add up to 300km when completed.

PCN routes are planned to maximise recreational experience along the route while striving to provide the most convenient and possibly shortest distance between parks and nature reserves. From experience,

Figure 6: People using the park connectors for jogging
Source: NParks

paths along water edges (drains, canals, and along the coast) are preferred by PCN users. A preliminary site survey is an essential part of the planning process to assess the suitability of the route. Potential obstacles and challenges along the way, as well as future plans for the surrounding areas are other practical and planning criteria for consideration. It is not uncommon to have to explore a number of different routes before making a considered decision on the most appropriate one. It is also not unusual that the chosen route does not fully meet the planning criteria. When that situation arises, design and management solutions would be sought.

Due to land scarcity and high population density in Singapore, land optimisation has to be a key strategy in the planning of the network. It constantly challenges planners to think 'out of the box'. Park connectors capitalise on readily available and under-utilised land, such as drainage reserves, road reserves and Mass Rapid Transit (MRT) viaducts. For some stretches, they also meander through adjoining public housing land. These reserves or 'buffers' were originally set aside for operational requirements of the primary users, e.g., as maintenance access for canals or as an urban design requirement for the intended cityscape.

Figure 8: Seniors using the Puggol park connectors Source: NParks

Figure 7: People using the park connectors for inline skating Source: NParks

Figure 9: Young people using the park connectors Source: NParks

However, by doubling up as recreational space for PCN, it increases the land-use value of utility infrastructural land which was previously thought to be unavailable for any use. As these areas could be managed by the Housing and Development Board[6] (HDB), JTC Corporation[7] (JTC), the Land Transport Authority[8] (LTA), SMRT Corporation Ltd[9] (SMRT), PUB, Singapore Land Authority[10] (SLA), Town Councils, etc., NParks has to work with these agencies on the multi-layering of these spaces for recreational use.

Drainage reserves are typically 6m wide, of which 4m typically is converted into a shared cycling and jogging path, with a 2m planting strip. A minimum width of 4m is required to facilitate vehicular access for maintenance purposes. The basic typology for park connectors along road reserves consists of a 1.5m wide footpath, 2m wide cycling track and a 3 – 6m wide planting cum services strip. While on paper the planning width for park connectors may seem narrow as they are only a few meters wide, in reality on the ground, park connectors cleverly make use of the multi-layering of open spaces and landscaping of adjoining lands like open water canals, landscaped building setback, school compounds, to provide a visually much

Figure 10: People using park connectors for nature watching
Source: NParks

wider open space effect. Coupled with the multiple-use concept, PCN provides unique recreational experiences and open spaces effects with minimum uptake of additional land in Singapore.

A key challenge in linking these strips of buffer land is ensuring connectivity and maintaining a standard for quality recreational experience. While park connectors along drainage reserves are largely seamless, those along road reserves inevitably encounter traffic light crossings, overhead bridges, bus stops and covered walkways. NParks works with LTA and the Building and Construction Authority[11] (BCA) to facilitate the movements of cyclists and those in wheelchairs at these points.

The promotion of sustainable development policies by government agencies, coupled with the advent of a community-based pro-cycling culture, has resulted in the introduction of bicycle paths by LTA and other agencies.

These paths facilitate short-distance commuting trips, most commonly between residential areas and transport nodes or key neighbourhood amenities such as markets, food centres and community centres. While the objective of these intra-town paths is different from that of the PCN, the integration and interconnectivity of both systems have to be looked into holistically to maximise public accessibility. As the PCN and commuter cycling networks become more prevalent in Singapore, the best options are currently being explored to facilitate public enjoyment, movement and environmental sustainability.

Designing and Developing the PCN

The design guidelines for park connectors take into account three objectives, i.e., to link major parks and nature sites, to enhance recreational opportunities and to provide green nature corridors. As described in the section on planning above, a typical park connector consists of a cycling cum jogging track as well as a planting strip. Depending on the availability of space, other facilities like shelters, etc. may be provided.

There are 4 main categories of park connectors based on their locations, i.e. 1) within Drainage Reserves which are under PUB (see Figure 11); 2) within Road Reserves under LTA (see Figure 12); 3) within vacant State land and State land under viaducts supporting MRT train tracks which are under SLA, and 4) abutting or within residential areas which are under the purview of HDB.

Guidelines for the landscaping of park connectors include planting specifications such as: 1) species, preferably native plant species, that attract birds and other wildlife; 2) trees that are fast growing and able to provide instant

shade, hence shade trees should take priority over elaborate shrub planting; 3) trees that have large spreading crowns which would facilitate movement of birds as well as provide continuous shade, etc.

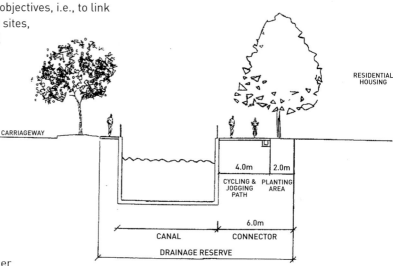

Figure 11: A typical cross section of a park connector along a Drainage Reserve. Source: NParks

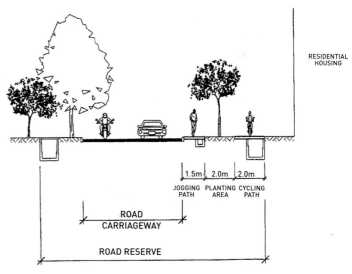

Figure 12: A typical cross section of a park connector within a Road Reserve. Source: NParks

The 6m width of drainage reserves in Singapore determines the land availability for the connector. The function of the drainage reserve is not diminished after the implementation of the park connector. On the contrary, the value and aesthetics of the drainage reserve are enhanced. Furthermore, the maintenance vehicles of PUB can now use the jogging/cycling track to carry out their maintenance works more effectively. It is a win-win situation for both government agencies.

While the 4m wide jogging and cycling track is wide enough for leisure activities, the 2m planting strip could limit its use as an ecological corridor and living space for birds. This constraint could be overcome by innovative design. Planting trees with large umbrella crowns, as stated in the landscaping guidelines given above, and edible fruits provides suitable bird habitats in a compromised space. Remnant spaces along the way may also be included in the design of the park connector, to provide small gathering places and also sites for installing small recreational facilities, e.g. fitness equipment, play equipment and small shelters.

Catering for the needs of the residents, some stretches of park connector are designed, developed, and used as linear parks for residents who live in the vicinity of the PCN. For the convenience of the residents, HDB and other property developers have also built tracks linking dwellings to the park connectors. Residents are commonly seen enjoying morning and evening strolls along the park connectors.

Another spin-off effect was created after the completion of the first few park connectors. Residents started using park connectors to gain easy and faster daily access to the transportation nodes (bus stops, MRT and Light Rail Transport stations) daily. More and more people are using the park connectors as their cycling routes to work, school, play or market.

As in planning, the key consideration for the design of park connectors is land optimisation. It is not about how to design a 'compact' or 'small park connector'; it is about how to design park connectors that will have multiple functions that, at first glance, could be seen as conflicting. Park connectors are designed without limiting them to serve only recreational purposes but also to include other non-recreational activities like drainage maintenance and inspection works, and daily commuting routes. This is crucial to a city state like Singapore where land is scarce and increasing efficiency of land usage is a necessity.

Park connectors are also designed for diversity of landscape, leveraging on their environmental setting. Those that are near residential areas are more horticulturally inclined and have basic facilities like benches for users. Some serve as access routes and these are rather basic in structure. Park connectors that are situated in more rustic settings are less manicured and these function more as refuges for wildlife.

Notwithstanding the above advantages and benefits that park connectors provide, the development of the park connector was initially not an easy and well-accepted process. In the early days of the park connectors, agencies were more focussed on their individual functions and remits, and consequently, combined use of land for different functions and purposes was seen as infringing on their areas of jurisdiction and viewed as unworkable.

Kallang Park Connector was the first pilot project, tested the feasibility of multi-agency and multi-function land use. This project was a great success and that led to a wider and faster pace of implementation compared with other places like Ulu Pandan River, Whampoa River and Geylang River. Following the success of these projects, more and more agencies like HDB, Town Councils, etc, started creating their own park linkages within their development sites. Eventually, it inspired an even bigger step by an agency to extend the idea of green park connector network to the blue waters. PUB initiated the ABC Waters Programme which harmonises well with the PCN.

Although the support of the people of Singapore and many agencies have helped to overcome most of the challenges of establishing the PCN, there is still a fundamental one that will grow in prominence. The issue of land limitation will intensify with a growing population. NParks has increasingly concentrated on developing park connectors along road reserves as most of the drainage reserves are either developed or are planned for projects under the ABC programme. Developing park connectors along the road reserve poses greater challenges than within the drainage reserve as unlike riverside, road reserves are not leisure environments for people. Moreover, road reserves are already being used for many other purposes such as utilities lines, roadside trees, bus stops.

Managing the PCN

To date 180 km of park connectors have been completed. By 2015, the rest of the PCN of Singapore will be completed, making a total of about 300 km of park connectors.

The Eastern Coastal PCN, a 42km loop is the longest loop to date, and was the first Park Connector Loop to be completed in December 2007. It links the popular 185 ha East Coast Park, which has the highest park visitorship of at least 7 million a year, to Changi Beach Park. As it is next to the coast, it is one of

the most attractive park connector loops for runners, skaters, roller bladers and cyclists. Added to this, there is the appeal of users who "ride to eat" from either end of the loop to and from Changi Village or East Coast Park, where there are locally renowned food centres.

The PCN by itself is an infrastructural hardscape. What brings vibrancy to it and improves the health and well-being of its population are the activities and programmes that are held in the PCN. In April 2011, 5,000 runners participated in the 42 km Sundown Marathon, followed by 800 runners who endured a 100 km Ultra Marathon along the Eastern Coastal PCN. Officers from government agencies go on night cycling trips along park connectors to socialise as well as resolve inter-agency concerns informally. Several cycling groups use the PCN for their regular outings. Community bonding activities are also common during weekends, public holidays and school holidays.

With such wide public usage, community engagement is key to the success of the PCN. Active citizenry - where users provide constructive feedback on such matters as defective lights, advice on appropriate spots to install more signage, etc. - makes it easier for us to serve the PCN users better and to ensure public safety. We also depend on PCN users to inform us of the condition of the tracks as it is quite difficult for park managers to cover entire lengths of the PCN regularly.

NParks, as the management agency of the PCN, has been working closely with important stakeholders, especially the cycling groups who use the park connectors frequently. To date, we have a number of cycling groups who provide us with constructive feedback in areas such as how to improve the connectivity, what amenities are necessary, etc. Such ongoing engagement establishes a healthy relationship which is beneficial to all.

The challenge is to maintain park connectors as linear parks while rising to the public's growing expectations for the park connectors to function increasingly as commuter routes. As the development of the park connectors progresses, PCN users would have embraced this product and enjoyed the recreational services that they provide. Many users now expect the PCN to connect not only park to park but also to link many other places of attraction and other commuting nodes like MRT stations, bus stops, etc. Integration of intra-town cycling paths to park connectors is already under discussion.

With space constraint and increasing usage for multiple purposes, it is inevitable that there will be conflicts arising from the shared use of the narrow strip of land. There is an on-going debate concerning shared track versus split tracks. Over the years we have made a decision, to construct shared tracks, and let users self-regulate the use of the tracks for cycling or running/walking. This has proven to work quite well.

A seamless connectivity throughout the PCN is not possible. Sometimes cyclists have to dismount and push or stop at a number of crossings along the PCN. While NParks does take heed of these connectivity issues, some are beyond the control of NParks as these gaps lie in areas outside NParks' jurisdiction. Public engagement in understanding these constraints is the only option.

Figure 13: Scaly-breasted Munia
Source: Sek Jun-Yan

Biodiversity of the PCN

Surveys of various park connectors have recorded a total of 90 species of birds (see Figures 13 and 14), 57 species of butterflies and 22 species of dragonflies. A diversity of reptiles like the Malayan Water Monitor, Changeable Lizard, Common Sun Skink, Common Flying Dragon, Reticulated Python,

Paradise Tree Snake and Oriental Whipsnake has been sighted occasionally. The Plantain Squirrel is frequently seen playing along the PCN. The deep resonance of the Banded Bull Frog and Asian Toad can be heard.

Generally, the birds seen are common to urban, park and disturbed forest edge habitats. Interestingly, some locally uncommon species typical of forest habitat have also been sighted. About a third of

Figure 14: Striated Heron
Source: Serene Chng

the birds recorded are migrant species. Butterfly species recorded can commonly be found in urban gardens and parks, but some interesting forest-associated species have been recorded too.

Bird species usually thought of as common park species (Pink-necked Green Pigeon, Common Iora, Blue-crowned Hanging Parrot, Brown-throated Sunbird) are stalwarts at all park connectors, as are species that have adapted to urban life (Asian Koel, Yellow-vented Bulbul, Black-naped Oriole, Olive-backed Sunbird, Common Tailorbird). Common park and garden butterfly species including the Grass Blue, Common Caerulean, Small Branded Swift, Common Grass Yellow, Lemon Emigrant, Chocolate Pansy, Common Mormon, Lime Butterfly, Plain Tiger (see

Figure 15) and Malayan Eggfly are regularly recorded. Transects along HDB estates are dominated by human-associated bird species such as Eurasian Tree Sparrow, Javan Myna, Rock Pigeon and House Crow, even though wildlife-attracting plants have been added (Kolam Ayer, Bukit Panjang Park Connector). Striated Heron, Little Egret, Grey Heron, Common Sandpiper, Collared Kingfisher, White-throated Kingfisher and Little Tern are regularly recorded at park connectors along water culverts.

Park connectors bordering areas of forested land were found to contain species commonly encountered at the edges of forests such as Greater Racket-tailed Drongo, Dark-necked Tailorbird, Laced Woodpecker, Greater Coucal and Pin-Striped-Tit Babbler (Ulu Pandan Park

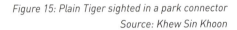

Figure 15: Plain Tiger sighted in a park connector
Source: Khew Sin Khoon

Figure 16: Crimson Sunbird in flight
Source: Cai Yixiong

Connector, Pangsua Park Connector). Rare raptors including Grey-headed Fish Eagle and Changeable Hawk Eagle have also been recorded in such forested areas. Forest-associated butterflies such as Bigg's Brownie, Forest Hopper, The Malayan, Commander, Anderson's Grass Yellow, Psyche and Banded Swallowtail are present.

Some unexpected surprises were found even along such narrow strips of vegetation. Nationally-endangered Black-crowned Night Herons have been seen feeding along the canals. Uncommon migrants such as Black-capped Kingfisher, Chestnut-winged Cuckoo, White Wagtail, Blue-winged Pitta and Asian Paradise Flycatcher have been recorded too. Although more often associated with forested habitats, it is likely these have dropped into

vegetation patches along park connectors to rest and feed en route to and from wintering grounds.

A key function of park connectors appears to be the provision of food resources; a large proportion of fauna are recorded to be foraging and feeding in park connector vegetation and even along the canals. It is expected that the presence of flowering or fruiting trees attracts large numbers of birds and observations support the effectiveness of such plants in enhancing urban biodiversity. Similarly, the planting of butterfly host and food plants and the presence of flowering trees attracts large numbers of butterflies; even flamboyant species that were previously restricted to more natural areas have now spread to urban parks and gardens with suitable planting schemes. The mere presence of food-providing plants is not sufficient; layers of mature trees and shrubs provide conductive feeding environments. A wide variety of plant species also provides a more complex habitat to support fauna. The planting guidelines listed in the design and development section above have proven to be appropriate as indicated by the observations in the field. Apart from just plants, the presence of healthy insect communities is also required to support birds.

It appears that some bird species defend home territories along park connectors – territorial calls of birds such as Olive-backed, Brown-throated and Crimson Sunbird (see Figure 16), Common and Dark-necked Tailorbird, Asian Koel, Striped Tit Babbler and Collared Kingfisher are regularly heard during surveys. A few bird species, notably those commonly found in urban parks, have been observed breeding along the park connector – nests of Striated Heron, Pink-necked Green Pigeon and Olive-backed Sunbird have been seen, as have juvenile Red Junglefowl hybrids, Black-naped Oriole, Javan Myna, Tailorbirds, White-bellied Sea Eagle, Brahminy Kite, Black-crowned Night Heron and Scaly-breasted Munia. This suggests that some urban-adapted species use the narrow park connector vegetation as breeding territories and thus are successfully colonising park connector vegetation as habitats. Caterpillars on host plants indicate successful reproduction, while dragonflies have been observed egg-laying along the canals.

The 2m wide planting edge may provide additional habitat for urban and park species, but is insufficient in providing a corridor for the movement of more sensitive species. Forest-edge species tend to be present only at park connectors bordering forest patches, and not at those merely connecting forest patches. If the full potential of park connectors as movement corridors is to be realised,

the planting width needs to be widened substantially or more innovative ways have to be devised.

The land use next to the park connector affects the species composition, diversity and abundance recorded along the park connector itself. Park connectors with lower levels of human activity, low-density land use and natural habitats adjacent to them have greater species diversity and a more equal spread of abundance across species compared to more urban Park connectors with high levels of human activity. Retaining existing natural habitat adjacent to park connectors is therefore as important as enhancing vegetation of the park connector itself.

Much has been done to enhance the biodiversity of park connectors. Efforts include the planting of butterfly host and food plants in butterfly gardens and fruiting trees to attract birds. Still, more can be done to fully realise the potential of park connectors as supplementary habitat and food resources and hence increase their biodiversity value. Viable habitat that can support fauna communities is required. Plantings should be continuous and multi-layered with mature trees and shrubs. On top of being fantastic for fauna, mature trees also provide users with shade.

Conservation of natural habitat patches adjacent to park connectors and the retention of existing vegetation during development is crucial to supporting wildlife. Park connectors can enhance such habitats as buffers and food sources. Species that cannot be sufficiently supported by linear park connector vegetation can colonise such patches and are likely to venture out to feed along park connectors. This will greatly enhance the biodiversity experience for park connector users too.

Sensitive management of the park connector vegetation is essential to the continued presence of fauna. Minimising the frequency and extent of maintenance will not only cut costs, but also increase the biodiversity value of park connectors. Less frequent grass-cutting and limiting major pruning work to non-breeding periods (September to February) will enable wildlife to thrive. At less urban areas, minimal maintenance limited to the path and non-mechanical methods will be less disruptive.

The accessibility of park connectors to the general public makes it an ideal outreach opportunity to highlight biodiversity to park connector users. Information boards on species found there are either in existence or will be put up at 'hotspots'. The PCN team also engages schools in stewardship schemes, for instance planting and caring for butterfly gardens. Such community involvement will increase awareness and concern for biodiversity and environmental sustainability issues.

jogging, cycling, nature watch, photography, marathons, family outings, community bonding, etc., indicate that it is well-used by people for their physical, psychological, social and mental well-being.

The diverse planting in the PCN, particularly large-crowned trees, facilitates the enhancement of wildlife in urban settings and the lowering of the ambient temperatures of surrounding hardscapes. These contribute positively to the environmental sustainability of the city.

As a network of park connectors running beside managed waterways, the PCN has integrated well into Singapore's scheme of being a biophilic City in A Garden, within twenty years of its inception.
Looking forward, there are plans to further innovatively enhance the greenery and biodiversity within the highly urbanised areas so as to make Singapore a sustainable, liveable and healthy city to live, work and play in.

Conclusion

Land scarcity is a key issue that needs to be addressed in the entire life cycle of the PCN, i.e., at the planning, design and development, and management stages. This is usually compounded by multi-agency jurisdiction of areas occupied by the PCN, and hence, could lead to conflicts of land-use. On the other hand, land scarcity has necessitated dialogue among agencies which has resulted in the optimization of space through the innovative multi-layering of uses. It has also challenged agencies to explore sites that were previously thought to be unusable. In developing the PCN, the land scarcity constraint in Singapore has been turned into an oasis of innovations, and opportunities for people and wildlife to enjoy.

The increasing use of the PCN by different users for various activities like walking,

Acknowledgement

The contributions of many NParks' officers, in particular, Nicole Anne Phillips, Bernard Lim, Serene Chng, Geoffrey Davison and Chia Seng Jiang are gratefully acknowledged. Rachel Lim, Jeremy Woon and Farhanah Hamid assisted in the preparations of the maps and figures. The authors would like to thank Khew Sin Khoon, Serene Chng, Sek Jun Yan, Mohammad Shairazi Idris, Cai Yixiong and NParks for the use of their photographs.

Common Name	Scientific Name
Birds	
Asian Koel	*Eudynamys scolopacea*
Asian Paradise Flycatcher	*Tersiphone paradisi*
Black-capped Kingfisher	*Halcyon pileata*
Black-crowned Night Heron	*Nycticorax nycticorax*
Black-naped Oriole	*Oriolus chinensis*
Blue-crowned Hanging Parrot	*Loriculus galgulus*
Blue-winged Pitta	*Pitta moluccensis*
Brahminy Kite	*Haliastur indus*
Brown-throated Sunbird	*Anthreptes malacensis*
Changeable Hawk Eagle	*Spizaetus cirrhatus*
Chestnut-winged Cuckoo	*Clamator coromandus*
Collared Kingfisher	*Todiramphus chloris*
Common Iora	*Aegithina tiphia*
Common Sandpiper	*Actitis hypoleucos*
Common Tailorbird	*Orthotomus sutorius*
Crimson Sunbird	*Aethopyga siparaja*
Dark-necked Tailorbird	*Orthotomus atrogularis*
Eurasian Tree Sparrow	*Passer montanus*
Rock Pigeon	*Columba livia*
Greater Coucal	*Centropus sinensis*
Greater Racket-tailed Drongo	*Dicrusrus paradiseus*
Grey Heron	*Ardea cinerea*
Grey-headed Fish Eagle	*Ichthyophaga ichthyaetus*
House Crow	*Corvus splendens*
Javan Myna	*Acridotheres javanicus*
Laced Woodpecker	*Picus vittatus*
Little Egret	*Egretta garzetta*
Little Tern	*Sterna albifrons*
Olive-backed Sunbird	*Nectarinia jugularis*
Pink-necked Green Pigeon	*Treron vernans*
Red Junglefowl (hybrid)	*Gallus gallus*
Scaly-breasted Munia	*Lonchura punctulata*
Striated Heron	*Butorides striatus*
Striped Tit Babbler	*Macronous gularis*
White Wagtail	*Motacilla alba*
White-bellied Sea Eagle	*Haliaeetus leucogaster*
White-throated Kingfisher	*Halcyon smyrnensis*
Yellow-vented Bulbul	*Pycnonotus goiavier*

Mammals

Plantain Squirrel	*Callosciurus notatus*

Reptiles

Malayan Water Monitor	*Varanus salvator*
Changeable Lizard	*Calotes versicolor*
Common Sun Skink	*Eutropis multifasciatus*
Common Flying Dragon	*Draco sumatranus*
Reticulated Python	*Python reticulatus*
Paradise Tree Snake	*Chrysopelea paradisi*
Oriental Whipsnake	*Ahaetulla prasina*

Amphibians

Banded Bull Frog	*Kaloula pulchra*
Asian Toad	*Duttaphrynus melanostictus*

Butterflies

Common Caerulean	*Jamides celeno aelianus*
Small Branded Swift	*Pelopidas mathias mathias*
Common Grass Yellow	*Eurema hecabe contubernalis*
Lemon Emigrant	*Catopsilia pomona pomona*
Chocolate Pansy	*Junonia hedonia ida*
Common Mormon	*Papilio polytes romulus*
Lime Butterfly	*Papilio demoleus malayanus*
Plain Tiger	*Danaus chrysippus chrysippus*
Malayan Eggfly	*Hypolimnas anomala anomala*
Bigg's Brownie	*Miletus biggsii biggsii*
Forest Hopper	*Astictopterus jama jama*
The Malayan	*Megisba malaya sikkima*
Commander	*Moduza procris milonia*
Anderson's Grass Yellow	*Eurema andersonii andersonii*
Psyche	*Leptosia nina malayana*
Banded Swallowtail	*Papilio demolion demolion*

Endnotes

1. The Malesian region is a biogeographical region which straddles the boundaries of the Indomalayan ecozone and Australia ecozone.

2. A dipterocarp forest harbours many species of *Dipterocarpus*, a prominent genus of timber trees.

3. The National Parks Board is the national agency responsible for conserving the natural environment and providing and enhancing the greenery of Singapore. It is Singapore's scientific authority on nature conservation.

4. The Urban Redevelopment Authority is Singapore's national land use planning authority, developing long term strategic plans as well as detailed local area plans for physical development.

5. PUB, the national water agency, is responsible for the collection, production, distribution and reclamation of water in Singapore.

6. The Housing and Development Board is Singapore's public housing authority, responsible for planning and developing public housing towns.

7. JTC Corporation is Singapore's leading industrial infrastructure specialist spearheading the planning, promotion and development of a dynamic industrial landscape.

8. The Land Transport Authority is the national authority overseeing the long-term transport needs of Singapore, for both private and public transport.

9. SMRT Corporation Ltd is Singapore's premier multi-modal public transport service provider offering integrated transport services island-wide.

10. The Singapore Land Authority manages the development of state land in Singapore and maintains the national land information database.

11. The Building and Construction Authority is the government agency responsible for ensuring that quality standards are met in the built up environment of Singapore.

References

Baker, N., Lim, K. (2008) Wild Animals of Singapore: A Photographic Guide to Mammals, Reptiles, Amphibians and Freshwater Fishes. Vertebrate Study Group, Nature Society, Singapore

Hails, C.J. (1985) Studies of the Habitat Requirements and Management of Wild Birds in Singapore: A report submitted to the Commissioner for Parks & Recreation, Ministry of National Development, Internal government report, Singapore

Khew S. K. (2010) A field guide to the Butterflies of Singapore. Ink on Paper Communications Pte Ltd.

National Parks Board (2009) Conserving Biodiversity: Singapore's National Biodiversity Strategy and Action Plan. National Parks Board, Singapore

Tan, W.K. (2004) A greenway network for Singapore, Landscape and Urban Planning, 76 (2006): 45-66
Urban Redevelopment Authority (1991) Living the Next lap: Towards a Tropical City of Excellence. Singapore

Urban Redevelopment Authority (2008) Singapore Masterplan, Special and Detailed Controls Plans, Parks and Waterbodies Plan www.ura.gov.sg/mp08/map.jsf, Singapore

Wang, L.K., Hails, C. (2007) "An annotated checklist of the birds of Singapore". Raffles Bulletin of Zoology Supplement 15, Singapore

Skolkovo:
City of the Future
as a Russian
Hi-Tech Hub

Fedor Kudryavtsev

Victoria Bannykh

Taking the Challenge: New City as an Innovation Locomotive

In spite of Russia's rich history of scientific and technical achievement, the last several decades of its development have been characterised by what might be called the "oil curse". The oil extraction industry has dominated the national economy, and other sectors such as manufacturing have declined unless oil-related. In a broader sense, it has become less interesting to develop new approaches, technologies and products that could achieve a leadership position in the global economic context.

Accepting the challenge, President Medvedev in his annual speech to the State Duma (Parliament) for 2009 initiated the Innovation Centre project as part of his policy of modernization that should back research and development activities in five key technological sectors:

- Energy efficiency, energy conservation and new types of fuel;
- Nuclear power technologies;
- Strategic information technologies and software;
- Space technologies, primarily as regards remote sensing, telecommunications and satellite navigation;
- Medical equipment and medicines.

According to the President, the new centre would "...offer attractive working conditions for leading researchers, engineers, designers, software programmers, managers and financial specialists, and ... produce new technology able to compete on the global market". Following this approach, the idea of the "city as an innovation" (see Figure 1) has been conceived as a part of a new "ecosystem", favourable to the development and marketing of new products and technologies.

All the activities of the city are determined by its main mission: to concentrate intellectual resources and produce innovations

Figure 1: Innovation City concept

Figure 2: Location map

Figure 3: Current use of
site (Satellite image from
Google Earth)

It is to be a compact urban space that provides conditions conducive to both work and life. It would also serve as an urban development benchmark both in Russia and worldwide.

Figure 4: Moscow School of Management Building

City of Innovations: Basic Ideas and Management

The place for the new city was the subject of intense debate between the stakeholders: politicians, government officials, scientists, businessmen and the general public. While there are many famous Russian cities with traditions as centres of science that date back to the Soviet era, the final selection fell upon a green field situated near the small village of Skolkovo 2 kilometres south-west of Moscow (see Figure 2).

Nowadays, this territory looks like a patch of pleasant natural hilly landscape almost 400 hectares in area that stretches along a small river among villages, cottages, gated communities and blocks of houses on the fringe of urban Moscow (see Figure 3).

In recent decades, the meadows and fields here have been used as a place for agricultural studies conducted by a State scientific institution that has protected them so far from inevitable suburbanization. Nevertheless, neither the landscape nor its good location near Moscow were driving forces in the selection, but rather its proximity to another project with global ambitions. The new Skolkovo division of the Moscow School of Management (see Figure 4), to be built nearby based on principles of combined public and private partnership, was perceived to have the proper "history of success" to back, facilitate and speed up development of the Innovation Centre.

Deriving its name from its location, a new brand, the Skolkovo Innovation Centre, has appeared. Although not officially stated, the intention to make it very distinct both from previous experience in town planning, urban management and economic development, and those of modern-day Russia, is evident from its management approach. This consideration seems to have played an important role in this selection, where an empty space in the Moscow metropolitan area was preferred over well-known R&D facilities and universities in Tomsk or Novosibirsk in Siberia, famed for their scientific achievements.

To allow the pursuit of this goal of creating extraordinary conditions for innovation, special laws were passed for Skolkovo, setting up special modes of taxation, city management, building regulations, etc. These laws are to simplify complicated bureaucratic procedures and to open the door for advanced methods, approaches and technologies. The Centre should become a testing area for new economic policies focused on overcoming the "oil-curse" problem.

While the law has defined the Skolkovo Innovation Centre as a "geographically separate facility," it definitely appears as an "island" in many other aspects too. It is an area where the building standards of other developed countries can be readily applied, including sanitation rules, should these be more stringent than the local ones. None of the State inspections of design documentation and building processes, compulsory for all remaining Russian territory, are applicable here. Medical and educational institutions are not obliged to get State accreditations and licenses that are mandatory elsewhere. Moreover, all such institutions are expected to be non-governmental. Unlike the existing Urban Planning Code, local plans are not subject to public debate with the local population or approval procedures by regional authorities.

The project is governed by only one institution – a management company named the Foundation for the Development of the Centre of Research and Commercialization of New Technologies in Skolkovo. It is a non-profit making organisation responsible for all issues related to the development and functioning of the Innovation Centre from selecting future street names to establishing the principles for medical services and the education system in the new city. It also has the power to introduce its own procedures for issuing building permits, as well as to develop and adopt the city's master plan and building regulations. The territory of the Skolkovo Innovation Centre will be beyond the bounds of power and responsibility of both regional and municipal authorities. Federal institutions like the police, the tax office, etc., must establish special divisions that answer directly to the central administration and not the regional one. The Foundation is the owner of the Innovation Centre's land and infrastructure, including the rental housing for future inhabitants. It is also responsible for the selection of the hi-tech companies that will settle in the Centre and for obtaining solid financial support from the State: zero profit tax for 10 years, halved social insurance tax, full reimbursement of Value Added Tax and customs duties on imported materials and equipment, grants for research, and the

possibility to use shared labs and facilities. Nevertheless, the Foundation is not intended to receive shares in or participate in the profits of the companies that will reside in Skolkovo.

While the management company is empowered with unprecedented responsibilities and privileges, it is only allowed to use them for developing the Skolkovo Innovation Centre and attracting research and development activities of the highest quality. There are two very important goals justifying its mandate:

- Developing and maintaining globally competitive conditions and an environment conducive to advanced and innovative research and commercialization of its results, as well as promoting the formation of a new generation of scholars in the priority fields of study.
- Organising a full cycle of research and development activities necessary for the production of technological innovations and their commercialization.

Exclusion from the routine and often complicated and inefficient administrative hierarchy and legal framework allows the Skolkovo Foundation to keep its activities open to the public. It also allows it to develop an internal management system adapted to working with international and local experts to effectively use the investments at its disposal and, on the other hand, to secure necessary political support and links to the financial and hi-tech sectors. The President of Russia is the Head of the Board of Trustees, while key ministers and other relevant top State officials are members. Multibillionaire Viktor Vekselberg and former Chairman of the Board of Intel Corporation, Craig Barrett, are co-chairmen of the Foundation Council. There is also a Science Consulting Council with two Nobel prize winners at its head, an Investment Committee, and a Town Planning Council that includes local and international specialists in planning, transportation, architecture, the environment, including two Pritzker award winners: Kazuyo Sejima and Pierre de Meuron.

The budget assigned to the Innovation Centre by the State is 15 billion rubles for 2011, 22 billion for 2012 and 17.1 billion for 2013 (~ 0.54, 0.79 and 0.6 billion USD respectively). In 2010, about 4 billion rubles were spent, 2.6 to support projects approved by the Presidential Commission for Modernization and 0.3 for projects selected by the Skolkovo Management Company itself. It is envisaged that the government will finance expenditure for the management of the project, development of city infrastructure and non-commercial buildings, and research and development facilities. Other issues will be co-financed by the State and investors.

In the end, the Innovation Centre should play the role of the "entrance gates" to the Russian market through which foreign investors can enter other regions and cities. Vice versa, Russian innovation companies can use its facilities to meet international venture investors and hi-tech corporations to enter international markets. At the moment, 275 applications for Skolkovo resident status have been submitted, with 57 approved. 16 companies have already received grants for research and development activities from the Skolkovo Foundation. In the future, it is planned to launch "virtual" Skolkovo companies that would be considered Innovation Centre residents while working in other cities and regions of Russia. If the project is successful, similar ones may be started in other parts of Russia too.

Master Plan for the Future

The Skolkovo Innovation Centre is envisaged as a pioneer project for the "city of the future." It is to promote modern approaches to town planning across Russia and to serve as an urban development role model for other cities. The city will gradually evolve and grow around the core infrastructure and public spaces, changing as the requirements of its inhabitants change. Nevertheless, its function and form should be focused on its mission of accumulating intellectual capital and generating technological innovation. The city is to have a techno park, scientific laboratories, a university and other educational institutions, hi-tech industries, housing, public spaces and cultural facilities like theatres, clubs, etc. The whole technological chain from research to the launch of new products on the global market is to be concentrated here in one place.

In the preliminary stages that were to lead to the drafting of the Skolkovo Innovation Centre master plan, four key principles were selected as guidelines for the area's design and development, known now as the "4 Es". They are environmentally friendly, ergonomic, energy efficient and economically effective.

Figure 5: Master plan of Skolkovo Innovation Centre by AREP

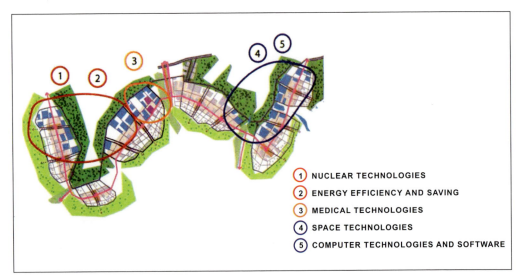

1. NUCLEAR TECHNOLOGIES
2. ENERGY EFFICIENCY AND SAVING
3. MEDICAL TECHNOLOGIES
4. SPACE TECHNOLOGIES
5. COMPUTER TECHNOLOGIES AND SOFTWARE

Figure 6: Innovation Centre land-use diagram

Any company that applies for resident status in Skolkovo is obliged to transfer its operations and staff to Skolkovo territory. Therefore, it is planned that the new city should have about 15,500 permanent residents (6,200 employees and university academic staff and 9,300 family members). In addition, about 7,000 people will come to work in Skolkovo every day as commuters and 2000 as "guests". About 22% of the total area of the buildings will be directly used for research and development functions, 60% for housing, and the rest for other functions.

Based on the principles developed during the preparatory stages, the Skolkovo Foundation announced an international contest for the drawing up of a master plan. It is pertinent to say that such a competition is not usual in modern-day Russia. It is especially true for projects financed by the State, as current legislation only allows tenders where the cheapest bid always wins. After the qualification stage among 27 international teams, six

were allowed to develop their proposals. Each entry was to be prepared within a budget of 195,000 euros.

In February, 2011, the winner was announced after six weeks of debates and Internet voting. It was the French team AREP Ville, Michelle Desvigne Paysagiste and SETEC (see Figure 5).

The principal idea of the layout is to organise a system of separate "clusters" or "city villages" which will be incorporated into system of green spaces carefully following the existing natural landscape. The number of clusters corresponds to the main fields of work the Skolkovo Innovation Centre must focus on (see Figure 6).

A green boulevard connects all parts of the city and is its backbone. A guest zone near the railway station combines key public areas of the city such as a congress hall, a business centre, religious buildings, hotels and medical institutions. It is linked to the adjacent area of

Figure 7: Green network

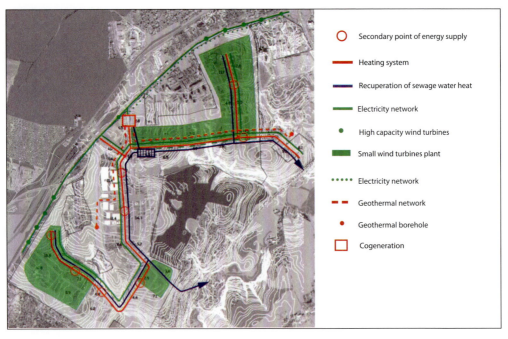

○	Secondary point of energy supply
▬	Heating system
▬	Recuperation of sewage water heat
▬	Electricity network
●	High capacity wind turbines
▬	Small wind turbines plant
•••••	Electricity network
▬ ▬	Geothermal network
●	Geothermal borehole
☐	Cogeneration

Figure 8: Engineering infrastructure

the university. Each "village" occupies a river terrace providing impressive and picturesque views over the surrounding areas and a landscape park to be developed along the river (see Figure 7).

At the same time, sections of the natural landscape will be a part of the engineering system and used for drainage and collecting of rainfall and water from melted snow (see Figure 8).

Each cluster presents a multifunctional structure (see Figure 9) consisting of three main linear zones: "manufacturing", where labs and other research and development facilities are concentrated, "public" or "social," and residential.

Due to the abundance of greenery, the urban areas are always within walking distance of a natural landscape, so the comfort of a modern city and elements of rural life become integrated (see Figure 10).

The transportation scheme envisages three main access points to the city for cars from roads leading to Moscow. Electric cars will be used for internal movement. The city will also be connected by express trains to two Moscow terminals.

Figure 9: Land-use principles: efficient city, modular and flexible, mixture of functions, evolutionary development

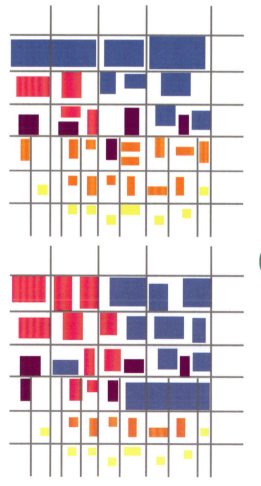

Figure 10: Principles of natural and urban environment interaction. Access to high quality natural landscape, regulation of city microclimate, maintenance of biodiversity, variety of natural resources utilization

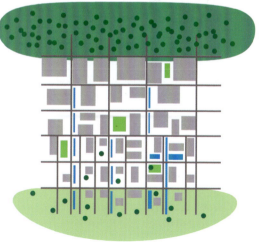

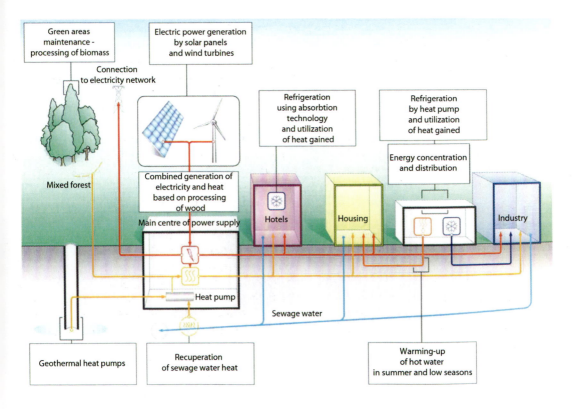

Figure 11: Principles of utilization of renewable sources of power supply

One of Skolkovo's objectives is to be an energy efficient city with zero or a minimized amount of waste, including carbon emissions. It is striving for the position of the first city in Russia that will not consume energy from external sources. The competition focused on the use of such renewable sources of energy as geothermal, solar panels and wind turbines. Nevertheless, taking local climate conditions into account, significant importance is now attached to the processing of biomass and the use of biofuels as part of the planned energy supply (Figure 11).

Additional significant features that impressed the jury were compliance with the "culture of a scientific city" and flexibility of the planning scheme, which would allow modifications and alterations as the project developed. Later, about 20 architectural competitions targeting both big design firms and particularly focused on young architects are planned. The total budget to complete the project in 2015 is estimated at 120 billion rubles (4.3 billion USD). Half of it should comprise private investments.

Reporting on the results of the competition, Mr.Vekselberg, the President of the Skolkovo Foundation, indicated that Skolkovo's town planning project will pursue the following principles:

- Compactness of the "urban tissue" and a mixed land-use structure: work places, residential and recreational spaces are to be within walking distance, creating diverse and intensive living spaces.
- High-density low-rise residential areas as simultaneously energy efficient and a human-friendly urban environment;
- Provision of public spaces that serve as multifunctional areas for work, rest and communication 24 hours a day.
- An efficient and effective transportation system based on the "smart" technology concept, which means active data flows between all its components and the possibility of managing it on-line.
- A polycentric structure of independent "islands" connected by infrastructural corridors and separated by natural landscapes.
- The intense use of telecommunications systems and related remote forms of access to work, educational and other activities and services.
- Last but not least is the requirement that the city should have low carbon emissions and a low or zero amount of waste released into the natural environment. Energy-efficient buildings, smart grids of engineering facilities, environmentally friendly waste recycling systems and a city layout adapted to the use of natural light are among the most important approaches to be applied.

Conclusions

The very idea of the Innovation Centre as a tool to push the whole country in the direction of a more effective economy, away from its dependency on raw material production, seems to be "green" in itself. Moreover, one of the Skolkovo Centre's strategic fields of research is energy efficiency. This is especially important for Russia, where the abundance of fossil fuels is always balanced by severe and long winters. The concepts of the master plan selected, such as a pedestrian friendly environment, the human scale of built-up areas, and the mixed use and integration of urban and natural landscapes, seem to promise that the new city will be livable. Nevertheless, some issues should be further analysed and carefully scrutinised in order to achieve this goal:

- While being proclaimed a "city," its status is questionable from some points of view. The new Centre is situated in a suburban area of Moscow and, in this respect, could equally be considered as a part of the urban sprawl that large corporate campuses and R&D centres usually form a part of. This threat is also backed by the low-density housing clearly selected by the authors of the project as the main form of urban residential areas. Its structure of random "integration" into green areas looks very attractive, but presents the risk of a gradual incursion of growing housing estates into green areas.
- Pedestrian accessibility and a clear transport scheme inside the designated area are not supported by similar regional development plans. For example, there are no plans yet for high-speed connections between the new city and its surroundings, such as international airports or other cities nearby, that should perform an important role in the functioning of an international hi-tech cluster.

• Concerning social life, the main question is whether a scientific city is capable of constantly maintaining a high percentage of its inhabitants actually working in hi-tech sectors or scientific laboratories. This problem has been experienced by a large number of such cities constructed in 60s and 70s around Moscow. Examples are the nuclear research centre in Dubna and cities in other regions, such as the famous Academgorodok near Novosibirsk. Children of the "first settlers" are not obliged to continue family traditions by working in the same industries or academic institutions. In the case of Skolkovo, this issue may be even more acute because of the attractiveness of Moscow as a metropolis, and the proximity of high-income suburbs in the western part of the Moscow region. From another point of view, to create a livable city with a population that is not permanent, but constantly changing, is a challenge that may not yet have been taken into account.

• Regarding the urban milieu provided for in the master plan, one may think about the character of the urban spaces formed by large-scale laboratories and assembly facilities. These buildings are not the same as the palaces and rich merchants' houses of the past. It is unlikely that Silicon Valley, or any other less famous suburban office parks, for that matter, is an example of an architecturally impressive city. Some new principles of "creative" urban space still have to be developed to avoid breaking up the Innovation Centre into purely functional zones similar to Tony Garnier's industrial city of more than a century ago, or Nikolay Milutin's linear city of Magnitogorsk proposed in the 30s. The AREP concept tends to be very similar to the latter in that functional zones stretch along a main transport backbone.

• Some sources of renewable energy appeared to be ineffective and insignificant in view of the local climate, for example solar panels or wind turbines. The use of low-rise housing, the density of which is anyway limited by its typology, is questionable. It has always been associated with a lifestyle built around the private car. The perfect solution for the city must be "green" in terms of energy consumption and not just due to an abundance of lawn grass.

Further criticisms could be made, but at the same time, they may be mitigated as the project moves forward and gradually becomes more detailed. The principal question that seems to remain on the agenda is paradoxical. Can the building of a new "green" and "hi-tech" city in a natural "green" environment that has fortuitously survived near a tremendous metropolis still be regarded as a "green" approach? The Skolkovo project has already started and is unlikely to be discontinued, but the pros and cons still have to be scrutinized in the continuing attempt to make better and more liveable cities, especially the new ones.

Fedor Kudryavtsev | Victoria Bannykh

References

"Foundation for the Development of the Centre of Research and Commercialization of New Technologies in Skolkovo". Innovation Centre Skolkovo: Urban Concept Contest. 2011

Federal Law #243-FZ of September 28, 2010 "On Amending Certain Legislative Acts of the Russian Federation in Connection with the Adoption of the Federal Law on the Innovation Centre Skolkovo". *Rossiyskaya Gazeta. September 30, 2010*

Federal Law #244-FZ of September 28, 2010 "On the Innovation Centre Skolkovo". *Rossiyskaya Gazeta. September 30, 2010.*

President D.A.Medvedev "Message to the Federal Parliament for 2009". *Rossiyskaya Gazeta. September 11.2009*

The Official Website of Skolkovo Foundation. http://www.i-gorod.com

The London 2012 Olympic Park: Planning for a Sustainable Legacy

Dan Epstein

Jo Carris

Emily Moore

Judith Sykes

Vision for the Olympic Park after the Games (computer generated image)

London 2012 took the lessons learnt from previous major sporting events on board when planning for the Games, by focusing planning and design on legacy rather than just the event.

A commitment to be the most sustainable Games ever and to leave a lasting legacy was initially established in the bid. The undertaking of such an ambitious commitment was carried out through two approaches. The first approach was to ensure that the development of the Games Masterplan had legacy at the forefront of its design. The second was to produce and implement a Sustainable Development Strategy for the delivery of the Olympic Park[xii].

The Sustainable Development Strategy set overarching sustainability targets that needed to be met on all aspects of the Park during construction. In conjunction with this, individual venues also set their own bespoke targets and objectives for achieving sustainable, legacy-driven designs. We cite as three examples of these venues and schemes the Community Utilities Infrastructure established, the Olympic Velopark and the Aquatics Centre.

The Olympic Delivery Authority [1] (ODA) is on track to deliver its challenging Sustainable Development Strategy and the construction of the Park is on programme, on budget and on course to meet its commitments to quality. The planning, design and delivery approach is widely regarded to have set new levels of best practice for major event construction and large scale regeneration projects. However the development does not come without criticism. Inevitably on such a large project there has been disruption to existing businesses and communities and the character of the place has been utterly transformed.

The measure of success will be how mixed, vibrant and inclusive the Olympic Park and surrounding areas have become in the decades after the Olympic Games. This will be measured in economic, social and environmental terms.

Lessons Learnt From Past Major Sporting Events

Major sporting events provide a unique opportunity to transform cities and even nations. A review of many of the most recent Olympic Games and World Cups, however, has revealed that whilst the events themselves have been successful, they have left proverbial white elephants. Stadia are underused or disused, Olympic Parks are wind swept and derelict and there has been little in the way of long-term social, economic or environmental regeneration.

In the city of Athens, of the 22 venues located in the city, 21 were in a state of disrepair in 2008 and under costly surveillance to prevent further vandalism.[i] In a statement to the media, Spyros Doukakis, General Secretary for Olympic Utilization, explained future host cities should "learn from our past mistakes and have a post-utilization Olympic plan that will invite mixed public and private schemes, these tenders should be organised well before the beginning of the event."[ii] Even the Barcelona Olympics, which is credited by many for helping to transform Barcelona into a thriving and confident city, has a poorly used Olympic Park that has not been fully integrated into the city as a whole.

It has taken Sydney nearly a decade to transform its Olympic Park from a soulless space into a bustling new suburb on the west of the city. The transformation has largely been achieved because the Park is now home to an active events and conference programme, which, in turn, has stimulated investment in a new hotel, offices and restaurants. There is still however much more to do. The development hiatus was largely caused by the lack of foresight and planning for legacy during the original design and construction period. The planning for the Games had been all-consuming and there was an unwillingness to invest in the social and physical infrastructure to support long-term development.[iii]

The experience of Sydney, Athens and even Beijing, where the Birds Nest Stadium has only been used a handful of times, was a lesson to London. London's focus therefore moved to planning for legacy and ensuring that the investment in stadia and facilities was based on their long-term economic viability.

Figure 1: Article on the importance of legacy
Source: The Evening Standard, 2009 [iv]

Vision for London 2012 – Focus on Legacy

From the outset, London was determined to host the Olympics only if it could demonstrate that investment in the Olympics would stimulate urban renewal. The Mayor of London, in agreeing to support the bid for the 2012 Olympics made it clear that his primary objective was to attract political support and funding for the regeneration of the Lower Lea Valley – an area in East London with recognised environmental and socio-economic issues.

The local economy within the Lower Lea Valley was traditionally dominated by manufacturing, waste management, warehousing, and other industrial uses, including a major landfill site. It was an area of great innovation in the industrial era of the mid 1800s and early 1900s. For example it was home to the famous Bryant and May's match factory [v] during this period, as well as a fireworks factory petrol station and electricity generating plant. Britain's first radio valve factory was established in the Lea Valley in 1916, and the first television tube factory following in 1936 [vi].

The site was also crossed by major urban infrastructure including high voltage power lines and other engineering structures which made development very difficult and expensive and inhibited movement across the site. Many of the factories and businesses went into decline from the 1970s onwards (when the docks closed), leaving a site that was contaminated and derelict, and resulted in major job losses. There were limited opportunities for higher wage employment and the physical neglect of the area had a negative impact on inward investment.

The site was also under multiple ownerships, and contained parts of five London boroughs which collectively experience high levels of

Figure 2: View of the Olympic Park before demolition

poverty, deprivation and socio-economic disadvantage. Data compiled by the Department for Work and Pensions in 2009 showed that two of the host boroughs' (Tower Hamlets and Hackney) rates of claiming housing benefits were more than double the national average of 17.6%. [vii]

Whilst the site was earmarked for development, there was no opportunity to deliver the scale of change needed to achieve economic restructuring and physical regeneration, due to a disparate and complex patchwork of infrastructure challenges.

Figure 3: Vision of the Olympic Park in legacy (computer generated images)

With all of these challenges in mind, the London 2012 bid presented a vision for change in an area of London that needed it the most.

Change involved preparing for the Games in 2012 with the clean up and re-profiling of approximately 2.5 km² of contaminated and derelict land and waterways. The objective is to deliver a legacy of between 8000 – 10,000 new jobs in modern workspaces, and up to 11,000 homes arranged around a 102 ha urban park and improved waterways. This will take

several decades to complete but a significant start has been made.

Sitting behind the vision to regenerate the area and create a new thriving community was a commitment to create a mixed use development, which would become part of London's urban fabric and be fully integrated into the neighbourhoods surrounding the Olympic Park. There is, rightly, great sensitivity about creating an inclusive new quarter for London that does not drive out existing residents,

whilst also inviting new communities to form. For this reason a mix of housing tenures is to be created, with 35% of the housing being affordable and largely managed by partner housing associations, who are investing in the development.

The site was also selected strategically for its growth potential, in order to help London meet its growing demand for housing, fuelled largely by migration both from within the UK and from around the world. The Lower Lea Valley has been identified as an important growth pole because it is a brown field site, is close to the City of London, was relatively under-utilised, is located next to excellent public transport connections (following major investment over the last 25 years), is located close to the largest shopping centre in Europe and to other community and social facilities and, as a result, could support a high density development[viii].

Figure 4: Vision of the Olympic Park in legacy (computer generated images)

Regeneration could only be successfully achieved if there was political support and sufficient funding to:

• Enable the biggest single compulsory purchase and land assembly scheme ever attempted in the UK;
• Create a single planning authority to deliver the planning approvals in time to meet the demanding Olympic programme without relaxing the planning requirements; and
• Support the programme of capital works required to deliver the Olympic Park and legacy project by 2012.

The opportunity to stage the Olympics therefore provided the political momentum and support for the project. It allowed the Olympic Park to be developed in under seven years from award of the Olympic Games, and in four years from planning permission. The planning and regeneration of such a large area would not have happened in such efficient time without the Olympic Games as a catalyst.

The Development of the London 2012 Masterplan

The vision for the London 2012 Masterplan was, first, to deliver a long-term sustainable community and then, secondly, to create a park to host the Olympics.

There were many challenges associated with this task, one being the complications with designing infrastructure for two very different purposes. The Olympic Games impose all sorts of constraints and requirements that are very specific to a one-off event and necessitate facilities and infrastructure that will never be required again. An example here is the creation of a fixed impermeable boundary, to ensure the security of the Park, access to which would be by ticket only. At the same time, the legacy development is specifically designed to be as open and permeable as possible and to provide a safe, well connected and fully accessible site as represented in Figure 5. The boundary fences and entrance designs for the Games therefore would be temporary but wherever possible aligned to the long term points of access and egress to the site.

During the Olympics   Games mode

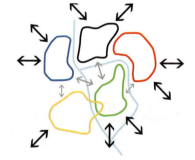

After the Olympics   Legacy mode

Figure 5: Masterplanning for the Olympic Games and Legacy Source: Design for London [ix]

Other examples of temporary design included bridges and concourses designed to cater for crowds of 400,000 people at peak times. After the Games the largest events are unlikely to exceed 100,000 people. Bridges and the main concourse were therefore designed with permanent and temporary components. The temporary components were designed in such a way that they could easily be removed and reused or recycled after the Games to create space for new development or extensions to the Parklands.

To cater for the changes in requirement from Games to legacy, a sequence of three masterplans were created to facilitate the smooth transition from the Games to legacy mode; these are listed below, and shown in Figure 6.

• The Games-time plan; designed to meet the needs of the Olympics and Paralympics.
• The transformation plan; which was the Olympic Park with all the temporary overlay structures required to meet Games needs

removed. This left a site with the permanent elements of the development in place including infrastructure, venues and Park, but also with a large number of serviced development plots and facilities that would be developed over the longer term.
• The legacy plan; showing a conceptual model of the site fully developed over a period of 20-30 years, depending on market conditions.[x]

A key driver of the masterplan was to ensure that only facilities that had a long term viable role in legacy master planning were created. Where facilities were needed for the Games but could not be justified in legacy, a temporary solution was found. One of the best examples of this was the 12,000 seat Basketball Arena. A business planning exercise was commissioned that demonstrated that there were no long term viable uses for this venue, but at the same time there were no existing venues within easy reach of the Olympic Village that could fulfil the brief. A fully demountable sta-

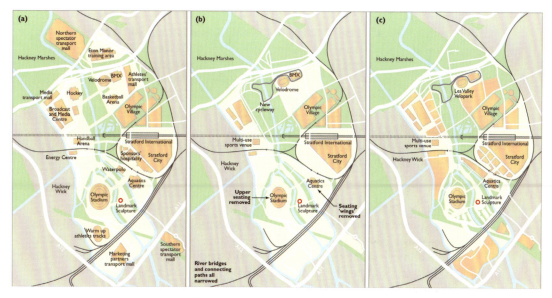

Figure 6: a) Masterplan for Games time in 2012, b) transformation in May 2014 and c) legacy framework under development by the Olympic Park Legacy Company. Source: Nimmo et al., 2011

Figure 7: The Olympic Stadium, which was originally designed to be dismantled to become a 25,000 seat Athletic Stadium after the Games

dium was designed that will be taken away by the contractor and reused on other sites after the Games.

The result of this approach is that London 2012 will have more temporary facilities than any previous Games. All the permanent venues have been specifically sized to meet their legacy requirements, with additional capacity only for the Games mode.

It is worth highlighting here that the Olympic Stadium was designed to have an 80,000 seat capacity during the Games, demounting to a 25,000 seat, world-class athletics stadium in legacy. This strategy was developed following extensive discussions in 2005-2007 with potential legacy tenants for the 80,000 seat stadium. At that time none of the major

football teams made what the Government considered to be an economically viable offer for the Stadium and the Government therefore decided that, as there was no apparent long term use for a major new stadium in London, it would leave a purpose built athletics venue capable of hosting international sporting events as part of the legacy.

The Olympic Park Legacy Company [2] (OPLC) however decided to test the market again in 2010 as they were concerned that the proposed 25,000 seat stadium would not be economically viable and they wanted to attract other users. OPLC established a bidding process to find a solution for the long-term lease of the Stadium. Over 100 expressions of interest were received. It became clear that the most economically viable operating model was to have a football club as the anchor tenant. West Ham United Football Club was selected to assume ownership of the Stadium after the Games. This was a joint bid with Newham Council, one of the host boroughs. In legacy, the Olympic Stadium is to be converted into a 60,000 seat stadium for football and athletics, as well as other sporting, cultural and community events. The costs of the transformation are estimated to be in the order of £100m and many people are sceptical that a football stadium can work with an athletics track around it. This demonstrates that even where the client focuses on legacy, developing fully adaptable and flexible venues is invariably a complex and expensive challenge, particularly where different interests have to be accommodated.

Unlike most masterplans, the Olympic Games and transformation plans were designed as tools for both planning and delivery. As soon as the plans were approved by the planning authority, work started on site. They were used by all the designers and contractors on the Park to designate site boundaries and interfaces with other contractors, to develop the Park operation plans and for event planning.

The masterplan, together with a number of supplementary documents set out the design language for the site. This was a very sensitive issue as the site was completely levelled, every building (240) but one was demolished, a new topography was created, the canals were opened up and the Park radically changed over the course of two years. The new buildings, Park and infrastructure, all built over a four year period, therefore created a completely new sense of place.

In terms of design challenges, the Olympic Delivery Authority (ODA) was very careful to invest in quality and diversity and to encourage architectural flare, whilst at the same time creating a degree of coherence and consistency across the site. This was achieved by setting the Olympic Park in distinctive new ecological parkland. The venues were all very different from one another, each having its own distinctive character, and the architectural quality was extended to the permanent utility buildings and other permanent facilities on site. Whilst the form and aesthetic of each project varied, a common philosophy underpinned all of the briefs, namely:

• The need to establish the most efficient and adaptable forms possible;
• The binding influence of parklands and landscapes; and
• The requirement to create the most environmentally sustainable, accessible and inclusive venues ever created.

Whilst the ODA was developing its plans for the Olympic Park site, the London Development Agency [3] (LDA) focused on making improvements to the areas immediately adjacent to the site, in advance of the 2012 Games. The LDA's £12.4 million Olympic Fringe Delivery Programme was established to ensure that existing communities benefited fully in socioeconomic terms from the investment in the Olympic site and Stratford City. As part of this programme of work, masterplans were developed for the six areas adjacent to the site, Hackney Wick and Fish Island, Hackney Marshes, Leyton, Stratford Town Centre, Stratford High Street and Sugarhouse Lane. The masterplans were designed so that these areas retained their individual character and history, while adapting to their new neighbour.

Embedding Sustainable Development into Games and Legacy Phases

In the bid, London committed to create the most sustainable Olympics ever, and to create a blueprint for sustainable living. This commitment was seen to comprise two elements:

- Ensuring the Park delivered a viable long term legacy; and
- Delivering an Olympic Park that met exacting environmental, social and economic objectives.

Figure 8: The ODA's Sustainable Development Strategy

The first element was addressed in the approach taken to develop a masterplan that had legacy requirements as its key driver in venue and facility designs. The second was addressed through developing a sustainability strategy for the construction and operation of the Games.

As part of the bid process, London's bid team worked closely with the World Wide Fund for Nature (WWF) and BioRegional, a London based consultancy practice, to develop London's approach to sustainable development and the Olympics. This followed a set of principles that WWF had been promoting around 'One Planet Living', which were based on the premise that the average UK citizen currently has a three-planet lifestyle; or put another way, if everyone in the world lived like the average UK citizen we would need three planets to sustain our level of resource consumption. The term 'Towards a One Planet Olympics'[xi] was coined, to encapsulate this idea, and the approach taken was to try to design and construct a Park that would support one planet lifestyles in legacy.

Following the award of the Games in 2005, the ODA, in consultation with key stakeholders such as the Olympic Board, the specially formed Government Olympic Executive [4], the Greater London Authority, and the London Organising Committee of the Olympic and Paralympic Games [5] (LOCOG), translated these commitments into a Sustainable Development Strategy.[xii] The Strategy aimed to set new standards for sustainable design and construction and covered all aspects of the project from the initial land acquisition and demolition, to the earthworks and design and construction of the venues, utilities, civil works, landscape, transport, offices and homes. There were 12 'Strategy Themes' of carbon, water, materials, waste, biodiversity and environmental impacts etc, and within each theme environmental targets were set.

Figure 9 shows these themes and how they align with both the Mayor's vision for London and the ODA's vision.

The Mayor of London's Vision:
"To create a major new sustainable urban quarter for London on a previously derelict site in a depressed area of the city."

ODA's vision:
"To deliver venues. facilities, infrastructure and transport on time for the London 2012 Olympic and Paralympic Games that are fit-for-purpose and in a way that maximises the delivery of a sustainable legacy within the available budget."

ODA's 12 Sustainable Development Strategy Themes:
• Carbon
• Water
• Waste
• Materials
• Biodiversity
• Environmental impacts (land, air, water, noise)
• Supporting Communities
• Transport and Mobility
• Access
• Employment and Business
• Health and Well-being
• Inclusion

For each of the 12 themes, London 2012 set performance requirements which could be included in contracts and audited.

Figure 9: Policy and Strategy Development from the Mayor's vision to the Sustainable Development Strategy

The 12 Strategy Themes each have corresponding high level objectives and requirements that collectively work towards achieving the Mayor's vision for London and the ODA's vision for the Games. The outcomes that are expected or already occurring as a result of integrating the Sustainable Development Strategy and the three-phase masterplan process include:

• The opportunity for the Olympic Park to be transformed into a neighbourhood, properly integrated into the fabric of Stratford and east London. The Park will create a family-focused environment and will see up to 11,000 new homes (including flats being built within the Olympic Village), developed over the next 25 years. 35% of the housing will be affordable and 90% of the new homes will be built to meet the 'lifetime homes' standard of accommodation, to be easily adaptable for older and disabled people. 10% of these will be wheelchair accessible.

• The opportunity to employ local people, and particularly people who had been unemployed long-term or within sectors of society that were often excluded from the construction industry (it is anticipated that there could be between 8,000 and 10,000 jobs created on the site over the long term).

• The establishment of accessible and inclusive facilities within the area to support the growing communities, including new schools, nurseries, health centres, and faith and community spaces that will also improve local employment opportunities.

• Buildings that have low energy and water use, and are 'healthy' to live in. The latest 'green' technologies and utilities infrastructure are being installed to minimise the overall environmental impact of the Park and to reduce utility bills for building occupants in legacy.

• High quality parklands (including 45 ha of biodiverse habitat), play areas and waterways that encourage outdoor activity and healthy lifestyles. Residents and visitors will be encouraged to cycle and walk, using the 25 km of new cycleways and footpaths that cover the Park. Cyclists will be able to use the Velodrome, outdoor road circuits and off-road trails at the Velopark. The Stadium, and the Aquatics, Tennis and Hockey Centres will also be open for people to keep fit and watch events. These venues will be

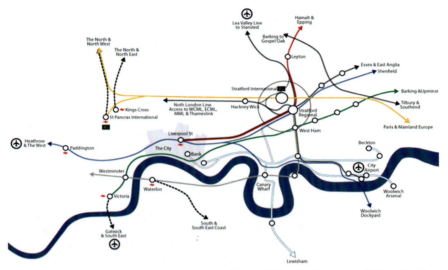

Figure 10: Upgraded transport links to the Olympic Park site

managed by the Lea Valley Regional Park Authority [6] (LVRPA).

- The upgrade and investment in new public transport infrastructure which will dramatically enhance the transport links to and within the Lower Lea Valley and reduce travel times to Central London. With nine rail lines serving the Park, it will be one of the best-conected destinations in London (Figure 10).

Case Studies – Venues and Schemes Designed for Legacy

As detailed in the previous section, the Sustainable Development Strategy sets over-arching sustainability targets that needed to be met for all aspects of the Park during construction.
Individual venues were also set their own bespoke targets and objectives for achieving sustainable, legacy-driven designs. The following three case studies provide examples of how specific venues and schemes were designed for legacy.

Sustainable community utilities infrastructure

Designing the Olympic Park utilities infrastructure for legacy rather than Games demands was a key strategic and sustainable decision. The greatest peak day demand for energy and water will occur during the Games period, during a period of intensive use by hundreds of thousands of spectators. However, demand for energy and water would be nothing like as high during legacy. Rather than over-sizing energy and water infrastructure to meet the extreme peak during the Games (to be followed by under-use in legacy), infrastructure was sized to meet demands over the operational life of the legacy development. This approach is much more sustainable.

Energy

The Olympic Park will be home to the largest community heating and cooling scheme

Figure 11: Computer generated image of the Olympic Park Energy Centre

to be built so far in the UK that will reduce carbon emissions by at least 20% compared to a 2006 baseline energy supply (equivalent to over 2200 tonnes CO_2 per year). This privately financed scheme has two Energy Centres with combined cooling heat and power systems (CCHP), one on the Olympic Park and one in Stratford. The CCHP engines convert natural gas into electricity, and hot and chilled water. The water is stored or piped directly underground to individual venues and buildings for domestic hot water, heating and air conditioning, via a 40 km network.

The Energy Centres have been designed to be flexible and modular so they can be upgraded over time to accommodate new low to zero carbon sources of fuel if and when they become available. The current gas boilers can also be replaced in the future as zero carbon technologies develop. Moreover, the heat network has been designed to be expanded in legacy, to supply low carbon and affordable heat to surrounding communities. This has set a benchmark for future regeneration schemes [xiii, xiv].

Water

The ODA set a challenging target to reduce potable (drinking) water consumption by 40% against a 2006 baseline across the Olympic Park, to be achieved by installing water efficient fittings and supplying water from non-potable sources (e.g. rainwater, surface water run-off and wastewater).

To help meet this target, the first large scale wastewater recycling scheme in the UK (Old Ford Water Recycling Treatment Works) has been installed on the Olympic Park, as part of a seven year research and development project with Thames Water. Membrane Bioreactor (MBR) technology will recycle raw sewage, greywater and surface water run-off from communities in North London (extracted from the Northern Outfall Sewer) into a non-potable supply of water for toilet flushing in venues, irrigation of the parklands and cooling the water in the Energy Centre. Non-potable water will be supplied to Olympic Park venues via a non-potable water distribution network approximately 3.65 km long.

This R&D project will reap important learning about this technology for future projects, particularly in relation to environmental, economic and social impact compared with other systems [xv, xvi].

London 2012 Olympic VeloPark

The Olympic VeloPark, which comprises the Velodrome and BMX track, was designed to be a thriving, economically viable legacy facility from the outset. After the Games, the Lea Valley Regional Parks Authority (LVRPA) will own, fund and run the VeloPark. A new mountain bike course and road-cycle circuit will be added to create a facility for the local community, sports clubs and elite athletes. It will include a café, bike hire and cycle workshop facilities, making it London's cycling hub.

net roof, lean design and using materials with lower environmental impact (e.g. concrete with cement and aggregate substitutions). The Velodrome was also designed to be inclusive and accessible.

The Velodrome's distinctive and aesthetically appealing design with extensive use of timber has already won many awards. In summary, the VeloPark delivers against the three pillars of sustainability and is a best practice example of venue design.

Aquatics Centre

The Zaha Hadid designed Aquatics Centre with its iconic wave-like roof will be the gateway to the Olympic Park.

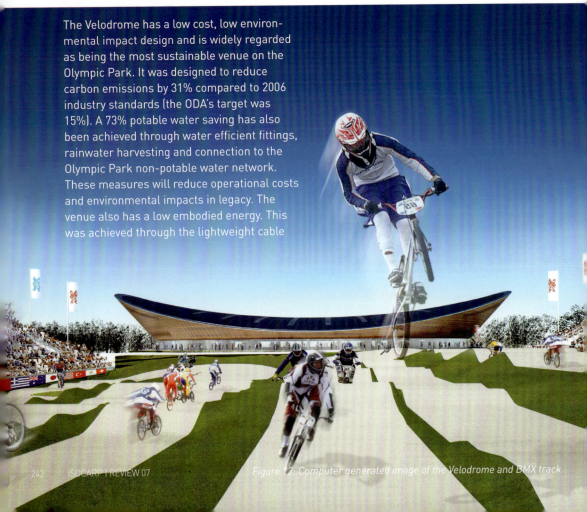

The Velodrome has a low cost, low environmental impact design and is widely regarded as being the most sustainable venue on the Olympic Park. It was designed to reduce carbon emissions by 31% compared to 2006 industry standards (the ODA's target was 15%). A 73% potable water saving has also been achieved through water efficient fittings, rainwater harvesting and connection to the Olympic Park non-potable water network. These measures will reduce operational costs and environmental impacts in legacy. The venue also has a low embodied energy. This was achieved through the lightweight cable

Figure 12: Computer generated image of the Velodrome and BMX track

The high number of spectators watching aquatic events during the Olympic Games dwarfs spectator numbers for swimming events in legacy. To avoid building an over-sized venue, the Aquatics Centre was de-signed with two temporary seating wings that would be removed after the Games. The venue capacity will be 17,500 during the Games. After the Games, the wings are to be removed, leaving a capacity of 2,500 seats, with the ability to add 1000 for major events.

In legacy, the Aquatics Centre will provide elite and community facilities that London did not previously have, including two 50m swimming pools, a 25m diving pool and diving facilities. The Centre will also have a crèche, family-friendly changing facilities and a cafe, alongside a new public plaza in front of the building.

Figure 14: Computer generated image of the Aquatics Centre in Legacy (2,500 seats)

Figure 13: Aquatics Centre in construction. During the Games it will have 17,500 seats

Figure 15: The Olympic Park in July 2011: one year to go to the 2012 Games

Measuring Success

At the time of writing, it is one year to go until the 2012 Olympic Games. The ODA is on track to deliver its challenging Sustainable Development Strategy and the construction of the Park is on programme, on budget and the quality of the work is very high. The planning, design and delivery approach has largely met the commitments that were set out in the original bid. Cumulatively, these set new standards for sustainability on major events and large scale regeneration projects. However, there are also concerns from members of the local community and critics of the Olympic Games and Park regeneration scheme (e.g. the writer Iain Sinclair[7]) about the negative effect of the large scale Olympic development on the community. Their criticisms are wide ranging and include: (1) the loss of established communities and businesses; (2) fear that an anonymous single land owner will fail to recognise the importance of community led bottom up development; (3) lack of community involvement or diversity of decision makers in the long term development of the area; (4) the impact the development will have on land prices and cost of living, which could exclude certain groups etc.

The real successes will only become apparent once the Games have occurred, the Park and its buildings become fully operational, and the legacy plans come into fruition. It will be vital to maintain momentum for sustainability through the transitions from the ODA, to the London Organising Committee of the Games (LOCOG), to the legacy owners.

The focus on legacy from the beginning of the project should put it on the trajectory for success. Establishing the Olympic Park Legacy Company (OPLC) in May 2009 – three years before the Games, was a key move. The OPLC is a public sector, not-for-profit organisation responsible for the long-term planning, development, management and maintenance of the Olympic Park and its facilities after the London 2012 Games. It is OPLC's task to transform and integrate one of the most challenged areas in the UK into world-class, sustainable, integrated and thriving neighbourhoods [xvii].

OPLC's Sustainability Policy [xviii] has three overarching objectives:

• Enable low carbon and resource efficient lifestyles
• Adapt to a changing climate
• Make the most of our green assets

It also has three enabling objectives:

• Procure sustainably
• Support environmental innovation
• Make sustainability a commercial success

OPLC was established by the Mayor of London, and two Government Ministries, the Department for Culture, Media and Sport, and the Department of Communities and Local Government. OPLC works with a wide range of partners from both the public and private sectors to ensure a successful legacy from the Games. Those partners include the five host boroughs, LOCOG, ODA, LDA, London Thames Gateway Development Corporation[8] (LTGDC) and the LVRPA. However, in 2010, in recognition of the multiplicity of development bodies working on the same patch, the Mayor of London launched proposals for a new urban development corporation to replace OPLC, LTGDC and other delivery agencies. The proposed corporation would have greater powers, including planning powers, and would work over a wider area than that covered by the existing OPLC. The Mayor believes that the new Corporation would boost the effectiveness of the Legacy Company, help make the very most of Games-related investment and, most importantly, ensure that the success of the Olympic Park will permeate into all the surrounding communities and beyond [xix].

The Olympic Park and the surrounding area (the Lower Lea Valley) is one of the largest regeneration opportunities in Europe and the largest remaining regeneration opportunity in inner London. The past 25 years have seen the creation of Canary Wharf, the regeneration of the Greenwich peninsular and the construction of the Jubilee Line and Docklands Light Railway in east London. The Olympics will act as the next major economic driver for the area. The Mayor of London, host boroughs and the regeneration agencies are taking legacy planning for east London very seriously. They have a vision to attract investment into the area, and to create a metropolitan quarter in east London that will turn around the fortunes of one of the poorest parts of the capital.

Examples of initiatives to drive legacy benefits include:

- Launch of the Green Enterprise District in 2010, which covers 48 km² of land in east London. The principle behind it is to transform the vast and unused industrial plots of land into a thriving area of low carbon, innovative organisations. It is hoped that the influx of new businesses will have massive benefits for London's economy and secure London's position as a leader of the global low-carbon economy [xx].
- Capitalising on the investment in the Olympic Park energy utilities infrastructure, by investigating opportunities to extend the heating network to serve low carbon heat to surrounding communities. The LDA and LTGDC are to provide £480,000 to Cofely, the energy services company, to install hot water pipework connecting the Energy Centres on the Olympic Park and at Stratford City through to Stratford High Street and beyond. This will mean that, in future, developers can tap into the low carbon heat source [xxi].
- Launch of the London Assembly's Economy Culture and Sport (ECS) Committee investigation focusing on the legacy plans for the 2012 Aquatics Centre, Handball Arena,

VeloPark, Eton Manor and the Hockey Centre, questioning: will these Olympic Park venues pay for themselves in the long run and if so how?; are the right decisions being made now to ensure fair access for the local community?; and will each venue strike the right balance between cost to the taxpayer, community access and elite use [xxii].

Conclusion

London seized the opportunity to regenerate a deprived area of the City when planning for the 2012 Olympic Games. From the outset, the masterplan was focused on leaving a long term legacy of environmental, social and economic improvement as well as world-class sporting assets. The London 2012 Olympic Board has worked hard to ensure that it delivers against those commitments and creates a successful regeneration project.

It will be impossible to determine whether this huge project which is transforming the Lower Lea Valley has been successful until long after the Games and legacy transformation has occurred.

The real test of success will be: how successful and vibrant the community is; how Londoners and other visitors see the Park, and whether it has a sense of place and individual character; whether it supports sustainable lifestyles; whether it is affordable, diverse and accessible; and whether it is economically sustainable.

The host boroughs of Hackney, Greenwich, Newham, Tower Hamlets and Waltham Forest have developed their own Strategic Regeneration Framework in which they aim to ensure that the communities who host the London 2012 Olympic and Paralympic Games will enjoy the same social and economic chances as their neighbours across London over the next

20 years – they have termed this convergence. If the investment in London 2012 helps realise this vision, the project will have made a very considerable contribution to London, and to the Lower Lea Valley in particular.

Acknowledgement

Images courtesy of London 2012 unless stated otherwise.

Endnotes

1 The Olympic Delivery Authority (ODA) is the public body responsible for developing and building the new venues and infrastructure for the Games and their use after 2012.

2 The Olympic Park Legacy Company (OPLC) is a public sector, not-for-profit organisation responsible for the long-term planning, development, management and maintenance of the Olympic Park and its facilities after the London 2012 Games.

3 The London Development Agency (LDA) is the Mayor of London's agency responsible for driving London's sustainable economic growth. It is a functional body of the Greater London Authority (GLA).

4 The Government Olympic Executive (GOE) is the lead government body for coordinating the London 2012 Olympics. It focuses on oversight of the Games and the 2012 legacy before and after the Games that will benefit London and the UK.

5 The London Organising Committee of the Olympic and Paralympic Games (LOCOG) is the private company responsible for preparing and staging the 2012 Games.

6 LVRPA is the statutory body responsible for managing and developing the Lee Valley Regional Park, in which the Olympic Park sits.

7 The British writer and filmmaker Iain Sinclair recently published a book, 'Ghost Milk' in which he strongly criticises the Olympic Park development and the regeneration plans.

8 LTGDC is the Government agency responsible for delivering social and economic growth to transform the London Thames Gateway.

References

i   Moore, M. 2008. Athens' deserted Games sites a warning to London Olympics. The Telegraph, 1 Jun.

ii   Taberner, P. 2005. The Athens Olympics Aftermath: Lessons Learned. London 2012, Olympics Forum, 8 Sep. Available from: http://www.the2012londonolympics.com/forum/olympics-olympians-past/ 187-athens-olympics-aftermath-lessons-learned.html

iii Woods, I. 2010. London 2012 To Learn From Sydney's Mistakes. Sky news, 14 Sep.

iv   The Evening Standard, 2009. The 2004 Olympic legacy that London must avoid. Available from: http://www.thisislondon.co.uk/standard/article-23636200-the-2004-olympic-legacy-that-london-must-avoid.do

v   Bryant and May. Wikipedia. Available from: http://en.wikipedia.org/wiki/Bryant_and_May

vi   Lea Valley History. Available from: http://eastlondonhistory.com/lea-valley-history/

vii Rose, E. 2009. East End benefit claims double the national average. Available from: http://www.eastlondonlines.co.uk/2009/11/east-end-benefit-claims-double-national-average/

viii Nimmo, A, Frost, J, Shaw, S. 2011. Delivering London 2012: master planning. Civil Engineering 162, pater 10-00043, pages 13-19.

ix   Design for London, London Development Agency: http://www.designforlondon.gov.uk/

x   Nimmo, A, Frost, J, Shaw, S. 2011. Delivering London 2012: master planning. Civil Engineering 162, pater 10-00043, pages 13-19.

xi   Bioregional and WWF, Towards a One Planet 2012. Available from: assets.panda.org/downloads/opl_ olympics_brochure.pdf

xii Olympic Delivery Authority, 2007. Sustainable Development Strategy. Available from: http://www.london2012.com/documents/oda-publications/oda-sustainable-development-strategy-full-version.pdf

xiii Carris, J. Epstein, D & Young, A. 2011. The Olympic Park Energy Strategy. London 2012 Sustainability Learning Legacy paper. Available from ODA Learning Legacy website.

xiv ODA, 2009. Work powers ahead on mean, lean and green Olympic Park Energy Centre. Available from: http://www.london2012.com/press/media-releases/2009/11/work-powers-ahead-on-mean-lean-and-green-olympic-park-energy-centre.php

xv   Carris, J. Epstein, E. Knight, H & Sykes, J. The Olympic Park Water Strategy. London 2012 Sustainability Learning Legacy paper. Available from ODA Learning Legacy website.

xvi ODA, 2009. Water recycling facility planning update. Available from: http://www.london2012.com/documents/oda-publications/water-recycling-facility-planning-update.pdf

xvii Olympic Park Legacy Company. Available from: http://www.legacycompany.co.uk/about-us/

xviii McNevin, N. 2010. Beyond the Games: The future of the London 2012 Olympic Park (presentation). Available from: http://www.legacycompany.co.uk/media/NM-Sustainability-Lecture-251110.pdf

xix Greater London Authority. 2011. Mayor consults on development corporation to drive Olympic Park legacy. Available from: http://www.london.gov.uk/media/press_releases_mayoral/mayor-consults-development-corporation-drive-olympic-park-legacy

xx Greater London Authority. 2010. Kickstarting London's Green Enterprise District. Available from: http://www.london.gov.uk/blog/kickstarting-londons-green-enterprise-district

xxi News Distribution Service. 2011. Olympic Park to provide green power to Stratford homes and businesses. Available from: http://nds.coi.gov.uk/content/Detail.aspx?ReleaseID=418894&NewsAreaID=2

xxii Greater London Authority. 2011. Assembly to probe Olympic Park venues legacy plans. Available from: http://www.london.gov.uk/media/press_releases_london_assembly/assembly-probe-olympic-park-venues-legacy-plans

03

CHINA
REPORTS

Planning the Ecological Spatial System of the Megacity of Wuhan

Liu Qizhi

He Mei

Wang Yun

Wuhan, the centre of central China, is a riverside and lakeside megacity. As urbanization develops rapidly, the contradiction between excessive expansion of urban land space and a limited resource capacity, as well as a vulnerable eco-environment, is now escalating. In the key period of establishing a new pattern of spatial development, Wuhan has advanced the idea of building an eco-system covering its administrative boundary characterized by "two axes, two rings, six wedges and multiple corridors". The City has identified construction-prohibited zones, controlled development zones and developable zones, formulated relevant management policies, and through a comprehensive range of urban function allocation such as eco-parks, scenic points, and leisure resorts, explored the path from the planning of the eco-spatial system protection to its practice.

Part of the East Lake Scenic Spot

Introduction

Through the first decade of the 21st century, China has been undergoing accelerating urbanization at an unprecedented rate. While promoting economic and social development, cities are also faced with such problems as traffic jams, ecological destruction and environmental pollution. "Ecology", "green", and "low carbon" have become key words in respect of the sustainable development of cities around the world, against the backdrop of accelerating economic globalization and the deteriorating crisis of global climate change. In this context, the Chinese Government has advanced national development strategies aimed at protecting the eco-environment and constructing a resource-conserving and environmentally friendly society.

Wuhan, the capital of Hubei Province, is at the center of central China, and a riverside and lakeside megacity. At the end of 2007, Wuhan City Circle[1] was approved as the "National Pilot Region for Comprehensive Supporting Reforms of Building a Resource-conserving and Environmentally-friendly Society", which enables Wuhan to take the lead in the exploration of materializing resource-conserving and environmentally friendly development.

Figure 1: The Yangtze River Ecological Axis - Hankou Beach Park

Figure 2: The cross-shape ecological axes formed by mountains and waters - The convergence of two rivers and the juxtaposition of three towns

Wuhan's Ecological Resources

Historical development and urban spatial characteristics

The urban prosperity of Wuhan depends largely on its water resource. Wuhan's remarkable progress is closely associated with the water: from the rise and fall of the Ancient Town of Panlong 3,500 years ago, to the rise of Wuchang City blessed with the natural barrier of the Yangtze River during the period of the Three Kingdoms, then to the prosperity of Hankou after the diversion of the Han River, followed by the emergence of the "Great Wuhan" stemming from the 'golden shipping channel' of the Yangtze River.

Converging in the downtown area of Wuhan, the Yangtze River, the 3rd longest river in the world, and the Han River, its largest tributary, divide the City into three parts, Wuhan's 'Three Towns' of Hankou, Wuchang and Hanyang, thus forming a unique layout based upon the convergence of two rivers and the juxtaposition of three towns. From this stems Wuhan's name of "River City"; this is a distinctive place, characterized by its great rivers, as well as its pervasive lakes.

Landscape resources

In terms of its freshwater resources per capita, Wuhan joins the front ranks of world cities. Foremost amongst China's major cities in this respect, Wuhan's total water area amounts to over 2,100 km², covering about 25% of its administrative area which measures 8,494 km²; that includes nearly 200 lakes scattered about the city. Four groups of those lakes spread around the central city. Wuhan also boasts a number of mountains and over one hundred hills of various heights. These

features complement the water environment, providing beautiful settings for the City.

To make the most of its exceptional ecological resources, Wuhan has been transformed into a "National Garden City of China"[2] characterized by riverside and lakeside in accordance with the planning vision - "Each river or mountain makes a scenic point in a complete development". The magnificent spectacle of "the Tortoise Mountain and the Snake Mountain guarding the Yangtze River", the beautiful panorama of "two rivers, four banks" and the picturesque landscape of "broad East Lake" together present a powerful image to people.

Figure 3: The classic image of Wuhan - The Scenic Spot of the Snake Hill and the Yellow Crane Tower

The city's current development stage

Wuhan has entered a rapid development phase of urbanization. The total population exceeds 9,780,000. The urbanization level is more than 70%. Wuhan's main built-up area measures close to 500km^2.

Being densely populated, the central city of Wuhan suffers badly from the heat island effect. The resident population in the central city totals 5,400,000 and the population density in the core city reaches a level of 40-50,000 per km^2. Arising from its intensive construction, the heat island effect makes the temperature in the central city area 2°C higher than that of the suburban areas.

Meanwhile, the peripheral suburban areas are expanding and sprawling at considerable speed close to the central city. However, arising in part from a lack of efficient land management methods, this area still follows an extensive, dispersed, pattern of growth which exhausts environmental resources to a considerable extent. Since 2005, the built-up area of Wuhan has increased by nearly 30 km^2 annually.

Difficulties and challenges of ecological protection

It is undeniable that in the rapid process of urbanization, the urban development and ecological protection of Wuhan will encounter unavoidable contradictions and conflicts similar to those of developing megacities generally. These manifest themselves as follows:

- Ecological resources are repeatedly damaged, making it difficult to protect them. In terms of water quality, of the 69 lakes under monitoring in 2010, 35 fell into the lowest quality categories of "Grade V or Below Grade V"[3], accounting for about half of the sample. Other types of ecological damage

arise from quarrying activities within the mountain areas and that frequently impinges upon the suburban areas.

- Superior landscape zones along the mountain and watersides are favored by the developers, and they are thus difficult to protect. People tend to prefer to build beside the mountains and live by the water. A psychological need that has made these areas the first choice for real estate and resort projects. A frequent consequence of such development is that there can be no public footpaths or other access to the lakeside as the lake becomes fully surrounded by development projects.

- In ecological areas, the farmers' right to development is restrained and there are conflicts between ecological protection and the interests of this group. Also there are a lot of rural settlements in these areas where residents' aspirations to develop can hardly be satisfied. For its part, the development of tourism tends to have a negative influence on the eco-environment, since much of this is in its preliminary development phase.

- The pollution arising from production activities in rural areas cannot be ignored. Although there is no very concentrated urban construction, pollution still exists. It results, for example, from the considerable use of fertilizer and pesticides. Moreover, in the absence of sewage treatment plant, the wastewater from production activities and the domestic effluent from rural settlements are further sources of pollution to the eco-environment.

At the same time, for a city with such an abundance of both mountains and water resources, another difficulty in eco-protection is the fact that in all directions in Wuhan one can find some or all of the elements which could influence the expansion of urban space, First, the City's ecological resources - its large-and-medium-sized lakes and its mountains - are evenly spread outside the central city area.

Secondly, its transportation and other crucial urban infrastructure are distributed in all directions; notably its deep-water harbor, its global airline hub, and the stations serving national high-speed railways. Thirdly, the distribution of the three vital industry clusters is also even. The three economic development zones at state-level, which are of great importance to the regional economy, are developing rapidly, alongside fast spatial expansion. Fourthly, Wuhan's administrative area is dispersed on all directions. All the outer suburban areas and development zones are connected to the central city area and thus have the access to its favorable opportunities and conditions.

Now is the crucial time for Wuhan to expand its urban space structure to secure the needed rapid development. The City needs to formulate promptly a proper spatial approach to urban space expansion and through effective management to protect the ecological environment, so that the urban expansion can shift from sprawling to expanding in an orderly way that will protect the ecological environment. In that light, it is a major project for us, the planners to choose a sustainable route to constructing an eco-city in line with the conditions of Wuhan, which is conducive not only to the city's sound and rapid development, but also to its ecological security.

Planning of Wuhan's Ecological Spatial System

Objective and mission

The planning of Wuhan's ecological spatial system is expected to shape an ecological network for the administrative area, which integrates the comprehensive protection of landscape resources and other ecological elements, lays equal emphasis on ecological conservation, restoration and ecological construction, with a complete spatial system, clearly divided functions, distinguished features of landscape and clear regulatory strategies. It aims to improve the living environment of Wuhan's citizens, facilitate intensive, economic and sustainable development, and lay the foundation for the construction of an eco-city. On one hand, by protecting the planned ecological area, the system can promote the urban space development strategy of: "Develop while conserve"; strengthen the control of the urban growth boundary; establish an intensive urban space structure; prevent disordered urban sprawl and; safeguard urban ecological security. On the other hand, it is also expected that while delimiting ecology control zones, the system can take implementation initiatives for the planned ecological area and give consideration to the needs for development in rural areas through land function allocations and active policy implementation. Therefore, the main mission for Wuhan's Ecological Spatial System focuses on four priorities:

• Build an ecological network system on the basis of natural ecological elements, which is complete, multi-functioned and distinguishes ecological character areas;
• Delimit the City's ecological boundary, strengthen the control of the urban growth boundary, and establish a spatial pattern of urban ecological security;
• Build upon the multiple functions of the ecological area to promote implementation initiatives for the planned ecological area;
• Aim for low carbon urban development, promote intensive expansion along urban axes and push forward the strategy of "Develop while conserve" by protecting the planned ecological area.

The prediction of gross ecological area

The new round of the Comprehensive Planning of Wuhan delimits more than 3,000 km² of the metropolitan development area as space for future expansion. In order to establish the urban ecological spatial component within this mega dimension, we must first scientifically calculate the gross ecological area.

The City's research concluded that the ecological area accounts for about 83% of the total land within the Wuhan administrative boundary. In terms of the metropolitan development area, the ecological area should take up two thirds of the total land.

At the same time, we applied a dynamic simulation approach (Cellular Automata) to ascertain the likely shape of the city construction area in Wuhan City, which in turn would reflect the potential harm of city sprawl upon the ecological environment and sustainable development. Also the technique provides technological support for the establishment of the development area boundary in cities and towns. This led us to the conclusion that the ratio of the planned ecological area to that of the city construction area should be about 2:1. This sets an important goal for the planning of Wuhan's ecological spatial system.

The planning of ecological spatial system

The new round of the Comprehensive Planning of Wuhan divides the City into two functional development areas - a metropolitan development area and an agricultural ecological area - for the overall arrangement of urban space at all levels and the strict protection of the

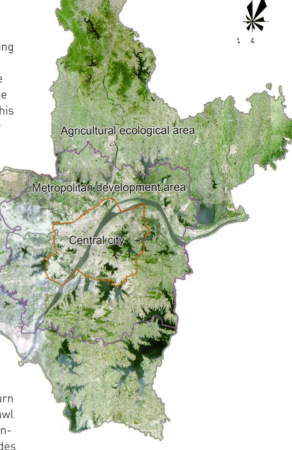

Figure 4: Wuhan's boundaries: Administrative Area, Metropolitan Development Area, and Central City

farmland and ecological resources (see Figure 4). The metropolitan development area, which consists of two major parts - the central city area and the new town clusters, serves as the main concentration area for the urban function and construction space of Wuhan. The central city area focuses on developing the core function of production and service in central China, with an emphasis on the functional and structural readjustment and optimization. The new town clusters take urban development and ecological protection as the leading factors, and determine the layout of industry, residence, eco-recreation, transportation and logistics industry, which are the key development areas for the future urban space of Wuhan.

As for the overall spatial structure, a strategy for development that is based on the core of the central city, forming a layout with six wedges interlaying six axes has been formulated, having regard to the unique natural and ecological context of Wuhan, and the developmental reality of its industrial space. The urban expansion areas are mainly along the six main axes beyond the central city. Based upon high capacity rail transportation and traffic corridors containing regional arterial roads, six new town clusters are to be constructed to achieve the intensive development of urban space. Each cluster is to include several new towns, and is to be provided with a high-standard transportation system and a range of public services.

In terms of the international practical experience of the middle and late 20th century, cities such as London, Moscow, Paris, and Chicago have played leading roles in establishing systems of protection for their urban ecological areas. The now widely-adopted models include: "round-the-city green belt", "wedge ecological belt", "wedge-ring ecological belt", "network ecological belt", etc. Based upon this experience, the ecological spatial system in Wuhan complements the

development model of cluster expansion along six main axes. Given the distribution of the various ecological resources, we have chosen an ecological network pattern of "axes-wedge-ring-corridor", which most suits the Wuhan context. It comprises the establishment of a sophisticated urban ecological system of "two axes, two rings, six wedges, and multiple corridors" inside the metropolitan development area (see Figure 5).

The "two axes" comprise the Yangtze River, the Han River and the transmeridional mountain system, whose junction forms a natural

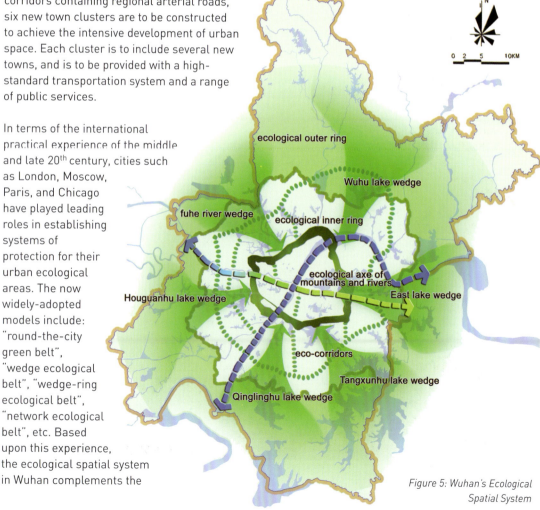

Figure 5: Wuhan's Ecological Spatial System

Figure 6: The Han River Ecological Axis - Hanyang Ancient Heptachord Terrace Park

cross. The "two axes" is a unique feature and classic image of Wuhan, and highlights its important urban ecology.

The "six wedges" refers to six green spaces extending from the peripheral suburban areas inwards to the central city. Integrated with the distribution of large and medium-sized lake and mountain systems to the east, southeast, west, southwest, south and north of those suburban areas, the six wedges include the water systems of Fuhe River, Wuhu Lake, East Lake, Tangxun Lake, Qingling Lake and Houguan Lake, each of which contains wetlands around water areas and forest lands on the mountain sides as its structural framework. To the northeast of Wuhan is the green wedge of the Wuhu Lake water system and to the southeast is that of the Tangxun Lake water system. These two green wedges serve as the "air channel" of Wuhan city, and play an important role in alleviating the heat island effect. In the ecological spatial system of Wuhan, the maintenance of the "six wedges" will be the key to the success of urban expansion along the direction of axes.

The first ring of the "two rings" refers to an inner ecological ring which is formed around a forest protection belt and the small and

medium-sized lakes and parks along the ring. It forms not only a green corridor outside the central city area integrated with natural landscape, ecological landscape and gardens as "one ring with multi-pearls", but it is also seen as a "green necklace". Its core significance lies in forming an ecological barrier which separates the main city and the outer new towns, and prevents disorderly sprawl. The second ring, located outside the metropolitan development area, is a wide, 'flaky' belt, and is primarily an agricultural/ecological area. It includes ecological elements, a large city forest, lakes, country parks, wetland nature reserve, scenic spots and farmland, and it functions as an ecological barrier, thus separating the whole metropolitan development area from the neighboring cities.

"Multi-corridors" refers to "green corridors" which serve as the channel between each ecological area, as barriers between new towns and as essential components of the overall ecological network. Lying between the new town clusters and the six ecological wedges, the corridors form zonal parks flexibly laid out in accordance with natural water or mountain systems.

Our planned, comprehensive Ecological Spatial System, for the Wuhan City Circle combines all the above elements, with the river system as the backbone, the mountains, forests, rivers, and lakes as the features, and connects the entire ecological system within the City Circle area, an area of about 60,000 km^2. This creates a macro, three-layer planned ecological system which consists of the 'central city-ecological inner ring', 'metropolitan development area-ecological outer ring', 'Wuhan City Circle-ecological barrier' and achieves the structural integration of the entire ecological area at a regional level.

Currently, the newly-elected Wuhan Municipal CPC Committee and the Municipal Government have proposed an important policy in the starting year of the Twelfth Five-year Plan. The policy explicitly stipulates that we should "construct an ecological barrier along the third ring, delimit the urban growth boundary, and prevent the city form sprawling in a disorderly way". The strategic thinking behind this policy promotes attaching equal importance to economic development and environmental protection.

Figure 7: The ecological outer ring - Bird's eye view of the Meidian Scenic Spot in the Mulan Ecological Tourism Area

Protecting and Establishing the Ecological Spatial System

Defining the boundaries

In order to protect and establish the ecological spatial structure, Wuhan City has divided the metropolitan development area into three types of zone: construction-prohibited zones, controlled development zones and developable zones.

We have established an evaluation system of land suitability for ecological use in the metropolitan development area based on three sub-systems, these comprising, land resources, 'other natural resources' and social and human resources system. The 16 factors considered in the evaluation include sub-grade bearing capacity, geological condition, elevation, landform, slope gradient, soil sensitivity, water environment, and flood risk; these are analyzed using GIS and other technical means. Based on the evaluation system, the metropolitan development area is divided into five grades: 'unsuitable for construction'; 'less suitable for construction'; 'basically suitable for construction'; 'suitable for construction' and 'most suitable for construction'. This division provides important support for the delimitation of construction-prohibited zones and controlled development zones.

In parallel, based on our comprehensive research on local climate conditions, we have provided technical support for delimiting the major urban ecological corridor, and ventilation channel, opening the way for an improved climate and a reduced heat-island effect.

On this basis, we have delimited construction-prohibited zones according to different elements as follows: first, the six core green wedge areas; second, major watershed preservation areas for the Han River and Sheshui River, etc.; third, mountains, waters and surrounding protection areas; fourthly, management of ecological corridors between six wedges and clusters in accordance with the requirement of planned ecological areas; fifthly, protected greenbelt along highways, railways and administrative infrastructure.

By establishing the construction-prohibited zone in this way, we can then complete the delimitation of the controlled development zone and developable zone, taking into consideration the ecological sensitivity and the requirement for managing urban spatial structure (see Figure 8).

Strategy of ecological area management

The scientific formulation of a spatial management strategy for the three zone types is at the core of the planned ecological system protection, and it has required the technical information to be translated into public policies. Its fundamental guiding ideology is to guarantee the protection of the city's ecological elements, the integrity of ecological systems and the balance of the ecological contribution, having regard to the requirements for ecological protection, and city, town or village construction in each area.

In the construction-prohibited zones, new urban construction land and any other construction program are under strict control. Only necessary roads, public facilities, ecological agricultural facilities, or core facilities for tourism and necessary special purposes are allowed and such projects receive strict scrutiny. In principle, operational projects such as industry, commercial, and residences

Figure 8: Ecological area designations within Wuhan's Metropolitan Development Area

Legends

mountains	lakes and rivers	construction-prohibited zone	controlled development zone	reserved development land
developable zone	planned roads	planned railways	boundary of central city	boundary of metropolitan developmental area

are forbidden. Beyond historical and culturally important villages, existing rural residents are encouraged to move out and there can be no increase upon the current scale of village construction.

In the controlled development zones, it is forbidden to construct new industrial areas and high-intensity development projects. On the condition that the environment will not suffer, certain low intensity activities and projects may be allowed, such as roads, public services, eco-agricultural facilities, tourism areas and their supporting facilities, parks and other green space. The approvals procedure for necessary projects must comprise a site selection study, environment impact assessment, a hearing, examination by the planning committee and governments' permission. Existing rural settlements may remain, but village relocation and combination are encouraged. No permitted construction project should harm natural scenic resources such as mountains and water areas. They should fit the criteria of being low-intensity and low-density and guarantee an ecological area proportion of 60% to 70%.

In the developable zones, we will set up corresponding procedures for the initiation of reserved development land, which can be planned and constructed after going through feasibility studies and attaining government approval.

To sum up, the management strategy for the zones involves: establishing the appropriate management requirement, deciding upon the classes of project that may be permitted, establishing permit procedure, deciding on the future of existing buildings in construction-prohibited zones and controlled development zones, and setting requirements on rural settlement construction according to different zones.

Implementation

It is difficult to protect the ecological spatial system if we merely delimit the ecological boundary on the map without taking actions. Therefore, on the basis of the defined construction-prohibited zones and controlled development zones in planned ecological

areas, Wuhan seeks to promote the realization of the ecological area in various ways.

Firstly, we will define and manage areas for disaster prevention and risk avoidance following the ecological spatial layout. In suitable ecological areas, the construction of such areas can improve urban function and ensure that the land will not be used for any other purpose.

Secondly, we plan to shape the country park system and actively protect the six core green wedges. These are the most sensitive areas in ecological terms and action there will have a decisive impact on the urban ecological structure. Within them, more than 20 eco-parks, in the form of nature preservation areas, scenic spots, forest parks, wetland parks, country parks and eco-agricultural gardens are to be constructed. We will also facilitate the construction of model eco-parks and large ecological leisure resorts to improve the landscape in the peripheral suburban areas and enhance its function as an area for relaxation and as a tourist destination.

Thirdly, through the greenway development plan we will promote the construction of ecological corridors. In tandem with the provision of cycleways, we plan to build a network of greenways forming, metaphorically, a 'green necklace' connecting such 'green pearls, as urban parks and large and medium sized eco-parks, and an important measure to make our city more livable.

Fourthly, we will implement projects relating to the water network and the protection and restoration of the water ecosystem. As Wuhan has abundant water resources, there is the scope to construct four sections of water channel and carry out projects to connect different water areas. Currently, there are special plans for the large ecological water network of East Lake, the water ecosystem of six connected lakes in Hanyang, that seek to promote water flow and upgrade water quality by diverting water from Yangtze River into the lakes. Alongside this, we will aim to conduct pollution treatment utilizing artificial ecological wetland and adopt the ecological approach to rain water drainage by relying primarily on natural water channels.

Figure 9: The East Lake Ecological Green Wedge - The Bird's Eye View of the East Lake Scenic Spot

In these four ways the planned ecological spatial landscape environment can be created, and costs can be reduced at the same time.

There is to be a compensation mechanism to protect the interests of farmers in ecological areas and to provide them with the necessary incentive to protect the ecological environment. This will involve a combination of compensation by government and through the market and it will be specially tailored to meet the needs of those living in different areas.

The Ecological Spatial System – The Future

While there remains much still to do in terms of the related planning research, in order to secure the protection and strengthening of the ecological spatial system, the following steps need to be taken immediately:

Firstly, the ecological boundary line needs to be defined and the areas within it protected through legislation. The urban ecological boundary needs to be marked on the city map (whose scale is 1:2000) and the areas within this boundary would be managed through local legislation so as to provide the regulations to be observed by the whole community. To that end, the aim will be to establish a real-time monitoring mechanism for construction projects by using satellite remote sensing technology, as an aid to planning and management according to the law, as well as to strict law enforcement.

Secondly, the achievements in terms of ecological protection should be taken into account in local government's evaluation system of GDP and the local government should further enhance people's awareness of and responsibility for protecting the ecological environment. Government evaluation should consider both the GDP growth of an area and how well the ecological environment is protected.

Thirdly, a public participation mechanism is to be set up to make Wuhan's planning better known to the public through planning exhibitions, the internet, and other media so that the public could participate in the authority's planning work. In so doing, a sound cooperation and interaction would be established between the Wuhan government and its people.

Conclusion

In the context of the current rapid urbanization, the planning and protection of the urban ecological system is a crucial part of the work needed to define an effective urban development boundary, as an element of sustainable development. Against the current backdrop, with "development" as the present theme, only by ensuring the fundamental improvement of the ecological spatial system, with resource preservation as precondition, reasonable utilization as key, and flexible and varied management as guarantee can we expect the real advance of ecological protection and utilization.

Endnotes

1. Wuhan City Circle comprises 8 surrounding cities including Huangshi, E'zhou and so on with Wuhan as the core.

2. The' National Garden City of China' is a safe and livable city with a balanced distribution of uses, a coherent structure, a complete range of functions, beautiful scenery and a good social and ecological environment. The winning cities are selected by China's Ministry of Housing and Urban-Rural Construction (MHURC) according to the State Standard for Garden City.

3. The statistics come from the Report on Wuhan's 2010 Environmental Status. According to the Environmental Quality Standards for Surface Water of the People's Republic of China and based on the environmental functions of surface waters and the target of protection, water bodies are divided into 5 categories. Grade V is the lowest grade of surface water; its use is restricted to the irrigation of agricultural areas and common landscape scenery.

References

Shen, Qingji (2009) *Urban Ecology & Urban Environment,* Shanghai: Tongji University Press

Bi, Linglan (2007) *The Spatial Form and Planning of Urban Ecosystem,* Beijing: China Architecture & Building Press

Zhang, Lang (2009) *The Research of the Great space System's layout structure and construction of hyper-megapolis,* Beijing: China Architecture & Building Press

He Mei, Wang Yun, Xia Wei, Li Haijun and Lin Jianwei (2010) *Ecological Spatial System Planning and Management Study of Megacity,* Beijing: China Architecture & Building Press

Wuhan Municipal Government. *The Comprehensive Planning of Wuhan City (2010-2020)*

Wuhan Planning and Design Institute and China Urban Planning and Design Institute. *The Planning on the Conservation of the Eco-framework in Wuhan City,* 2008

Local Governance of Low Carbon Cities: Is our Local Planning System Ready yet?

Stanley C. T. Yip

Recently considerable interest has been shown by researchers on the role of local governance in respect of climate change issues at sub-national and local government levels. There is a need to understand the various modes of governance for low carbon cities including self –governance, governing by enabling, provision and authority. The need to localize the global climate change issue and develop co-benefits in order to gain local political and community support is raised. This paper reviews the discussion framework, and then assesses the current Chinese statutory planning system, raising the concern that our planning governance and decision making processes need further enhancement to meet the challenge of climate change at local city and municipality level. The statutory planning framework should be reviewed and enhanced to expand the planning policy and action areas, establish horizontal and vertical collaborations, and set up a consistent planning governance model.

Stanley C. T. Yip

Cities: the Forefront of the Climate Change Challenge

The Intergovernmental Panel on Climate Change (IPCC) Fourth Assessment Report (AR4) contains the latest assessment of the impact of climate change (IPCC, 2007). The warming of the climate system is unequivocal. Cities are at the forefront of the climate change challenge for several reasons (Lindseth, 2004; ICURR, 2008). First of all, cities are the main sources of greenhouse gas emissions (GHG), mostly through energy consumption and waste management. Secondly, local governments are the frontline entities facing the various stakeholders such as private enterprises, the public and the non-governmental organizations in the implementation of mitigation and adaptation action plans. Thirdly, local governments have considerable direct experience in dealing with environmental issues associated with emissions generated from economic and development activities such as transport emissions, power generation, and industrial production. Finally, amongst the various emission abatement opportunities to reduce the global GHG emissions, the most cost-effective strategies are those most commonly available and applicable in cities (McKinsey & Company, 2009).

The recent focus by local governments in different parts of the world has been on building low carbon cities through various urban planning policies. For example, in 2007 the City of New York issued its city planning strategy up to the year 2030. This plan, the PlanNY, maps out the various planning policies for the city to meet its growth challenge for the next decades such as housing, open space, brown-fields, water quality, water networks, transportation, energy and air quality. It has included a specific strategy on climate change

(The City of New York, 2007, 2008). The Tokyo Metropolitan Government (TMG) announced its Climate Change Strategy in June 2007. It includes basic policies for a "10-Year Project for Carbon-Minus Tokyo," part of its 10-year plan (Tokyo Metropolitan Government, 2007). The strategy has included a target to reduce overall emissions by 25% between 2000 and 2050. Singapore's Climate Change Policy (NCCS) announced in 2008 summarizes the key policy framework (The Government of Singapore, 2008). The NCCS represents Singapore's comprehensive and holistic response to climate change. It documents Singapore's ongoing efforts and future plans to address climate change in terms of vulnerability and adaptation, mitigation of greenhouse gas emissions, local competency-building efforts, and international participation on climate change discussion.

Low Carbon Cities and the Issue of Local Governance

The issue of governance is critical to the achievement of an effective and successful society-wide collaborative effort to manage the climate change issues. Governance is the use of political authority and institutional resources to manage the problems of society (World Bank, 1991; Bell, 2002). The governance of low carbon cities concerns the ways local municipal governments use their political and legislative authority, make the choice of institutional tools, and collaborate with various stakeholders in the community in order to plan, build and manage the cities based on low carbon principles.

The studies on the governance models of carbon emission mitigation policies started back in the 1990s and recent research efforts have been focused on how cities in various countries responded to climate change governance. Betsill (2001) examined the ways US cities responded to the Cities for Climate Protection (CCP) programme supported by the then International Council for Local Environmental Initiatives (ICLEI). Bulkeley and Kern (2006) compared the governing of climate change by local governments in Germany and the UK. An analysis of the local governance experience in Sweden was undertaken by Granberg and Elander (2007), and Kern (2008) studied the various governance issues in Germany. This growing interest in looking at the local governance issue has expanded into examining local and sub-national politics. Schreurs (2008) has examined why local governments may set the local climate change policy agenda in case studies relating to California, Germany Tokyo, Kyoto, as well as some provinces and prefectures within China. Qi et. al. (2008) examined the ways local governments responded to central government climate change policies in China.

Modes of Local Governance for Mitigation and Adaptation

Alber and Kern (2008) in their study on cities in the OECD have adopted the four different modes of governance for climate change issues in cities proposed by Bulkeley and Kern (2006). This classification of various local government mitigation and adaptation actions based on the four modes is further expanded and summarized by the author in Table 1.

Table 1: Local Governance Mitigation and Adaptation Actions
Source: Bulkeley and Kern, 2006; Author's Analysis

Modes of Local Governance	Mitigation Actions	Adaptation Actions
Self Governing (local governments governing their own activities):	• Municipal building energy efficiency improvement schemes; • Energy efficient appliances and recycled goods procured by municipal government; • Government funded demonstration projects; • Municipal employees mobility management; • Municipal government offices waste recycling and reuse schemes; • New government buildings adopting high energy efficiency standards.	• Planning and design of public and government buildings for flood prevention; • Government building heating and cooling facilities to allow for emergency during weather extremities; • Employees' emergency action plans during extreme weather events.

Governing by Enabling (local governments facilitating the private sector and the community through incentives and persuasion)	• Energy efficiency campaign; • Technical advice to citizens; • Promotion and education programmes; • Economic incentives such as tax reduction; • Public participation programmes; • Planning guidance to developers and architects on building energy design.	• Provision of financial incentive to relocate buildings from future flood risk areas; • Provision of incentives such as tax breaks to encourage private sector to develop new food production systems / food species against global warming.
Governing by Provision (Local governments deliver particular forms of services and resources)	• Clean energy services; • Public transport services; • Open space and green infrastructure; • Waste recycling and composting; • Municipal waste to energy projects.	• Relocating municipal facilities such as water supply and power distribution facilities from flood risk areas; • City wide emergency support plan and life line services; • Weather extremities warning system; • Flooding prevention and coastal protection works.
Governing by Authority (local governments use regulations and sanctions)	• Statutory plans; • Building codes; • Zoning requirements; • Planning conditions as part of planning approval or planning permits; • Mandatory control of renewable energy; • Transport related mandatory control such as congestion charges; • Control of emissions from landfill or waste water treatment facilities.	• Review statutory planning control on development close to flood plain areas; • Develop land information systems on flood and extreme weather impacts as part of land use and development control monitoring; • Review building codes and engineering design codes to adapt to impacts.

This range of local government actions under the various modes of governance emphasized the different roles to be played by the municipal governments in the pursuit of low carbon city development pathways. Schroeder and Bulkeley (2009) have further pointed out that there may be differences in the relative importance of these modes when used by various local governments.

Localize the Global Issues – Identifying Co-benefits

One of the key issues in local governance of low carbon city policies is that climate change has been framed as a global issue and the issue of governance has been focused on studying international regimes (Betsill and Bulkeley, 2006). It was argued that traditional approaches to international negotiation and relations offer limited scope for efficient governance for managing climate change. In fact, economists have long been stressing the global public interest nature of GHG emissions in the atmosphere against the background that the social costs of carbon emissions do not equate with the private costs of the emission sources, no matter where the gases are emitted. Once locally emitted, GHG is a global problem (Tietenberg T. H., 2000; van Kooten C., 2004). The results are that GHG emissions are not always regarded as a local issue. The implication is that local governments and also the local community at large may not think the climate change issue is their concern. It has been suggested that it is necessary to reframe the global climate issue locally by identifying the co-benefits generated by the local mitigation plans, in order to ensure local political and bureaucratic support (Betsill, M., 2001; Sippel and Jenssen, 2009). Local co-benefits are developed by aligning mitigation or

adaptation actions with those issues already accepted by local governments and communities as their immediate concerns. These may include air quality issues (carbon dioxide emission reduction and lower sulphur dioxide emission into the atmosphere), energy saving (reducing energy consumption lower carbon dioxide emissions but also helps to lower electricity costs), compact transport oriented development TOD (compact city forms make urban living more convenient and promote public transportation , while at the same time reduce the burning of fossil fuels by cars).

Co-benefits are important because they provide the local political incentive to further the implementation of low carbon city development plans, and greatly enhance the effectiveness of the public education programme on climate change now that the issues are localized.

Building Multi-level Local Networks

Multi-level networks emerge as one of the modes of governance in the promotion of local actions on climate change. One of the earlier initiatives has been the setting up of transnational municipal networks. Examples include the earlier Cities for Climate Protection (CCP) programme. A recent world renowned transnational city network initiative is the C40. The C40 is a group of large cities committed to tackling climate change.

Kern and Bulkeley (2009) studied similar networks in the European context, and summarized the fundamental internal functions of transnational municipal or city networks as: (1) information and communication; (2) project funding and coordination; and (3) recognition, benchmarking and certification. Information is important as the participants can share experience, data and best practice examples to learn from each other. Project funding and cooperation opportunities are provided by the networks for their members to collaborate and identify funding for joint efforts. Recognition, benchmarking and certification are means provided by the network to accredit members who have attained good performance or standards. Transnational municipal and city networks provide, in general, opportunities which are not available internally to individual local governments.

Apart from transnational networks, national multi-level governance networks also prove to be of significant value. Alber and Kern (2008) pointed out that within a country, local government climate change governance networks are an effective mode of governance for two purposes: (1) horizontal collaboration that works amongst cities at metro-regional level; and (2) vertical collaboration within the country between different levels of governments (national, sub-national, and local) and modes of cooperation.

Horizontal collaboration is particularly relevant because GHG emissions in the local geographical context would not be limited to administrative city boundaries. The issue is spatial mismatch. GHG emission arising from the activities and demands from within a city may be generated outside the city boundaries (the most common examples include: regional transportation, electricity supply from power plants located outside the city boundary, and landfill sites located outside the city boundaries but serving the disposal of waste from the city, and a flooding risks management plan usually follows the natural boundary of watershed instead of municipal boundaries). By working together, local governments within a region can collaborate to implement cross boundary mitigation and adaptation plans, provide examples of best practices and learn from each other, and potentially work together to lobby for senior government fund-

ing support for regional programmes (see diagram 1).

Vertical collaboration works to link up the initiatives between different levels of government from the central national government to the sub-national and local city governments. The commonest forms of collaborations in this context include the passing of national climate change legislation that is legally binding on all local governments; central government special grants and funding support for demonstration projects at local levels; provision by senior governments of professional guidance and expertise to assist the local governments in assessing the local climate change risks; local government capacity building through training programmes organized by the national government; as well as certification such as the national green building certification systems. Within a local government at sub-national and local levels, similar vertical collaboration can also mean concerted and consistent effort implemented by different levels of government departments at various stages of performing their functions. Provincial governments can work closely with the cities and counties at lower levels, legislate sub-national laws or mandatory guidelines, provide technical guidelines, technical capacity support, and cooperate in areas of multi-level government concerns.

In summary, successful and effective local governance of low carbon cities' policies depend on understanding the above issues, and on a coordinated effort by the local municipal governments both inside the individual cities as well as among the cities. The different modes of governance inside the cities include self governing, governing by enabling, provision and authority. Externally, regional horizontal networks between cities as well as vertical collaboration between national, sub-national and local governments are important modes of operations.

Diagram 1: Local Governance – Regional Urban System Plan as a platform for horizontal collaboration (example of Zhengbian Regional Urban System Concept Plan)

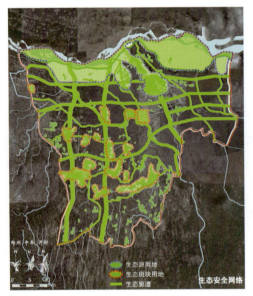

Ecology System

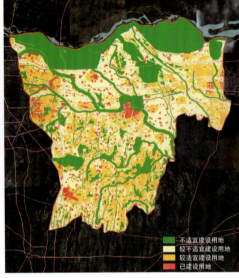

Site Assessment

China's Statutory Planning System: Proposed Responses to Effective Local Governance for Climate Change

Local planning is an important city function that has a great impact on successful implementation of climate change policies through effective local governance. This section of

the paper examines if the existing statutory planning system in China responds effectively to the issue of local governance. The current legal basis of the Chinese statutory planning system is founded on the recently revised Urban and Rural Planning Law that came into effect in 2008 (Standing Committee of the National People's Congress, the People's Republic of China, 2007). The Chinese statutory planning system encompasses a hierarchy of three-tier statutory plans from a regional scale Urban System Plan, to city-wide Master Land Use Plan and the Detailed Plans.

The Provincial Urban System Plans are prepared by provincial governments covering

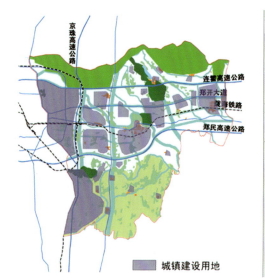

Future Urban System Concept

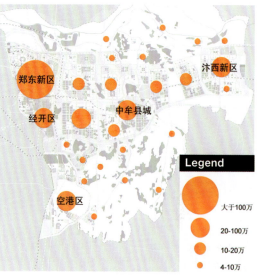

Managing horizontal collaboration among Urban centers in a Regional Plan

areas in regional scale, and depict the future system of urban, town, rural centers and villages. City Urban System Plans can also be prepared by cities and cover the urban and rural areas within the municipal boundary. It provides a strategic plan for the urban and rural systems in the planning area. as well as ecological green space, major roads, rails and infrastructure. The Master Land Use Plan covers the urban areas of cities and provides the legal basis for the scale of the cities (extent of urban area) and the general distribution of major land uses such as residential, industrial, commercial and open space. Master Land Use Plans usually have a planning time horizon of 20 years. The Detailed Plans include both Regulatory Plans (zoning plans) as well as Site Plans. The Regulatory Plans are a refinement of the Master Land Use Plan down to street block level. They are the fundamental development control tools employed to regulate and control site specific development (density, coverage and uses). The Regulatory Plans also act as the fundamental basis for the preparation of planning conditions for individual sites. These conditions are normally enforced as specific terms in the land use lease agreement signed between the Government and the developer for the land use right transfer. The Site Plans are the basis for controlling urban design, architectural massing and building forms, as well as local pedestrian

Figure 1: Overview of the Statuory Planning System of China

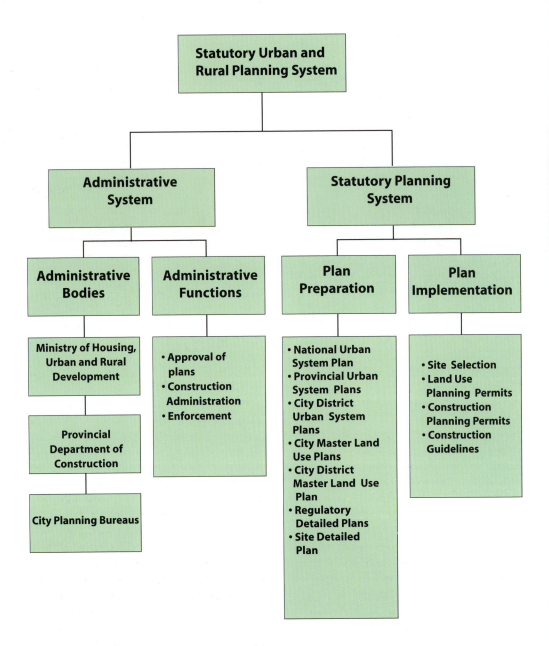

and vehicular circulations. Figure 1 illustrates the legal framework of the statutory planning system in China.

In the pursuit of innovative planning policies and approaches to planning, building and managing low carbon cities, different project based initiatives have been undertaken by the various levels of government in China recently. The concept of planning demonstration "Low Carbon Eco-Cities or Communities" has been a direct response to the climate change issues. Examples of these projects include the Sino-Singapore Tianjin Eco-City, Tangshan Caofeidian International Eco-City, Bejing Changxingdian Low Carbon Community (see diagram 2), the WWF Low Carbon City projects in partnership with the City of Boading and Shanghai, etc. Low carbon eco-communities in China are a concept to achieve ecological balance in urbanization, by taking the carbon emission reduction as the central driving principles for the planning of cities. Typically, the low carbon eco-city demonstration projects in China have adopted low carbon planning and design approaches (Yip, 2008).

While demonstration low carbon city projects have their role to play in terms of experimenting innovations in city planning, design and implementation, the issue of local governance is best examined by assessing the statutory planning system and its related functions. The following three aspects of local governance are used as the framework for discussion:

- Use of different modes of local governance
- Multi-level horizontal city networks as support to local governance
- Vertical collaboration

Modes of governance in the statutory planning system and climate change

The Chinese Planning System provides local governments with two main planning functions: plan preparation and development control through planning permits. So conventionally, local planning functions have focused on preparing the Master Land Use Plans and Detailed Plans for the cities, as well as issuing planning permits based on satisfactory fulfillment of site specific planning conditions by the developers. In terms of local governance modes, the current planning system is very much focused on governing by authority such as the preparation of the 'blue print' statutory plans, granting of the planning permits, setting up planning conditions, and monitoring actions to identify illegal developments. Even so, the scope of governing by authority is relatively narrow, primarily covering spatial and physical issues such as: the ultimate scale of city growth in terms of the planned size of the urban land area, different types of land uses in terms of area and locations, the supply of municipal facilities and services such as water and utilities to support urban growth, and co-ordinated transportation services and routing. The law does not explicitly identify other local governance modes (such as self-governing, enabling and provision) directly as part of the planning systems.

In order to promote better local governance, the local planning system can further focus on policies or actions that expand the scope of governance modes beyond governing by authority, into governing by enabling and provision as well as direct municipal actions. Table 2 outlines the author's proposed local planning actions under the four modes of local governance.

Diagram 2: Governing by Authority - Zoning codes for Detailed Plans to cover low carbon planning conditions
(example of Beijing Changxindian Low Carbon Community Plan)

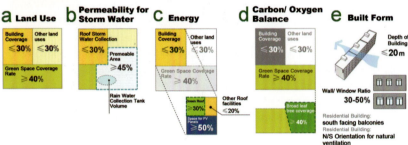

SITE B-39
Land Use: R2
Site Area: 3.09Ha
F.A.R. : 2.2
G.F.A. : 67,980m²
Max.Building Height : 45m

A

a Land Use

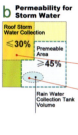

b Permeability for Storm Water

c Energy

d Carbon/ Oxygen Balance

Table 2: Local Governance and the Statutory Planning System

Modes of Local Governance	Possible Statutory Urban-Rural Planning Functions and Initiatives
Self Governing (local governments governing their own activities):	• Specifying in statutory plans that all municipal buildings and public facilities must meet energy efficiency standards beyond the existing building codes. • Identify demonstration low carbon government building projects and undertake site search
Governing by Enabling (local governments facilitating the private sector and the community through incentives and persuasion)	• Highlight the issues of climate change and local impacts in the public participation programme for statutory plans • Technical planning advisory services to citizens on mitigation and adaptation actions; • Promotion and education programmes on local planning and climate change issues; • Provide fast-track planning permit processing arrangements for green buildings; • Granting plot ratio bonus for projects meeting a high level of GHG emission reduction target; • Planning guidance to developers and architects on building energy design.
Governing by Provision (Local governments deliver particular forms of services and resources)	• Incorporate specific low carbon objectives and GHG emission reduction targets for municipal services and facilities in the statutory Master Land Use Plan statement (including power supply, public transit, open space and greening standards, energy recapture facilities for water treatment/supply plants and land fill sites) • Compile city GHG inventory in support of the preparation of statutory plans and future monitoring. • Incorporate low carbon performance indicators as part of the statutory plans.

Governing by Authority (local governments use regulations and sanctions)	• Low carbon city policies and special sector study incorporated as part of the statutory planning documents • Building codes to cover low carbon design requirements; • Zoning codes for Detailed Plans to cover low carbon planning conditions; • Mandatory code of renewable energy usage levels in statutory plan and as conditions for issue of planning permits; • Identifying social, environmental and economic co-benefits and outline them in statutory planning documents as specific low carbon policies – localizing the global issue of climate change

Statutory plans as platform for horizontal collaboration

As discussed before, horizontal collaboration through city networks set up within a region is an important governance tool. Horizontal collaboration will address the issue that GHG emissions in a local geographical context would not be limited to administrative city boundaries. The issue of spatial mismatch is best resolved by bringing together various local governments located within the region and working in collaboration. This is for three reasons.

Firstly, the statutory Urban System Plan (whether at regional or city region levels) is the best spatial platform for the formation of the horizontal collaboration. The Urban System Plan covers a wider spatial scale of a system of cities and towns and, therefore, has already provided the political justification for the local governments to work together to reduce the impact of climate change.

Secondly, with the Urban System Plan area, most of the sources of emissions associated with the urban-rural activities would be covered (such as regional landfill sites, power plants, rural land uses, district heating, regional transportation, major infrastructure works, regional airports, flood plains etc). This spatial match will facilitate collection and analysis of data, as well as the development and implementation of joint mitigation and adaptation strategies.

Finally, as the local governments are from cities in the same region, they in general would share common physical and climate conditions, as well as a cultural affinity. The local governments could therefore easily share their relevant experience in climate change policies and their success stories and best practice examples. Leading and successful cities within the region may set benchmarks for others to follow, while problems encountered by some cities may find their solutions from the experience of the others.

This proposed trans-city network can provide six key collaborative governance functions including (see Figure 2):

• Cross municipal boundary joint mitigation and adaptation actions
• Benchmarking and promotion of best practices
• Regional municipal leadership in managing climate change
• Regional GHG inventory database
• Exchange of experience and expertise, training and capacity building
• Funding cooperation and joint financing

Trans–City Network
Based on the Provincial
Urban System Plan

Figure 2: Provincial System Plan: Horizontal Collaboration Among Cities

An Integrated Planning Process for Vertical Collaboration in Local Governance of Low Carbon Cities

In order to develop a decision making framework for the planning, building and management of low carbon cities, an integrated framework for the preparation of a Low Carbon City Plan based on strong vertical collaboration is needed. The vertical collaboration could be approached from two aspects: the joint collaboration between provincial planning authorities (the Department of Construction), the City Planning Bureau, as well as the District sub-offices of the Planning Bureau. Moreover, the Low Carbon City Plan is a set of strategies and steps to be implemented at various stages of the planning and development control process for a city. The planning systems need to incorporate governance actions at different stages of the planning process in a consistent manner.

The proposed vertical governance framework is outlined below and it includes recommended strategies and action plans associated with the different stages of the current Chinese statutory planning decision process. The outline below will cover the six major components of an integrated planning governance framework.

1. City vision and goals
2. Regional and City Urban System Plans
3. Master Land Use Plans
4. Detailed Plans: development control / planning permits
5. Urban design / building design guidelines
6. Monitoring and research

City vision and goals: setting emission reduction targets

Cities are vulnerable to the negative impacts of global warming. Cities and local municipal governments are obliged to provide vision and leadership to their local communities in this respect. Cities should undertake to understand the real and potential impact of global warming on their economy, society, environment and infrastructure investment, through the carrying out of city GHG inventory assessment. The GHG inventory would provide a comprehensive assessment of the various scenarios of global warming and their local impact on the city. This will lead the way in the development of city vision on managing climate change, supported by specific GHG emissions reduction targets.

Regional and city urban system plans: ensuring multi-level spatial consistency in climate change goals

Deriving from the city's vision and goals, and based on the GHG inventory studies, the city should also align its goals with the climate change action incorporated in the Regional or City Urban System Plans. The latter are regional plans and should have incorporated regional level targets and action strategies. The climate change strategies in the Urban System Plan should guide the preparation of mitigation and adaptation measures in the City Master Land Use Plans. This consistency would ensure multi-level spatial consistency in climate change governance actions, and regional collaboration in future implementation.

City master land use plans: mitigation and adaptation strategies

Based on the Urban System Plans and the GHG inventory analysis, the City Master Land

Use Plan can now identify the various means to reduce carbon emissions throughout the urban development process and the adaptation measures, as well as their effectiveness. These possibilities may then be formulated as a sector document of Integrated Low Carbon City Planning Strategies for the City Master Land Use Plan. Typically these may include, but are not limited to:

• Renewable energy and clean power generation
• Combined heating, cooling and power generation
• Restructuring of industry
• Clean industrial production and low carbon economy
• Compact development and urban form
• Transit oriented development
• Energy efficient building codes
• Consumer education and energy labelling
• City adaptation plans : flooding, weather extremities, ecological changes
• Carbon tax and other fiscal incentives
• Food and agriculture policies

The above planning principles and strategies should be integrated as part of the current statutory City Master Land Use Plan, making it effective and enforceable by law.

Detailed regulatory plans: development control for mitigation

The City Master Land Use plan provides the statutory basis for implementing the mitigation and adaptation actions. Energy reduction, renewable energy supply and carbon emissions are the key indicators to be incorporated in the Detailed Plans, particularly the Regulatory Plans (zoning), as the zoning codes for individual sites in the statutory plans. Examples of these have already been recommended to be piloted through development control in some cities.

The Regulatory Plans (zoning plans) under the current Chinese statutory planning system have placed great emphasis on setting out site specific physical development parameters such as maximum density, plot ratios, setback requirements etc. as a means to control development forms, scale and physical dimensions. These mandatory day to day planning standards and site specific planning parameters in the Regulatory Plan usually include:

• Land use types;
• Building coverage;
• Building height;
• Plot ratio;
• Green space coverage
• Vehicular access and egress; and
• Parking and other facilities

This limited list of mandatory planning parameters do not have adequate breadth and depth to make them fully relevant to planning issues in the context of low carbon cities. Low carbon cities are built upon the management of resources use, energy efficiency and renewable energy supply. The zoning codes for the regulatory plans should be expanded to include specific planning parameters for a low carbon plan such as: energy usage reduction, use of renewable energy sources, rain water re-cycling, storm water management best practices, waste management as well as water treatment and re-use.

Low carbon urban design and building design guidelines

To assist the development industry to move towards designing communities and buildings that meet the low carbon or sustainability objectives, different systems of design guidelines and a certification system have been proposed. Typically these systems adopt an array of points or scoring systems that can be used to assess the performance of a plan or a building during design and also the operation stages. The total score will represent the standard or level achieved and is then certified. The certification is done by qualified professionals or designated institutes. These are important components of the overall local governance framework.

These guidelines can be used by low carbon cities as a benchmark for comparison purposes, for example by specifying the levels of local green building standards, or by providing local urban design guidelines to achieve the proposed mitigation measures. They can also be used as benchmark referencing by the stakeholders (either through trade associations, professional bodies, non-government organizations, certified individuals or qualified assessors, or directly by a designated government agency or department.

Monitoring and research

The last component of the integrated planning governance framework is the need for a programme of on-going project monitoring and research. The implementation of the land use plans or development projects will usually take a certain time span. During the time from initial commencement to final completion, the performance of the plan based on the GHG emission control targets set out at the planning making stage, as well as the various technical criteria and the measurement of performance should be covered by an ongoing monitoring programme. Ongoing research work is also an important part of the governance as the city would need objective GHJG emissions data and assessment methods to measure the efficiency of the various policies during implementation

Conclusions

Managing the challenge of climate change has compelled national and city governments to explore the pathways for the planning of low carbon cities. Our cities and our economies will all need to be enhanced in order to adapt and mitigate the impact of climate change. Recently there has been considerable interest by researchers in the effects of local governance practices on climate change at sub-national and local government levels. There is a need to understand the various modes of governance for low carbon cities including self–governance, governing by enabling, provision and authority. It is suggested that there is a need to localize the global climate change issue and develop co-benefits in order to gain local, political and community support. Specifically, city leaders, politicians and planners will need to review whether our current governance modes, our knowledge base, the statutory planning process, the planning tools and decision making framework are sufficiently ready.

This paper also reviews the current Chinese statutory planning system, and raises the concern that our planning governance and decision making processes need to be enhanced to meet the challenge of governance of climate change at local, city and municipality level. The statutory planning framework needs to be reviewed and enhanced to expand the planning policy and action areas, establish horizontal and vertical collaborations, and set up a consistent planning governance model.

References

Alber, G., Kern, K. (2008) "Governing Climate Change in Cities: Modes of Urban Climate Governance in Multi-level Systems". *Conference on Competitive Cities and Climate Change Conference, Milan 9-10 October 2008.* Available at www.oecd.org

Bell, S (2002) *Economic Governance and Institutional Dynamics,* Melbourne, Oxford University Press

Betsill, M. (2001) "Mitigating Climate Change in the US Cities: Opportunities and Obstacles", *Local Environment, 6(4), 393-406*

Betsill, M., Bulkeley, H. (2006) "Cities and the Multilevel Governance of Global Climate Change", *Global Governance*, 12, 141-159

Bulkeley, H., Kern, K. (2006) "Local government and the governing of climate change in Germany and the UK", *Urban Studies, 43 (12), 2237-2259*

Granberg, M., Elander, I. (2007) "Local Governance and Climate Change: Reflections on the Swedish Experience", *Local Environment, 12 (5), 537-548.*

Intergovernmental Committee on Urban and Regional Research (ICURR) (2008) "Climate Change: Canadian Cities are doing their share", *Plan Canada, Vol. 48 No. 1, 2008.*

Intergovernmental Panel on Climate Change (IPCC) (2007) "Climate Change 2007 - The Fourth IPCC Assessment Report (Synthesis Report)". *IPCC, 2007. Available at: www.ipcc.ch*

Kern, K. (2008) "Sustainable Development Initiatives in Federal States in Germany", in Baker S., Eckerberg, K. (eds.) *In Pursuit of Sustainable Development: New Governance Practices at the Subnational Level in Europe,* London/New York, Routledge

Kern, K., Bulkeley, H. (2009) "Cities, Europeanization and Multi-level Governance: Governing Climate Change through Transnational Municipal Networks", *Journal of Common Market Studies, 47(2), 309-332*

Lindseth, G (2004) "The Cities for Climate Protection Campaign (CCPC) and the Framing of Local Climate Policy", *Local Environment, Vol. 9, No. 4, 325–336, August 2004*

McKinsey & Company (2009) "Pathways to a Low Carbon Economy – Version 2 of the Global Greenhouse Gas Abatement Cost Curve", *Available at: www.mckinsey.com/globalGHGcostcurve*

Qi, Ye. et. al. (2008) "Translating a global issue Into Local Priority: China's Local Government Response to Climate Change", *The Journal of Environment & Development, 17(4), 379-400*

Schreurs, M. A. (2008) "From the Bottom Up: Local and Subnational Climate Change Politics", *The Journal of Environment & Development, 17 (4), 343-355*

Schroeder, H. and Bulkeley, H. (2009) "Global Cities and the Governance of Climate Change: what is the role of law in cities?" *Fordham Urban Law Journal*, *XXXVI (2). pp. 313-359.*

Sippel, M., Jenssen, T. (2009) *What about Local Climate Governance? A Review of Promise and Problems. MPRA Paper.* Available at: mpra.ub.uni-muenchen.de

The City of New York (2007) *PlanNY: A Greener, Greater New York,* New York, the City of New York

The City of New York (2008*) PlanNY: Progress Report 2008*, New York, the City of New York

The Government of Singapore (2008) *Singapore's National Climate Change Policy*. Singapore, The Government of Singapore

The People's Republic of China, Standing Committee of the National People's Congress (2007) *The Urban and Rural Planning Law*. Promulgated on 28 October, 2007. Effective date: 1 January 2008.

Tietenberg T. H. (2000) *Environment Economics and Policy* . Addison-Wesley

Tokyo Metropolitan Government (TMG) (2007) *Tokyo Climate Change Strategy - A Basic Policy for the 10-Year Project for a Carbon-Minus Tokyo*. Tokyo, Tokyo Metropolitan Government

van Kooten C. (2004) *Climate Change Economics - Why International Accords Fail*. Cheltenham : Edward Elgar

World Bank (1991) *Managing Development – The Governance Dimension*. Washington D.C., World Bank

Yip, Stanley C. T., (2008). "Planning for Eco-Cities in China: Visions, Approaches and Challenges". *The 44th ISOCARP Congress 2008, Dalian, China*

Industrial Heritage as a Cultural Infrastructure

Dong Wei

Meaning of Cultural Infrastructure

Urban infrastructure forms the basic supporting platform of the city. The cities where we live and work are undergoing tremendous changes, but any long term and sustainable change has to rely upon the upgrading of the urban infrastructure. Besides the traditional infrastructure, such as transportation, electricity, communication, water supply and drainage, education and health facilities, etc., there exists another kind of infrastructure, which includes culture, the urban pattern and the environment. These ingredients make a city different from any others, and make the world rich and diverse in cultures and life styles. As one of the crucial parts of culture, industrial heritage reflects the origins of urban modernization, and it is very important for us to understand it in depth in the context of social development.

China's industrialization began after the 1840s, when Western military force invaded the country in the Opium War. The process of industrialization made dramatic changes to many traditional cities in China, and as a result many new cities and towns, industrial blocks and buildings were created. During the past decades, the industrial facilities have contributed greatly to the city, and they have become the cultural infrastructure as the former production went into decline.

Process of Industrialization and Typology of Industrial Heritage in China

To study the development of industrial heritage development in China, one must understand the industrial history of China.

Phase one: Invasion by foreign forces and the beginnings of domestic industrialization, 1840-1949

The first Opium War in 1840 signified an upheaval in China over the next one hundred years. On the one hand, China was split and colonized by foreign powers and the population suffered great hardship. On the other hand, some new ideas and advanced techniques were introduced. Modern factories and wharves were first established in the coastal cities and then gradually infiltrated the inland cities, so ensuring that the western powers took a firm grip of the economic and social life of the country. These new formations changed the traditional way of production as well as the approach to urban development. Just as modern urban planning and management developed and changed the cities greatly, so did the new national industries, especially in the fields of textiles, mining and military industry,

although these started in a very small scale way with new and unproven technologies.

Phase two: The beginnings of large scale industrialization, 1950-1970s

From the 1950s, and supported by Soviet Russia, China began the first five-year program with 156 important national projects and many other local ones. With these projects many heavy industrial bases were established in different regions. During the 1960-1970s, more industrial projects were located in the inland cities and countryside due to the difficult international situation. However, this shift in location made the industrial development more balanced in China in general. Great developments took place not only in the coastal areas, but also inland and in the western part of the country. All of them established a solid foundation for the well-being and modernization of the new China. It would have been impossible to launch the state reforms in the later 1970s without the industrialization of this period.

Phase three: Ubiquitous and advanced industrialization, 1980s-today

In the era of reform, China developed rapidly. More and more industries started up, and "industrial heritage" began to emerge through the growing obsolescence and replacement of many old factories and equipment.

Of course, only those buildings/structures with the greatest cultural significance were at the outset recognized as "industrial heritage", and these pioneer projects have set important benchmarks which help decision makers today identify what is worthy industrial heritage. In recent years, more and more cities have endeavoured to conserve their industrial past as one of the significant strategies for future development.

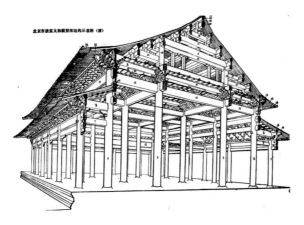

北京市故宫太和殿梁架结构示意图（清）

Figure 1: The timber-structure of the Hall of Taihe, Forbidden City, Beijing. 1368-today

Typology of Industrial Heritage

1. Industrial period

- 1840-1949: Most industrial heritage of this period is located in the coastal areas, such as in Guangzhou, Fuzhou, Shanghai, Qingdao, and Tianjin, with some in the cities inland along the major water ways, such as in Suzhou, Wuxi, Nanjing, and Wuhan. The specific feature of the industrial heritage of this period is that many industries grew up as a result of foreign investment and technology.
- 1950-1970s: The industrial heritage of this period forms the major part of the industrial heritage of China as a whole. The specific features are that the industrialization in the country takes place more gradually, while the industrial heritage is distributed more evenly throughout different regions;
- 1950-60s: Many leading projects were supported by Soviet Russia, while afterwards a national industrial network was set up by the Chinese. To many people the industrial heritage of this time reflects the spirit of self-dependence and also reminds them of a difficult time in the establishment of key domestic industries.

- 1980s-today: The industrial heritage of this period is rare but emerging rapidly, especially when the renewal of industrial technology is getting faster.

2. Mode of production

Key examples are:

- The mining and metallurgical industry, the basis of many other industries;
- Transportation and energy: all kinds of facilities and factories related to transportation and energy production and supply;
- Types of manufacture: from food to textiles, from light industries to chemical industries, special kinds of industrial projects, etc.

3. Regional base

Even though all levels of government have endeavoured to balance industrial development in different regions, the social and economic gap is still a major issue for China. For instance, the industrial heritage in the western region is mostly related to mining and heavy industry, while that in the eastern region is mostly related to the production of precision goods.

Figure 2: The timber-structure of Naign Shrine, Japan. The 7th century-today

Figure 3: Stone-structured Colosseum of Rome, the 1st century

Figure 4: Adapted reuse of industrial heritage in Vanke
Crystal City, Tianjin, 2005
天津万科水晶城中保留的原天津玻璃厂工业遗产
Photo: Dong Wei 摄影：董卫

Figure 5: Entrance of Kailuan Mining Museum,
Tangshan, 2008 开滦煤矿-矿山博物馆入口
Photo: Dong Wei 摄影：董卫

Theoretical Approach

The conservation of industrial heritage has a theoretical importance in China.

There is much evidence of the tension between the "theory" and "practice" of heritage conservation. For example, having the "knowledge" of heritage on the one hand and being able to "understand" the "meaning" of it on the other, end up as contrary positions: people from different disciplines have different concepts of this issue. This is especially the case when the "theory" is "international" while "practice" is "local". It is clear that a theoretical inadaptability appears when international conservation principles are understood doctrinally and rigidly. This is, to a large extent, due to the fact that the "international" principles of the West are mostly developed from a stone and brick building tradition while Chinese and Eastern architectural ideals are mostly from a timber-tradition. Stone endures for a long time but wood is always growing and changing. To those in the West, it is reasonable that a building could last for hundreds and thousands of years, while in the Eastern countries with their abundance of timber and long tradition of building in wood, it is reasonable to assume that the life-cycle of a building should be equivalent to that of human beings. Thus cities and buildings are constantly renewable and sustainable. Only in this way can each generation maintain and redevelop the cities and architecture according to its particular needs.

Thus, the Chinese and the Eastern urban and architectural conception is based on a thousand-year old timber-tradition, and today this has become an irreplaceable and intangible heritage in many countries in Asia and the Pacific Region. However, this does not mean that such a tradition is unconnected with modern conservation principles. On the contrary, this tradition is inextricably linked to both the present and the past. The custom of ancestor-

Figure 6: Urban Design for the central part of 751 Factory, Beijing, 2007.
The factory is transformed to be the center of
fashion design. Designed by Dong Wei Studio. 北京751工厂改造城市设计，董卫工作室，2007

worship and the worship of the natural spirits has been a common thread in traditional society. But people focus on the spirit of a place rather than on the building itself. To them it is natural that the building cannot last indefinitely. Rather, it can be replaced and changed quite often according to the needs of each generation, which means that the spirit of a place is more important than a particular building or temple.

However, while the main proponents of today's conservation theory still stick to the significance of physical authenticity, the great debate on what is the "right way" in the interpretation of heritage means that the distinction between the theory of restoration and that of conservation will continue to exist amongst experts for many years to come. In 1993, Xi'an Municipality bid for three sites to be included in the tentative world heritage list , but two of them, the restoration of Daming Palace of the Tang Dynasty (618-907) and the old city wall

of the Ming and Qing Dynasties (1368-1911), were immediately turned down by western experts because both sites were believed to have lost their historical authenticity., Japan also faces the problem that its traditional restoration approach based on timber-tradition is not recognized by western experts. Naign Shrine is one of the most important Japanese monuments, and to conserve this national treasure, the state followed a method from the 7th century, that is to rebuild the building every 20 years. A new one was built just beside the old which was then pulled down when the new one was completed. Today this shrine has been rebuilt 60 times, and with such a tradition people developed a sophisticated means of maintaining the old craftsmanship. This architectural ideal as an intangible heritage makes the timber shrine vivid and understandable to each generation. And most important of all, this ideal can last much longer than any physical space or tangible heritage. In fact, because wood is one of the main build-

Figure 7: Redevelopment of 798 Factory, Beijing.
Two old factory buildings were connected with the new highrise office buildings (under construction).
Designed by Dong Wei and Du Xiaomin, Duocheng Studio of Architectural Design, 2007 北京国际电子城总部设计

ing materials in the East, a similar tradition has been generally accepted and handed down from one generation to another in the countries of Asia and the Pacific.

Anyhow, conservation of the industrial heritage has achieved a great breakthrough in the theoretical dilemma cited above. To deal with industrial heritage, one has to think about how it can be adaptably reused when carrying out conservation and restoration. For the first time, and in a broad sense, an academic balance has been struck between the purposes of conservation and urban redevelopment, and between theory and practice. Comparing this with other kinds of cultural heritage, this is largely due to the fact that the industrial heritage is mostly of high value in terms of reuse and restoration, given its scale, its comparative modernity, its structure and the space available. From the point of view of social and economic development, the old industrial sites have multiple value to the public, which readily creates a dynamic balance among the different driving forces at political, community and financial levels. Thus the results of conservation usually blend well with purposes of urban redevelopment. Moreover, the conservation of industrial heritage makes a great contribution to the general theory of heritage conservation, even though industrial heritage is only a small part of the total extent of cultural heritage in the world.

Since the last decade of the 20th century, conserving the intangible heritage has become noticeable and has come under the spotlight of mainstream heritage conservation theory. TICCIH (The International Committee for the Conservation of the Industrial Heritage) issued the Nizhny Tagil Charter in 2003 which put forward international criteria and became an academic reference for industrial heritage study and conservation throughout the world. This means that a leading international organization in industrial heritage conservation has gone into a new phase of activity following

Figure 8: Redevelopment of 798 Factory, Beijing. Two old factory building were connected with the new highrise office buildings (under construction). The old factory buildings have themselves been transformed into an international arts centre. Designed by Dong Wei and Du Xiaomin, Duocheng Studio of Architectural Design, 2007

北京国际电子城总部设计

its foundation 30years ago. Encouraged by this charter and the related research, a specifically design-based and creative approach to conserving industrial heritage has been developed. The aim is to see heritage buildings within an urban structure as an integrated whole. This approach marked a change from the traditional conservation principle of providing a protective umbrella over the heritage sites to make them "safe" and "untouched" by the wave of urban transformation. Creative and adaptive reuse but not "segregation" and "control" become the key words in industrial heritage conservation.

This is a great achievement in the history of urban conservation, and it will have a crucial impact sooner or later on the general theory of heritage conservation in the world. To be "safe" and "untouched" or "segregation" and "control" are only the elementary objectives in heritage conservation, while urban sustainability and cultural continuity through re-creation and adaptive reuse, generation by generation, is the ultimate focus of heritage conservation.

Large scale industrial heritage conservation in China started at the beginning of the 21st century when the famous 798 factory complex in the northeastern suburb of Beijing was transformed by a group of local artists to become an international arts center in 2001. During the last decade this factory has become very famous worldwide as the "wind vane" of China's modern art development.

In 2006 at the second Heritage Conservation Forum of Wuxi, at which the leader of the State Administration for Heritage Conservation in China and other participants were present, the Wuxi Proposal on Industrial Heritage Conservation was announced to the public. This is an important document in China which focuses on industrial heritage. The Proposal calls on governments at all level to do a better job in popularization, legislation,

planning and other works to protect industrial relics and heritages. "We appeal to the whole of society to raise awareness of conservation by implementing this proposal with an open-mind and long-term vision. More effort should be made to turn those potential cultural creations into the future cultural heritage". Delegates from different regions jointly made these proposals, which reflected the level of public concern on this issue. The Wuxi Forum has become the most influential domestic forum on the protection of cultural heritages.

Conclusion

The development of industrial heritage conservation offers opportunities for us to rethink the major theories and approaches we have used for years in the field of heritage conservation. This is really a turning point to re-making various ideas from different countries and regions that are related to their own cultures. In short, the emergence of heritage is culturally based, and conservation has to be culturally-oriented. In order for this to happen, a major issue is how and at what level the "international principles" could be accepted by local knowledge.

As one of the important cultural infrastructures, industrial heritage is now the newest cultural resource for cities and it is becoming increasingly important. From the very beginning, industrial heritage conservation in China has focused on urban redevelopment as well as the revitalization of cultural resources . Behind this approach is the dominant Chinese ideology of historical continuity and the handing down of tradition. This means, whether a historic site is to be handed down or not depends on its acceptance and reuse by future generations. This thousand-year tradition gives full scope for the conservation of the industrial heritage. The great achievement in conservation has inspired people to recognise that architectural tradition can be revitalized in the new situation and that the industrial heritage can be saved. In the meantime, it is also beyond all doubt that the timber-structure based tradition has a new lease of life both today and in the future, and will improve and enrich international heritage theory.

Devising an Adaptable Urban Shelter and Evacuation System in Disaster Situations

Su Jing-yu

Liu Chao-feng

Wang Wei

Figure1: Refugees in the streets

The shelter and evacuation system is an important measure to reduce losses caused by disasters and to respond to sudden disasters in cities. In the relief of recent major disasters, the shelter and evacuation system has played a positive role. However, it has also revealed a lack of adaptability. In the 2008 Wenchuan earthquake, for example, there was a severe shortage of emergency shelters. People afflicted by the earthquake had to settle in places not suitable as shelters, such as on the road (see Figure 1) and by river banks. Millions of refugees even had to set up shelters in the ruins of buildings. In addition, primary and middle schools which are supposed to serve as shelters were seriously damaged. The shelters did not have the emergency facilities needed for earthquake relief *(Ye Ming-wu et al. 2010 and Huang Dian-jian et al. 2006)*. The Haiti earthquake of 2010 also witnessed a shortage of shelters and the shelters that did exist were in poor condition. Most refugees had to seek temporary shelter in the Haitian capital Port au Prince and nearby areas, or even in temporary tents provided by the Americans in Guantanamo Bay[1]. On March 11th 2011, an earthquake of Magnitude (M) 9.0 hit Japan. Blackouts, interrupted water supply, oil shortage and the severe weather conditions affected the disaster-area. The heating facilities in some of the emergency shelters did not work properly, leading to some deaths. By the morning of March 18, the death toll had reached 21 after some refugees had been transferred from hospitals to the shelters[2]. All the above highlights the vulnerability and lack of adaptability of emergency shelters in the face of a major disaster, as the shelters are built according to normal environmental planning regulations. Therefore, the long-term planning of an adaptable shelter and evacuation system is very important *(Jin peng-hui et al. 2009 and Liu Yan-hua 2009)*.

The Adaptable Shelter and Evacuation System in Disaster Situations

Given the above, we first summarize the concepts surrounding a disaster situation and an adaptable shelter and evacuation system. Then we discuss planning strategies and measures for a shelter and evacuation system in the event of a disaster situation. We approach the topic from four aspects: the disaster prevention functions of the shelter; the standard of shelters and corresponding spatial features; the construction standards of shelters; and the configuration requirements for supporting facilities in shelters. We aim to provide guidance on the planning and construction of an urban shelter and evacuation system appropriate to a disaster. It is vital to reduce the response time of the urban shelter and evacuation system in the face of serious disasters, and to change the situation where there are no proper coping strategies for such events.

The disaster situation is a hybrid system consisting of the geographical environment of human habitat and its interaction with natural disasters, and manmade disasters. Depending on the timing and severity of disasters, human living conditions are divided into three stages: normal situations, common disaster situations and extreme disaster situations. In between, one stage can gradually or suddenly merge into another, as illustrated in Figure 2. Adapting to disaster situations is a complex issue. It not only involves disaster-causing factors and the natural ecological environment, but is also closely related to human social and economic systems. The adaptable shelter and evacuation system should respond to urban disaster situations. It should be an adaptable and hybrid system, a system consisting of different grades of shelters with the supporting facilities and rescue roads. The shelter

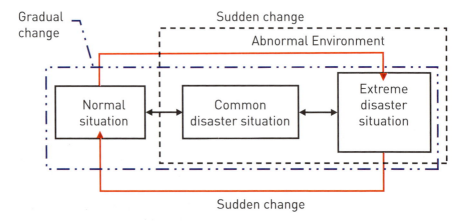

Figure 2: Three-state environment model

system should also be closely connected to other urban systems for disaster prevention and rescue, such as firefighting, public security, medical treatment, supply of goods and materials, emergency command, maintenance and management systems. Its purpose is to ensure the shelter, evacuation and resettlement of people affected by disasters. It is a multi-level, networked, and complex system.

The planning of an adaptable shelter and evacuation system involves establishing different models for various disaster situations, different stages in social and economic development, and different needs. The planning is an interactive, dynamic and adaptable process, constantly moving between the disaster situation and planning goals and effects, as illustrated in Figure 3. Moreover, the strategy of building a shelter and evacuation system should be systematic, the planning done in advance, the construction phased, and the implementation coordinated.

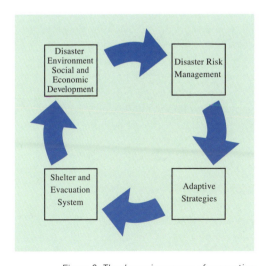

Figure 3: The dynamic process of evacuation system planning

Optimisation and Coordination of the Disaster-Prevention Functions in the Adaptable Urban Shelter and Evacuation System

The current concept of shelters used within and outside China mainly focuses on common disasters such as unexpected public events, earthquakes, secondary fires and so on. The types of disaster which can be prevented are limited. Such a concept of shelters does not take into account catastrophic risks, neither does it recognise regional differences. Moreover, there is no systematic thinking about the evolution of disasters in this concept. Urban disasters are diverse, frequent, interlocked, and often take place concurrently. When different disasters strike in parallel or in sequence, shelters designed for one kind of disaster might prove to be insufficient in disaster-prevention and mitigation, limiting the role of a shelter and evacuation system. Coastal cities in China with an advanced economy and dense population have built shelters suitable for earthquakes and/or fires. But they may be inappropriate for concurrent natural disasters, such as parallel or sequential incidences of earthquakes, tsunamis, and typhoons. In addition, the functions of the shelter and evacuation system do not adapt to the different stages of natural disasters. There is also a lack of coordination between different evacuation measures. In the Wenchuan earthquake, for example, the shelters in Mianyang City were insufficient, leading to a flood of refugees onto the street and road congestion. Some of the shelters could only provide temporary refuge during the disasters, and

Figure 4: Refugees settled in the streets in the rain

were not suitable for evacuating and resettling people in the post-disaster period. Many refugees had to settle on the streets (see Figure 4) and in the ruins of buildings . For this reason, it is necessary to optimize and coordinate the planning of a shelter and evacuation system from a risk-management perspective, taking into account the critical disasters, the range of disasters, and the sequence of disasters.

According to the urban disaster risk assessment and the urban development conditions, a city should be divided into several disaster-prevention areas which are relatively independent. In each disaster-prevention area the size of the impact (key points and the disaster area) and spatial distribution of major disasters should be examined. The types and functions of adaptable and optimal shelters should also be examined, according to the characteristics of the disasters. To cope with earthquakes, for example, a particular approach to sheltering within the area should be used; open fields or low-rise (one storey) buildings are suitable shelters. In rain or snow follow-

ing an earthquake, suitable shelter buildings can protect the refugees from freezing and can keep them warm. In cases of secondary fires, mudslides, leaks of toxic gas induced by earthquakes, it is better to apply a model of sheltering outside the area, placing refugees in open fields. Shelters should be built with fire barriers; they should be located above or by the side of areas hit by mudslides, and far away from the sources of toxic gases.

In areas prone to typhoons, floods, and rainstorms and waterlogging, the planning and construction of shelter and evacuation sites should take into account the shelter and evacuation needs of flood- and wind- prevention. Shelter sites should be located on high ground with a substantial flood discharge capacity. Alternatively, the sites could be in shelter buildings that are multi-storey, resilient to disasters, and with at least two evacuation exits. In the various stages of the disaster, although the disaster-prevention functions required for a shelter and evacuation system are different, they are also closely related. Therefore, the functions of an emergency shelter system should be adjusted to and coordinated with the needs of each stage in a disaster. In normal times, the buildings used as shelters serve their original purposes (such as entertainment, accommodation, events organization). Immediately before the emergency, their normal functions change so that they become emergency shelters, to meet the shelter needs of the refugees. During the emergency, they perform their shelter and evacuation functions, according to the pre-arranged plans. After the emergency, they

act as medium- to long-term settlements for refugees. In sum, the types and functions of shelters should be planned bearing in mind the characteristics and sequence of the disasters. It is necessary to optimize the types and functions of shelters, and adjust their functions to the needs of disaster prevention. The shelter system should be coordinated with and support other disaster-prevention and rescue systems. All the above requirements work together to create an adaptable and coordinated shelter and evacuation system (see Figure 5).

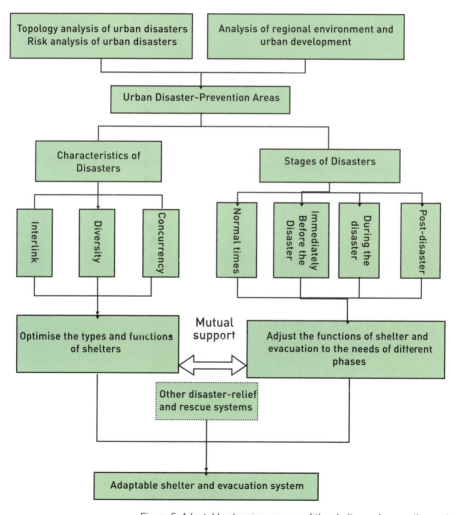

Figure 5: Adaptable planning process of the shelter and evacuation system

Classification of Shelters and Corresponding Spatial Layouts

In the Wenchuan earthquake, the shelters played a positive role. However this earthquake also exposed disorder in terms of the distribution and structural levels of the shelters. For example, the affected population in Mianyang had no other choice but to make their temporary home by the roadside or in an open field within residential communities. Some residents could not find an open field safe enough to put up tents, and were forced to take shelter under bridges *(Ye Na et al. 2009; Qiu Jian et al. 2008; Lin Shuzhi et al. 2008)*. A good shelter and evacuation system requires different grades of shelters. Existing shelters in China are inadequate to meet the challenges of the different stages of disasters. For this reason, we will discuss on a macro-level three models of a shelter and evacuation system that are suitable for different urban spatial features, taking into account the regional environment and the characteristics of the particular city (see Table 1).

Table1: Evacuation system models

Evacuation system models	Features	Suitable cities	Examples
Three-dimensional model	Sufficient shelters with balanced distribution; developed road and waterway networks, good airport; evacuation and rescue by land, sea, and air	Cities by the sea or the river	The Yangtzi river delta
Two-dimensional model	Sufficient shelters with balanced distribution; developed road networks, good airport; evacuation and rescue mainly by land, and complemented by rescue by air	Inland cities on plains	The Beijing-Tianjin-Tanggu area
Point- to- Point model	Insufficient shelters with scattered distribution; undeveloped road and waterway networks that are vulnerable and are difficult to repair; evacuation and rescue mainly by air, and complemented by rescue by land and by river	Highland	Panzhihua City

The three-dimensional model is for cities with shelters that are sufficient, evenly distributed, and with a diverse and closely connected means of transportation. Through air, land, and sea rescue, and by working with other disaster-prevention and rescue systems, this model helps facilitate the evacuation and settlement of displaced people, as well as the transport of materials. This model requires advanced road and waterway networks connecting different urban shelters. It also requires air corridors connecting helicopter landing areas in fields used to shelter people, and the city's airport. The two-dimensional model relates to cities with shelters that are sufficient, evenly distributed, and with a diverse and closely connected means of transportation. Through land and sea rescue, and by working with other disaster-prevention and rescue systems, this model secures the evacuation and re-settlement of displaced people, as well as the transport of materials. It requires advanced road networks connecting different urban shelters. Rescue through air corridors connecting helicopter landing areas and the city's airport is complementary. The point-to-point model is for cities with a lack of shelters or with shelters that are scattered, and with a single transportation connection. Through rescue by air and by working with other disaster-prevention and rescue systems, this model helps facilitate the evacuation and settlement of refugees, as well as the transport of materials..

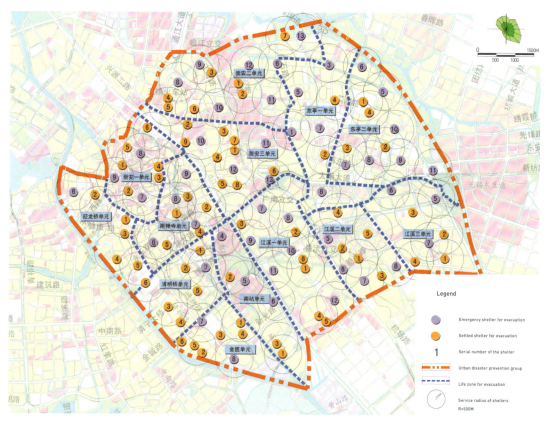

Figure 6: Seismic shelter for evacuation plan for a city

On a micro-level, the levels of emergency shelters should correspond to their spatial distribution; they should be mutually supportive and complementary. The needs of the people affected (the actual shelters and the services shelters provide) change with each stage of the disaster. Those particular needs then determine the type and corresponding functions of emergency shelters (Chen Zhi-fen et al. 2010; Chen Zhi-fen et al. 2010). To maximize the benefits of limited urban disaster-prevention and relief resources, the layout of shelters and their spatial distribution should be adapted to the needs of the evacuation, and the levels of shelters and the layout requirements should match Figure 6. Table 2 lists three levels of shelters, and summarizes the corresponding layout requirements. Their optimal distribution can be ascertained by mathematical modelling, with the help of computer technology. Within the constraints of safety, need, economic considerations and the environment, one can determine the shelter and evacuation objective, and then calculate through optimisation which shelter would be the most effective. This is how the optimal spatial distribution is achieved.

Table 2: Shelter classification and layout requirements

Level of shelters	Functions	Spatial features
Emergency shelters for evacuation	Shelter-in-place, self-help in emergency, temporary facilities	Adjacent to residential buildings, within ten minutes walk, small in size (1,000m² minimum), a large number, distributed according to the location of urban residences
Settled shelter for evacuation	Concentrated shelters, for medium- and long-term inhabitance, with emergency infrastructure and rescue equipments	Not far from urban residences (2~3km), within a one hour walk, relatively large size (5000m², minimum) in open areas that are big enough and located according to the distribution of the population, coordinated with the shelter buildings
Central shelters for evacuation	Shelters for longer term settlement at a distance from the disaster site and providing a complete infrastructure including a command centre for rescue and evacuation and stockpiles of disaster-relief materials	Faraway from urban residences, large scale (around 500,000m², few in number, on level land

Construction Standards for Adaptable Urban Shelters

Shelter sites consist of shelter fields and shelter buildings. Planned and equipped with the necessary supporting facilities, shelter fields can be used in the pre-disaster phase, post-disaster evacuation, and for settlement during the reconstruction and recovery phases. Areas suitable for shelter include sizeable parks, open fields, plazas and other open spaces. Shelter buildings fulfil the same roles and they too need to be properly planned and constructed. They include stadiums, primary and middle schools, and civil air defence and other buildings.

There are currently no unified planning and design standards for shelter and evacuation systems. The current construction standards and architectural specifications are suitable for the more normal disaster situations. There is a lack of clear thinking with regard to extreme disasters and urban regional disasters. The buildings constructed according to current standards cannot survive extreme disasters. The Wenchuan earthquake showed that the construction standards for primary and middle schools were quite low. A large number of school buildings collapsed immediately. Those still standing were severely damaged, and could not function as shelters (Lin Shuzhi, Huang Jiannan 2008; Sun Hui, Luan Bin 2009; Xue Yusheng 2006).

When constructing shelter sites and supporting facilities, the types and history of incidences of disaster in a region should be taken into account. The possibility of catastrophes should also be considered. It is important to define the standards for disaster prevention and defence, to give comprehensive consideration to disaster-prevention standards, defence systems and the area likely to be affected by disasters. We should also plan and design with a long-term vision in mind, in order to cope with unforeseeable and sudden major disasters and ensure the resilience of shelters so that they function well in an evacuation.

The Adaptation and Coordination of Supporting Systems in Shelters

In recent years, there have been numerous major and sudden disasters. Although many countries have instituted disaster-prevention and relief plans, as well as plans for shelter sites, the supporting facilities for shelter and evacuation systems are far from adequate to cope with extreme disasters. As stated earlier, that proved to be the case in connection with the recent Japanese earthquake where some shelters could not provide warm enough conditions to counter the extreme cold, leading to a number of deaths. But beyond that, and its direct impacts, the earthquake had two major 'knock on' effects. First, it triggered a tsunami, leading to a huge number of deaths, as well as blackouts, interrupted water supplies, an oil shortage and a shortage of materials. Secondly, it caused great damage to the Fukushima nuclear power plant leading to the release of radiation into the environment and the subsequent evacuation of housing within a certain radius. Those effects tested the emergency services to the limit.

In China, the Wenchuan (2008) and Yushu (2010) earthquakes exposed problems such as a shortage of medical aid facilities, sanitation and quarantine facilities and emergency material storage facilities in shelters. Those shelters also lacked a supply of electricity and water, as well as garbage and sewage disposal facilities for emergency use. Such problems demonstrate the lack of adaptability and coordination of the shelter system. It is, therefore, necessary to study the optimal co-ordination of the configuration for emergency shelters when disasters take place, and define the configuration requirements for supporting facilities.

The configuration systems for emergency shelters are planned by coordinating the sub-systems (command system, electricity system, communication system, water supply system, material storage system and so on) in a com-plex and dynamic way. This involves adaptable optimization within and between the subsys-tems, and coordination between subsystems and the types of shelters (see Figure 7). Based on the city master plan and other special-ized plans, and given the disaster-prevention needs and types of shelters, we propose the following planning and construction require-ments for supporting facilities, as listed in Table 3.

Figure 7: Functional planning of seismic shelter for evacuation for a city

Table 3: Shelter types and configuration requirements of facilities

Type of shelter	Functional requirements	Configuration requirements of facilities
Emergency shelter sites	Emergency shelter, temporary sites	Temporary water supply, sewage, electricity and lighting facilities, and temporary toilets. Meeting the basic living needs of refugees and fire prevention requirements
Fixed shelter sites	Medium- to long-term shelter, con-centrated shelter and evacuation sites	Water supply, sewage, electricity, lighting and sanitation facilities, dwellings for refu-gees with storage for living necessities and medicines, fire-fighting facilities, emergency communication and broadcasting facilities, temporary generators and lighting facilities, medical treatment facilities, and vehicles for transportation. Meeting the needs of the long-term liveli-hood of refugees; ensuring that the rescue functions of shelters are carried out, meeting the requirements of disaster-prevention and -relief.
Central shelter sites	Long-term shelter, concentrated evacu-ation, rescue, and settlement sites in post-disaster period	Water supply, electricity, lighting and sanita-tion facilities, dwellings for refugees with storage for living necessities and medicines, fire-fighting facilities, emergency communi-cation and broadcasting facilities, temporary generators and lighting facilities, medical treatment facilities, and vehicles. Disaster-relief command operations, information facili-ties, disaster-relief military camp, helicopter pads, medical treatment and rescue centre, transfer centre for the severely injured. Meeting the needs of long-term livelihood of refuges; and ensuring that the rescue func-tions of shelters are carried out, meeting the requirements of disaster-prevention and -relief.

Concluding Remarks

An urban emergency shelter and evacuation system is an important measure in disaster response. However, the system planned and constructed for normal situations or common disaster situations does not adapt well to extreme disasters. For this reason, we have proposed in this paper an adaptable shelter and evacuation system to meet the challenges of major disasters, and have put forward some preliminary ideas on adaptable planning strategies and measures in four categories. But the adaptable shelter and evacuation system in disaster situations deserves further, in depth study, especially in two directions. The first is in respect of disaster situations based on simulations. The second concerns the planning and construction indicators for an adaptable shelter and evacuation system; such indicators need to be quantified.

Endnotes

1. http://news.163.com/special/000143HI/
   Haitiearthquake0112.html

2. http://news.sina.com.cn/z/japanearthquake0311/
   index.shtml

References

Ye Ming-wu, Wang Jun, Huang Jing (2010) "Theoretical exploration and empirical analysis of construction of Urban Emergency Shelter", *Resources Environment and Development*, No.3

Huang Dian-jian, Wu Zong-zhi, Cai Si-jing, et al. (2006) "Emergency adaption of urban emergency shelter: analytic hierarchy process-based assessment method", *Journal of Natural Disasters*, Vol.15, No. 1, Feb.

Jin peng-hui, Fang Xiao, Zhang Xiao-ying, et al. (2009) *Getting started guide of cities for climate change adaptation,* Beijing: China Financial Publishing House.

Liu Yan-hua (2009) *Adaptation to climate change-the East Asia Summit member countries strategies, policies and actions*, Beijing: Science Press.

Ye Na, DengYun-lan, XiaYi-ping (2009) "Inspirations on the Disaster Prevention and Reduction of Public Green Space from Wenchuan Earthquake", *Urban Studies*, Vol.16, No. 5.

Qiu Jian, Jiang Junhao;Jia Liuqiang (2008) "Enlightenment of Disaster Prevention and Reduction of the Park System Construction with regard to Wenchuan Earthquake", *City Planning Review*, Vol.32, No.16.

Lin Shuzhi, Huang Jiannan (2008) "The Research on the Construction of Emergency Shelter after Wenchuan Earthquake", *Fujian Architecture & Construction*, Vol124, No 10.

Chen Zhi-fen, Gu Lin-sheng, Chen Jin, et al. (2010) "Study on hierarchical location of urban emergency shelters - hierarchy analysis", *Journal of Natural Disasters*, Vol. 19, No. 3.

Chen Zhi-fen, Chen-Jin, Li-Qiang (2010) "Study on hierarchical location of urban emergency shelters: three-hierarchical location models", *Journal of Natural Disasters*, Vol.19, No.5.

Sun Hui, Luan Bin (2009) "Analysis of spatial planning for urban disaster refuge space based on green space system design", *Journal of Dalian University of Technology*, Vol.49, No.5, Sept.

Xue Yusheng (2006) "Space-time Cooperative Framework for defending Blackouts Part III Optimization and Coordination of Defense-lines", *Automation of Electric Power Systems*, Vol.30, No.3, Feb.

A Study of Target Groups for Affordable Housing

Zhang Jie

Jiao Yang

In 1998 twenty years after the Reform associated with Deng Xiaoping was launched, China's welfare housing system, which had lasted for decades, was eventually converted into a commercial housing one, in order to adjust to the country's emerging market economy. This change was signalled by a milestone national policy statement entitled: *Further consolidation of the housing system reform with the aim of accelerating housing development (Zhang Jie, Li Li 2009).*

Over the last ten years, with a steady growth in commercial housing development, average housing conditions for urban residents have been greatly improved. According to the statistics published by the Ministry of Housing and Urban-Rural Development and the National Bureau of Statistics of China, by the end of 2006, housing floor area per capita in cities and towns reached 27.1 sq.m, while the latest data shows that the living area per capita in Beijing was 28.8 sq.m at the end of 2009 *(China Statistical Year Book 2010).*

While housing is fully commercialized and privatized, a real social issue has emerged which is that the housing needs of low-income families can hardly be met. Urban China is starting to see a new phenomenon described by academia as a 'structural shortage' of housing, or to put it in a more explicit way 'housing inequity'. In economic terms, the nature of the crisis of low-income housing is one of affordability.

In recent years, Chinese society has gradually realized that public housing programs of one kind or another may still be the most effective way of meeting the housing needs of low-income families. However, the failure of the operation and allocation of the newly developed public housing system has embarrassed local and central governments, mainly because of the resultant failure to identify the most needy citizens/groups. This is due to the lack of a clear definition of policies related to hous-

ing. With regard to the existing public housing system in China, this paper will concentrate on the target groups for affordable housing by examining the basic housing needs of ordinary citizens and the composition of costs for such types of housing.

Costs of Affordable Housing

The goal of affordable housing is primarily to meet the basic housing needs of urban families who cannot afford commercial housing. Research has been carried out to ascertain the basic housing needs of low-income families in cities such as Beijing *(Zhou Yanmin, Wang Fuqing 2009).* According to the research findings, design requirements for affordable housing can be summarized as follows:

- The provision of the basic rooms/spaces for sleeping, cooking, dining, storage and a quiet area for children to study.
- Children should have their own beds when they are grown up.
- A separate space for school-age children to ensure a comfortable learning environment.
- An indoor bathroom and kitchen for each household to ensure health and safety.
- A multifunction room which can be used for dining, and gatherings for family and guests.

In design terms, such needs can be met through the provision of small-sized apartments. On May 19, 2006, the central government of China issued 'The Results of a Surveying and Mapping Ordinance (Revised Draft)' calling for this category of housing and an increase in the supply of housing units of less than 90 sq.m.

Looking at international experience in housing standards, great similarities can be found. According to Japan's social housing program, the floor area of a housing unit is between 40 and 60 sq.m, the average floor area being 50 sq.m. *(Jin Yihua. 2008)*. In Hong Kong, the Home Ownership Scheme (HOS) has established a standard apartment unit which is between 50 and 80 sq.m, the average being 70 sq.m. *(see Hong Kong Housing Authority)* In China, the current apartment unit floor area for low-rent housing is between 40 and 60 sq.m, the average being 50 sq.m, while the floor area of affordable housing units is between 60 and 80 sq.m. with an average of 70 sq.m. *(Deng Zhongmei, 2008)*. In China under existing public housing policy and according to the basic housing conditions aspired to by households, a unit of affordable housing is composed of a bathroom, a kitchen and two or three bedrooms, with an average floor area of 70 sq.m. That standard meets the basic housing needs of the average family of three people in urban China.

As a consequence of the high cost of land, it is a common practice in Chinese cities to design affordable housing mostly in high FAR (Floor Area Ratio). In China, the cost of a commercial housing project typically includes: land purchase, survey and design, construction related product development, preliminary work, construction and installation, landscaping works, supporting projects, expenses during construction operations, management fees, interest, taxes, marketing costs and so on. According to incomplete statistics, the construction costs of high-rise housing range from ¥2,000 to ¥3,000 per sq.m. Accordingly, if land costs, taxes, interest and other related fees are put to one side, the general construction costs of affordable housing with basic interior decoration are on average about ¥3,000 per sq.m. Therefore, the construction cost of an ordinary apartment of around 70 sq.m floor area is about ¥210,000.

Residents Income Structure

In the last thirty years, along with China's reform and economic growth, the average living standards both of urban and rural sectors have been steadily rising. As shown in Figure 1, the balance of RMB[1] (bank) savings of urban and rural residents increased from ¥21 billion in 1978 to ¥26,077 billion in 2009. However, given China's large population of over 1.33 billion at the end of 2009, average RMB savings per capita are still very low. Those of the urban and rural residents in 2009 were only about ¥19,537

In terms of the changes in disposable income per capita a remarkable gap has grown between the urban and rural sectors over the last decades as shown in Figure 2, average urban disposable income per capita increased to ¥17,174.7 in 2009 from ¥343.4 in 1978, while those of rural residents reached ¥5,153.2 from ¥133.6 during the same period - far behind the urban sectors.

Within the urban sector too, increasing stratifications can be seen among different income groups. In China, low-income groups generally can be identified by three criteria: (1) the level of minimum wage; (2) average consumable expenditure per capita amongst the lowest 10% of urban households; and finally (3) record of unemployment insurance and social security.

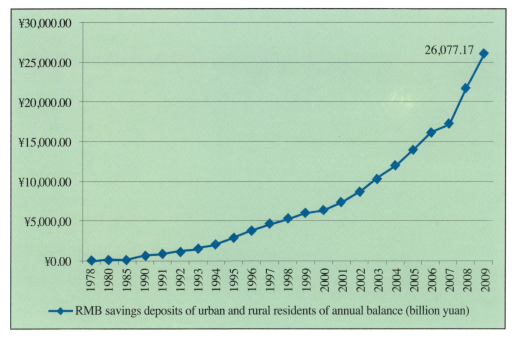

Figure1: Income increase of all sectors, from 1978 to 2009
Source: China Statistic Year Book 2011

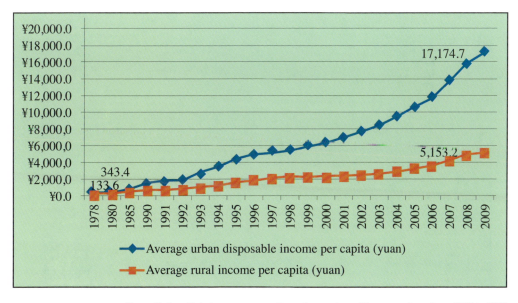

Figure 2: Growth in income per capita, urban and rural in comparison, from 1978 to 2009
Source: China Statistic Year Book 2010

Items	Total	By level of income							
		Lowest income households (10%)	Low-income households (10%)	Lower-middle income households (20%)	Middle-income households (20%)	Higher-middle income households (20%)	High-income households (10%)	Highest income households (10%)	
		Hardship households (5%)							
Ratio (%)	100.00	9.95	4.95	10.02	20.05	20.05	20.03	9.96	9.93
Average yearly income per capita (Yuan)	18858	5951	4936	8957	12345	16858	23051	31172	51350
Average disposable income per capita (Yuan)	17175	5253	4198	8162	11244	15400	21018	28386	46826

Table 1: Social income structure in urban sectors, 2009
Source: China Statistic Year Book 2010

The National Bureau of Statistics has adopted a seven grade method to separate the different incomes groups in the country, as shown in Table 1. Urban low-income groups generally include: urban retirees and workers who have been laid-off, low-income workers, unemployed workers, unemployed workers of bankrupt enterprises, elderly people with disabilities and without support, other incapacitated people, migrant workers and other migrants.

At present, inadequate housing, 'housing poor' in China is measured by the ratio of living area per capita of households to the local average. Households which fall into the 'lowest housing-poor' are defined as those where the average incomes per capita are below 20% of the local minimum wages, and the living area per capita is below 60% of the local average; while households in 'housing poor' are those whose average incomes per capita are between 20% and 30% of the local minimum wages, and their living area per capita is below 60% of the local average. Households both in the lowest housing poor category and in the housing poor category can be defined as households which cannot pay for minimum housing (Qin Hon 2007).

According to the above definitions, both the lowest-income and low-income households classified by the national statistics generally fall into housing poverty groups. The housing demands both of those groups should, we argue, be looked after by the government through low-rent housing, or other more practicable housing programs, because the ability of these households to purchase is extremely low, and cannot even match the prices of affordable housing. In general, those in these two groups should not be included in the target groups for affordable housing.

Target Groups for Affordable Housing

In order to better define those target groups, we should first examine the levels of savings and incomes of urban residents. Here we have used the latest relevant data released by the National Bureau of Statistics at the end of 2009. According to these data, the annual balance of RMB savings of the urban and rural residents nationwide was ¥26.08 trillion while the total population is ¥1.34 billion, and the average RMB savings per capita was about ¥19,500.

Comparing the average disposable income per capita of urban households with the average net income per capita of rural households from 1978 to 2009, the former was 3.32 times more than the latter. Therefore, it can be calculated that average RMB savings per capita in urban sectors by the end of 2009 was roughly ¥32,000. Given the average household size of 2.89 people in cities (China Statistical Year Book 2010), it was estimated that average RMB savings per household in urban sectors by the end of 2009 was approximately ¥92,000 as shown in Table 1.

The data of 2009 also showed that average disposable income per capita in the urban sector was ¥17,000. According to experience worldwide, households' expenditure on affordable housing usually accounts for one third of households' disposable incomes. If this is applied to the Chinese case, the average urban housing affordability per household in 2009 was around ¥16,500.

As shown in Table 1, incomes from different income groups are available from national statistics, as are the average annual balance of RMB savings per household. We assume that there is close practical link between households' incomes and their RMB saving balances. Therefore, we first compared the ratios of household incomes of different groups to the average income per household nationwide, and then applied these ratios to the average household annual balance of RMB savings in 2009 to calculate the RMB savings per household of all income groups.

The figures in Table 2 show the average annual balance of RMB savings per household and average housing affordability per household of the lowest income households, low-income households, lower-middle income households and middle-income households. Both the average RMB savings per household of the lowest income households and low-income households was less than ¥40,000, while average housing affordability per household in 2009 in both groups was less than ¥8,000. Average RMB savings per household both of lower-middle and middle-income households were more than ¥55,000, while average housing affordability per household in 2009 in each case was higher than ¥10,000.

	Average RMB savings per household by annual balance in 2009 (Yuan)	Average housing affordability per household in 2009 (Yuan)
Urban residents	91,682	16,545
Lowest income households	26,182	5,061
Low-income household	40,680	7,863
Lower-middle income households	56,038	10,831
Middle-income households	76,754	14,835

Table 2: Annual balance of savings and incomes per capita in cities and towns, 2009
Sources: China Statistical Yearbook - 2009

It is obvious that a unit of affordable housing with a floor area of 70 square meters and a total construction cost of ¥210,000 cannot be covered by the average RMB savings per household of all the low and middle-low income groups as shown in Table 2. Accordingly, we propose a financial scheme with an initial payment accounting for 20% to 30% of the total cost, with the residual amount being paid for by mortgage loans with lower interest rates (lower than the ordinary commercial residential mortgage rate), the loans to be repaid in equal monthly instalments.

Based on the assumption that the total cost of one unit of affordable housing is ¥210,000, it is proposed that the initial payment is ¥50,000 to ¥70,000 in the new financial scheme. The average annual interest rate of a commercial residential mortgage loan in China, based on the local governments' website, ranges from 6% to7%. The interest rate for housing saving funds ranges from 4% to 5%. The term of the mortgage loan for affordable housing can be about twenty years.

	Mortgage rate				
	3.0%	3.5%	4.0%	4.5%	5.0%
Initial payment (Yuan)	70,000	70,000	70,000	70,000	70,000
Monthly instalment (Yuan)	776	812	848	886	924
Annual instalment (Yuan)	9,317	9,743	10,180	10,629	11,087

Total cost = ¥210,000, Term=20yrs, Initial payment = ¥70,000, Residual amount = ¥14,000

Table 3: Mortgage rates and instalment changes with a fixed initial payment for the new financial scheme

	Mortgage rate				
	3.0%	3.5%	4.0%	4.5%	5.0%
Initial payment (Yuan)	50,000	50,000	50,000	50,000	50,000
Monthly instalment (Yuan)	887	928	970	1012	1056
Annual instalment (Yuan)	10,648	11,135	11,635	12,147	12,671

Table 4: Mortgage rates and initial payment changes with fixed instalments for the new financial scheme

Taking different incomes and the financial abilities of households of different income groups into consideration, Table 3 and Table 4 show the different mortgage rates, different initial payments and annual instalments for an affordable housing unit of 70 sq.m, at a total cost of ¥210,000. From the data in Table 2, it is clear that the lowest-income and low-income households cannot afford the instalments, or even the initial payments. An initial payment of ¥50,000 and an annual instalment of some ¥10,000 are both acceptable for the lower-middle income households in urban sectors.

Consideration should be given to processing mortgage loans for affordable housing where interest rates and repayment terms can be adjusted according to the needs of the different income groups. Each of the lower middle-income households can purchase one unit of affordable housing with the most suitable mortgage scheme according to his or her savings and income. Given the available statistics, an initial payment ranging from ¥50,000 to ¥70,000 is affordable for middle-income households.

To sum up, the target groups for affordable housing of 70 sq.m costing ¥210,000 per unit may be roughly defined as the lower-middle and middle-income households, and they account for 40% of the total urban households in

China. Moreover, when necessary, parts of the low-income households and higher-middle income households may also be included in the target groups by adjusting initial payments, repayment terms and mortgage rates. We clearly recognize that there are some limitations on the indirect data used in this research, but we think this does not detract from the general conclusion drawn.

Local differences exist in cities across the country in terms of construction costs, income levels and the general economic situation. For instance, the average RMB savings per household in Beijing in 2009 was estimated at around ¥275,000 which was three times the national average (China Statistical Year Book 2010). Therefore, the definition of target groups and the purchase scheme for each city needs to be adjusted according to its social and economic circumstances.

Supporting the System of Affordable Housing

It is necessary for the affordable housing scheme proposed by this paper to gain support from the whole of society, especially the government, if the controlled housing standards, construction costs and lower interest rate mortgage schemes are to be implemented.

Firstly, government control, guidance and assistance to build decent housing with limited space are essential at every stage of planning and design. As part of the whole social security program, the costs of affordable housing proposed in this paper only include construction costs and related fees, while the costs of public infrastructure and land have to be covered by the government, as is often the case in many countries and regions. Although affordable housing is mainly aimed at urban middle- and low-income households, it does not mean that such housing can be located anywhere. As urban middle- and low-income residents have to rely very much on public infrastructure and services, with affordable housing and assistance from the government. The result is that they have more security both in their lives and in their jobs. Linked to this, land for affordable housing projects should be sited close to bus or transit stations. Basic services such as hospitals, schools, shops also need to be available and well planned. We can learn a great deal from these experiences.

In the 1970s, a program named the Home Ownership Scheme (HOS) was started by the Hong Kong Government. The HOS housing was established by the Hong Kong Housing Authority with the assistance of a special fund and land provision by the Hong Kong Government. Identification of its target groups and regulation/supervision by the Government are critical for the success of the program.

The price of the HOS housing is about 60% to 70% of the market value, while the Housing Authority guarantees the mortgage loan with a loan ratio of 95% over a repayment term of 20 years. However, the property rights of HOS housing are limited. Within the first five years the housing can only be transferred at its original price to the Housing Authority if the owners wish to, and at its current price within the second five years. After ten years, the housing may be sold on the open market, but 45% to 55% of the increase in value belongs to the Housing Authority (see Hong Kong Housing Authority). Following the critical acclaim it has received, Hong Kong's Home Ownership Scheme may be adopted in mainland China.

In China there currently exists a housing financial system called the Housing Saving Fund which is designed to provide funds for urban residents to purchase housing. However, the balance of the funds was only ¥1.21 trillion at the end of 2008 (see People's Daily Online). About 310 million people were eligible for the Fund and it was estimated that the balance per household was less than ¥1.2. Therefore, the Housing Saving Fund alone is not sufficient to help urban families benefit from the affordable housing program. As a consequence, it is necessary to set up a specific nationwide banking system backed by the government.

Recently, in Tianjin, China, a financial institution called the Sino-German Bausparkasse, jointly established by the China Construction Bank and German Schwaebisch-Hall, has started this type of service. In 2008, the Sino-German Bausparkasse was allowed to expand its business scope on the basis of individual housing loans to support affordable housing and low-rent housing in that city. The applicants for affordable housing can enjoy the benefits of financial assistance for five years and a loan discount of 0.5%, which is equal to 60% of the Central Bank benchmark interest rate, with options of a maximum loan ratio of 80% and maximum repayment term of 30 years *(see Sino-German Bausparkasse).*

Based on the successful experience in Hong Kong, an effective entry and exit mechanism and operation is a crucial element of the affordable housing system. In China there is an urgent need to develop more sophisticated mechanisms to verify the qualification criteria for applications for affordable housing, and to ensure that the existing occupants of affordable housing can move out whenever their income levels have reached a certain level. Social supervision of certain legislation is required if such mechanisms are to be operated effectively, fairly and transparently.

Conclusion and Discussion

By analyzing the total cost of affordable housing and the state of the social income structure in China, the target groups for affordable housing can be broadly defined as urban lower-middle and middle-income households, which account for about 40% of the total urban population. Meanwhile, the adjustment on financial assistance of affordable housing can extend the target groups. If necessary, certain low-income and higher-middle income households can also be included in the target groups through adjusting initial payments, repayment terms and mortgage rates. To ensure the viability of the affordable housing system, it is necessary for the government to provide the land required and the supporting infrastructure, tax breaks, low-interest loans, effective and transparent entry and exit mechanisms and the legal and regulatory framework. Nevertheless, only a proportion of urban households qualify for the affordable housing system, which is one element of China's general public housing.

_____

Endnote

1. The Chinese currency is called Renminbi (People's money), often abbreviated as RMB. Issued by the People's Bank of China, it is the sole legal tender for both the Chinese nationals and foreign tourists. The unit of Renminbi is yuan and the smaller, jiao and fen. The conversion among the three is: 1 yuan = 10 jiao =100 fen. Retrieved from http://www.china.org.cn/english/LivinginChina/184832.htm

References

"China Statistical Year Book 2010" Statistic Bureau of P.R. China, Beijing, *China Statistical Publishing House*

Deng Zhongmei (2008) "The development of small-sized social housing", *Chinese Development Education*, 11:53-55.

Hong Kong Housing Authority. www.housingauthority.gov.hk.

Jin Yihua (2008) "Social housing in Japan", *Urban and Rural Development*, 06: 72-73

People's Daily Online. http://house.people.com.cn/GB/9008473.html.

Qin Hon (2007) "Low rent housing is the core of the social housing system", *China Reform*, 2007, 08: 21-23

Sino-German Bausparkasse. http://www.sgb.cn

Zhang Jie, Li Li (2009) "Changes in ten years: Analysis of Beijing housing development", Beijing Planning Review 05, 56-61

Zhou Yanmin, Wang Fuqing (2009) "Low-income households: housing needs in Beijing and their implications for low-rent housing design", *Architectural Journal*, Beijing, 2009.08, 6-9.

ABOUT THE EDITORS

Chris Gossop

Chris Gossop BSC MA PhD MRTPI is a chartered town planner with a broad range of experience that has embraced local and central government, a pressure group, the Town and Country Planning Association (TCPA), and voluntary organisations, including ISOCARP. As Deputy Director with the TCPA he was involved in numerous planning campaigns, from the local to that of the European Union. Between 1991 and 2011, he served with the Planning Inspectorate in England where he had responsibility of the scrutiny and determination of many major developments, including housing schemes, the Cambridgeshire Guided Busway and wind farms. During that period he also spent a period with the former Department of the Environment where he co-ordinated United Kingdom preparations for Habitat II, the United Nations Conference on Human Settlements. In 2009 he became a Vice President of ISOCARP with responsibility for publications, including the Review, and also in that year he was General Rapporteur for ISOCARP's 45th World Congress on Low Carbon Cities. In a second volunteer role, he is a trustee of the National Energy Foundation which is based in the new city of Milton Keynes where Chris has his home.

Shi Nan

Secretary General, Urban Planning Society of China (UPSC); Executive Chief Editor, City Planning Review (CPR); Associate Chief Editor, China City Planning Review (CCPR); Senior Planner, China Academy of Urban Planning and Design (CAUPD).

Dr. Shi Nan has 29 years of planning experience and is specialized in policy analysis and master planning. He has been very active in major planning and research projects including the Revision of National Planning Act. He has more than 15 years of experience working with major international organizations including the World Bank, UNDP, IFHP, the Rockefeller Foundations etc. He is currently a Member of the National Board for Planning Education Accreditation and the National Board for Certified Planner Examination and Registration. His major publications include *The State of China's City, Some Observations Concerning China's Urban Development, China Urban Development Report and Reader of Urban Planning, etc.*

ABOUT THE AUTHORS

Making Indian Cities Liveable: the Challenges of India's Urban Transformation

Shipra Narang Suri

Dr. Shipra Narang Suri is an urban planner with a Ph.D. in Post-War Recovery Studies from the University of York, U.K. She has worked with the United Nations for nearly fifteen years in different capacities and locations. She has wide-ranging experience in the areas of urban governance, urban planning and management, and post conflict recovery and development, across Asia, Africa, South Eastern Europe as well as the Middle-East.

Shipra is also an Associate of the Post-War Reconstruction and Development Unit (PRDU), University of York, where she convenes and teaches a module on project planning and management. She has been a guest lecturer in various universities in Europe and India, and is a member of the Board of Studies of the Department of Physical Planning, School of Planning and Architecture, New Delhi (India). She is an Editor (Special Features) of the international journal 'CITY'; a member of a global think tank on 'Liveable Cities' which has recently been set up by Philips; as well as a member of the Scientific Committee of ISO-CARP. Shipra has collaborated with numerous national and international agencies for development and execution of a variety of research and training projects and programmes, and has several publications to her credit.

The Urban Reform Agenda and the Struggle for Liveable Cities in Brazil

Edesio Fernandes

Jurist and urban planner; Member of DPU Associates (Development Planning Unit DPU/ University College London – UCL), associated with the Institute for Housing and Urban Studies (IHS), and member of the Teaching Faculty of the Lincoln Institute of Land Policy; during 2003, the author was Director of Land Affairs at the Ministry of Cities' National Secretariat for Urban Programmes, and in that capacity he co-ordinated the initial formulation and implementation of the National Programme to Support Sustainable Urban Land Regularisation.

The Netherlands in Transition The Planning Of Low Carbon, Sustainable and Liveable Cities in The Utrecht Region

Martin Dubbeling

Martin Dubbeling is a senior consultant, urban planner and urban designer at SAB in Arnhem, The Netherlands. SAB is a multi-disciplinary office active in the fields of spatial planning, urban lanning, landscape architecture and the environment in Arnhem, The Netherlands. Martin Dubbeling is bureau member of ISOCARP and board member of the Netherlands professional organisation of spatial planning and urban design As the co-chair of the comity on sustainable urban design and planning of the Netherlands professional organisations of landscape architecture and urban planning and design, Martin

Dubbeling is one of the authors of the book Sustainable 'Urban Design, Perspectives and Examples' (2005), for which he was awarded with the Gerd Albers Award on the 42nd ISOCARP Congress in Istanbul. The second and revised edition of this book is published in September 2011.

Martin Dubbeling was Rapporteur and member of the Congress Team on the 45th ISOCARP congress 'Low Carbon Cities' in Porto in 2009 and Young Planning Professionals workshop coordinator prior to the 46th ISOCARP congress 'Sustainable City -Developing World' in Nairobi in2010.

Martin Dubbeling studied Urban Planning and Design at the Delft University of Technology (1981-1988). He has a professional record in the consultancy, design and process of the regeneration of historic town and village centres, sustainable urban planning and design and the redevelopment of urban networks and retail districts. He has made several master plans for sustainable residential areas and sustainable residential urban renewal in The Netherlands. Many of those projects have been realised or are under construction. Recently he worked as a consultant for The Philips Center of Health and Well-being.

WikicitY
Open Planning for a Liveable Amsterdam 2004-2011

Zef Hemel

_____

Zef Hemel is deputy director of the Urban Planning Department of the City of Amsterdam. Prior to that he was director of the Academy of Architecture in Rotterdam, member of the think tank of the Ministry of Housing, Spatial Planning and the Environment in the Netherlands, editor of the Dutch

planning magazine Stedenbouw & Ruimtelijke Ordening and secretary of the Dutch Advisory Board on Spatial Planning. Among the books he published were: 'How to construct the camel. A new Architectural Museum for the Netherlands' (Delft 1989), 'Het landschap van de IJsselmeerpolders. Planning, inrichting en vormgeving' (Rotterdam 1994), 'Creatieve Steden/Creative Cities!' (The Hague 2001) and 'Vrijstaat Amsterdam/Free State of Amsterdam' (Amsterdam 2010). Zef Hemel studied human geography at the State University of Groningen and history of art at the University of Amsterdam.

Beyond Cities: Is An Urban Planet Even Possible?

Jeremy Dawkins

_____

Jeremy Dawkins has enjoyed a life in urban planning, alternating between academic and professional practice. He has played crucial and creative roles in city, provincial and national governments, undertaken and published international research into planning systems, and taught in good planning programs, including an innovative postgraduate program at the University of Technology Sydney which he founded and directed in the 1990s (it has just celebrated its 20th anniversary). Recently he completed a five year term as executive chairman of the Western Australian Planning Commission and now writes, researches and teaches in Sydney.

Towards A Liveable Urban Climate: Lessons from Stuttgart

Michael Hebbert
Brian Webb

————

Michael Hebbert, Professor of Town Planning at the University of Manchester since 1994, is a member of the Royal Town Planning Institute and an elected member of both the Academy of Urbanism and the Academy of Social Sciences. He read history at Oxford and obtained his doctorate in geography from the University of Reading. He has wide ranging research interests in the fields of town planning history, urban design, and city governance, as well as practical experience in community initiatives and building trusts in London and Manchester, and with design review of the London Crossrail project. His current research into the application of urban climate knowledge in urban design since 1950 is supported by the UK Economic and Social Research Council.

————

Brian Webb is a Research Associate with the Centre for Urban Policy Studies (CUPS) of the School of Environment & Development at the University of Manchester UK, where he is also completing his PhD in Planning. His topic is intergovernmental spatial policy coordination within federal government systems. He has previously worked with the City of Toronto's City Planning Department, where he specialised in developing heritage-planning policy, and for the Government of Ontario's Ministry of Municipal Affairs and Housing, working in both the disaster relief and planning unit and the planning education and training unit. His current interests explore understanding of spatial scale by policy makers.

Strategies for Integrated Spatial Development along the European North-South Railway Link

Bernd Scholl

————

Bernd Scholl is since 2006 a full professor for Spatial Planning and Development at the Institute for Spatial and Landscape Planning at the ETH Zurich. His teaching and research focal points are on land and spatial management in the local and regional development, space and infrastructure development, transnational tasks as well as development and organization of innovative planning processes and methods in spatial planning and regional development. From 1997 to 2006 Bernd Scholl directed the Institute for Urban Development and Regional Planning at the University of Karlsruhe as a full professor for the chair of the same name. During this time, Bernd Scholl acted as a chairman and member of numerous international expert commissions and Urban Development juries, such as: the development of long-term perspectives for the Zurich airport and the spatial planning and development of the canton Zurich, the «Europaviertel» Consortium of Frankfurt am Main, the development of the «Südbahn» in Austria, the integrated traffic and land development of the Grand Duchy of Luxembourg; in the context of a group project of the European Union for the promotion of the internal development of our cities, he took the scientific direction and led the test planning procedures in Milan, Budapest and Stuttgart.
Bernd Scholl is full member of the German Regional Studies and Planning Academy, member of the International Association for City and Regional Planning, as well as a founding member of the "Baukultur Foundation", in Berlin.

The Contribution of Mobility to Liveable Cities

Pierre Laconte

————————

Pierre Laconte specialises in urban and transport planning, and their links with environmental issues. He has Doctorates in Laws and in Economics from the Louvain University and is Dr h.c., Edinburgh Napier University. P. Laconte was one of the three planners in charge of the Louvain University "Groupe Urbanisme Architecture". This team was entrusted in 1969 with the planning and architectural coordination of the new university town of Louvain-la-Neuve, now a major growth pole south of Brussels. It includes a new underground railway station and numerous ecologic features such as separation of storm water and sewage water and its centre is entirely pedestrian. He is vice-chair of the European Environment Agency Scientific Committee, honorary Secretary General of the International Association of Public Transport - UITP, past-president of the International Society of City and Regional Planners (2006-2009) and president of the Foundation for the Urban Environment. About his publications visit: www.ffue.org

Linking People, Linking Nature: The Park Connector Network of Singapore

Lena Chan
Cheng Hai Sim
Meng Tong Yeo
Kartini Omar-Hor

————————

Lena Chan is the Deputy Director of the National Biodiversity Centre (NBC), National Parks Board of Singapore. NBC is a biodiversity hub that: a) formulates policies on biodiversity, b) documents Singapore's native biodiversity through surveys and in partnership with tertiary institutions, non-governmental organisations, and amateur naturalists, c) maintains a biodiversity database (BIOME), d) safeguards Singapore's native biodiversity through species conservation, recovery and enhancement programmes, e) provides biodiversity considerations to development projects, f) enhances education and public awareness through outreach activities and working with non-governmental organisations, schools, tertiary institutions, amateur naturalists, etc., and g) partakes in regional and international biodiversity fora. Singapore has spearheaded the development of a self-assessment tool, the City Biodiversity Index, also known as the Singapore Index on Cities' Biodiversity, in partnership with the Secretariat of the Convention on Biological Diversity and the Global Partnership on Cities and Biodiversity that Lena has helped to coordinate. Lena studied the behaviour of the black-handed gibbon, Hylobates agilis at Kuala Dal, Perak in Malaysia during her undergraduate vacation. She researched on parasitology at the Institute of Parasitology, McGill University, for her M.Sc. Her work on the design of cost effective chemotherapeutic soil-transmitted parasite control strategies for an urban slum community in Kampung Pandan, Kuala Lumpur, earned her a Ph. D. from Imperial College, London. Lena collaborated with State Governments of Malaysia to develop Conservation Strategies for Negeri Sembilan, Melaka, Terengganu, Kedah, Perlis, Sarawak, Selangor and Federal Territory.

————————

Cheng Hai Sim works as Director (Policy and Planning) in National Parks Board (NParks), Singapore. He is in charge of planning and securing all public park and greenery lands in Singapore. This includes securing of lands for the park connector network. He works with other land-use agencies in Singapore to secure park land through the land-use planning process. Whilst greenery lands are secured mainly through development regulatory process. In addition, Cheng Hai also works with the Conservation Division in NParks to conserve nature reserve and nature areas in Singapore. During his twenty years in NParks and its former organization Parks & Recreation Department, Cheng Hai had been involved in operational management of parks and roadside greenery, park development and park business management. He has also con-currently been in charge of corporate planning and research functions in NParks in the past. The scope of research covers horticultural, arboricultural, highrise-greenery, park recreation and inter-city comparison studies.

————————

Meng Tong Yeo heads the Parks Development Division which is in-charge of design and development of parks and park connectors. Annually, Meng Tong manages a development budget of over S$50mil. He has overseen the successful completion of highly visible projects such as the Park Connectors, Istana Park, Mt Faber Parks, Pasir Ris Park, Redevelopment of Singapore Botanic Gardens and East Coast Park and West Coast Park. He spearheaded the pilot park connector network (along Kallang River) in 1991 as well as the first Park Connector Masterplan in 1992 and is still overseeing the design and development of the park connectors.

Meng Tong had also pioneered the trans-planting of mangroves for the landscaping of Sungei Api Api (1990) which is a model for how nature could be brought back into Singapore. He has been actively involved in the landscaping components of the ABC programme by PUB. He has done oversea projects. He led the landscape projects in Doha, Qatar. He did the landscape masterplanning of Tianjin Ecocity (Tianjin, China), especially the Eco-valley

design. He has carried out the preliminary landscape masterplan for Knowledge City (Guangzhou,China). He developed the Rooftop Garden at the Singapore Pavilion in Shanghai World EXPO 2010.

————————

Kartini Omar-Hor is the General Manager (Parks) in National Parks Board (NParks), Singapore. She currently oversees the management of Riverine Parks, Community Parks, Nature Parks and the Park Connector Network in Singapore. In the more than 20 years that she has been with NParks, Kartini has had the opportunity to work in various sections of the organisation that include Parks Management, Parks Development, Horticulture Excellence, Procurement as well as Nursery Services. During her tenure as chairperson of the NParks Public Service Work Improvement Teams, she placed the organisation in the spotlight by spurring teams to win Gold and Million Dollar awards as part of the Government's productivity and innovation drive. She has also been actively involved in organising and participating in the various garden and flower shows organised by NParks, such as Skyrise Gardens Exhibition, GardenTech, Singapore Garden Festival and the 20th World Orchid Conference which will be held in Singapore in Nov 2011. During her stint with the Nursery Services, she co-authored a publication entitled '1001 Garden Plants In Singapore' which features some 2000 plants that are found in Singapore, and initiated the NParks online plant reference website 'NParks FloraWeb'. She was instrumental in sourcing for and propagating many plants that currently line our streetscape and form the backdrop of our city in a garden.

Skolkovo:
City of the Future as a Russian
Hi-Tech Hub

Fedor Kudryavtsev
Victoria Bannykh

––––––––

Fedor S. Kudryavtsev is an architect and town planner, through his entire carrier, started in 1993, keeps a link with his Alma Mater, Moscow Institute of Architecture, and now holds a position of associate professor of Town Planning Department. Since 2005 being also a head of the Laboratory of Urban Studies in that institution he researches problems of metropolitan areas growth, city strategic planning, self-organization processes in urban transformation and impacts of new technologies and infrastructure on urban development. As practicing architect, he is a partner and general director of ArchNOVA architectural bureau specializing in master planning, site potential analysis and building design. Among recent projects completed under his guidance for state and municipal agencies following can be mentioned:

• 2009-2010, "Principles of Forecast for Urban Territories Growth in Metropolitan Areas (Moscow Region Case)";
• 2009-2010, "Regularities of Urban Landscape Evolution as a Cumulative Result of Smaller Fragments
• Change";
• 2009, "International Airports Influence over Local and Regional Urban Networks";
• 2007-2008, "Impact of Private Real Estate Mega-Projects upon Moscow Region Urban Structure".
Fedor is also member of Town Planning Council of Russian Union of Architects.

––––––––

Victoria Bannykh graduated from Moscow Institute of Architecture, 2008, Department of Town Planning. Being especially interested in studies concerning sustainable urban development she also took part in several summer schools (2008, 2009) of Facoltà di Architettura di Alghero, Inalia, focused on new methods of planning and management of natural parks in urbanized regions. Since 2008, she works in Laboratory of Urban Studies of Moscow Institute of Architecture specializing on projects related to sustainability and green networks development.

The London 2012 Olympic Park:
Planning for a
Sustainable Legacy

Dan Epstein
Jo Carris
Emily Moore
Judith Sykes

––––––––

Dan Epstein is Director of Sustainability at the Useful Simple Trust. He was formerly Head of Sustainable Development and Regeneration for the London 2012 Olympic Park, the biggest sustainability job in the country, after a 30 year career in thinking, designing and delivering sustainable development in the UK and overseas. Dan's strengths are his knowledge of the whole sustainability agenda and how it applies to development, his reputation and knowledge of the market and the respect he commands within it, his ability to sell ideas and business, his experience in place making, urban regeneration and new development and the whole sustainable cities programme. Dan has participated in many government and agency panels and regularly gives talks on environmental policy and delivery, urban design, environmental planning, green space, health and other quality of life issues. In his current role, he is specialising in providing sustainability advice to major sporting event development projects, including the Rio 2016 Olympic Games, the Brazil 2014 World Cup and the Sochi 2014 Winter Olympics.

_____

Jo Carris holds a Masters in Environmental Technology and Energy Policy from Imperial College. For her thesis, Jo conducted a critical analysis of the sustainability of the Olympic Village. Since then, the majority of Jo's career has been focused on the sustainability of the London Olympic Park: first delivering the sustainability objectives through design, procurement and construction; then analysing achievements and lessons learnt for the Learning Legacy programme; followed by developing regeneration projects for communities surrounding the Olympic Park. Most recently, Jo has been transferring lessons learnt from the London Olympics to the Rio 2016 Olympics and the Brazil 2014 World Cup. Jo works for the Useful Simple Trust.

_____

Emily Moore is a sustainability researcher for the Useful Simple Trust. She has a background in urban and environmental planning, with particular experience in conducting and writing environmental assessments on sustainability-driven infrastructure projects. Most recently, Emily has been working for the Useful Simple Trust on research projects around the London Olympics and carbon footprinting methodologies for major sporting events.

_____

Judith Sykes is a chartered civil engineer whose expertise lies in the integrated design and delivery of sustainable infrastructure projects both in the UK and overseas. She holds a Masters in Sustainable Development from the University of Cambridge, lectures on sustainability masterplanning at University College London and is a Visiting Research Fellow at the University of Bath. Judith worked on the London Olympic Sustainability Team where she developed and implemented the Sustainable Water Strategy for the Olympic Park. She is currently developing the sustainability strategy for a 2500-home development in Brasilia and working with the 2014 Brazilian World Cup host cities in delivering carbon reduction requirements. Judith is Director of MustRD, the research and development arm of the Useful Simple Trust.

Planning the Ecological Spatial System of the Megacity of Wuhan

Liu Qizhi
He Mei
Wang Yun

_____

Liu Qizhi, Deputy Director and Chief Planner of Wuhan Land Resources and Planning Bureau, Deputy Director of the Academic Committee of Urban Planning Society of China, Professor Senior Planner, and National Registered Planner. He has taken charge of organized and given guidance to such major projects as the edition of The Comprehensive Panning of Wuhan of both 1996 and 2010 versions, and The Immediate Plan of Wuhan and the Overall Planning of Urban and Rural Construction of Wuhan. Among all the merits, The Comprehensive Panning of Wuhan (2010 version) is honoured with ISOCARP Awards for Excellence, the highest praise of the ISOCARP. Mr. LIU Qizhi is also the chief editor of Urban Water System Regulation and published over 10 essays about urban development strategy, renewal planning of industrial city and urban design in core journals.

He Mei, (1969-), Deputy Dean of Wuhan Planning and Design Institute, Professor Senior Planner, and National Registered Planner. Among all the planning projects she has undertaken or participated in, more than 30 are rated at provincial or ministerial level. Within them, the project of The Flood Control and Environmental Comprehensive Regulation Project of Jiangtan in Hankou has been in construction. The Comprehensive Planning of Wuhan City (2010 version) won the ISOCARP Awards for Excellence. Moreover, she has one book published by China Architecture & Building Press and 9 essays in Chinese core journals.

Wang Yun Deputy Chief Planner of Wuhan Planning and Design Institute, Senior Planner, National Registered Planner and the visiting scholar to the University of Illinois at Chicago (UIC)in 2006. Among all the planning projects he has undertaken and participated in, more than 15 are rated at the provincial or ministerial level. He has 2 books published by China Architecture & Building Press and 7 essays released in Chinese core journals.

Local Governance of Low Carbon Cities: Is Our Local Planning System Ready Yet?

Stanley C. T. Yip

Stanley Yip is a town planner, land economist and urban designer with in-depth professional and research experience. Over the last 25 years, he has been living and working in different cities around the world, and has led many major urban development projects in Hong Kong, Mainland China, Southeast Asia and North America.

Dr. Yip is currently the Director, Planning & Development with ARUP and is responsible for the development and implementation of planning practices in China. His recent experience in China includes a wide range of planning projects driven by sustainable development principles and innovative resource management approaches. He has been undertaking continuous research work in the areas of low carbon economy, eco-cities, circular economy, cost and benefits of green buildings and new institutional economics.

Dr. Yip is the Past President of the Hong Kong Institute of Planners and has been serving as advisor to various local governments in China. He speaks at major conferences and writes and publishes books and research papers on planning on a regular basis.

Industrial Heritage as a Cultural Infrastructure

Dong Wei

Dong Wei, Professor of Urban Planning at School of Architecture, Southeast University since 1997, is a member of the Urban Planning Society of China and an member of both the Academy of Historic Cities and the Academy of Ecological Urban Planning and Construction.

Professor Dong studied architecture and urban planning and obtained his doctorate in the Faculty of architecture, Norwegian University of Science and Technology in 1995. He has wide ranging research interests in urban planning history, urban design, and heritage conservation, as well as practical experiences in the fields above. He is the UNESCO Chair holder in Cultural Resource Management since 2001 and got twice UNESCO Heritage Conservation Awards in Asian and the Pacific for his urban conservation projects in Zhenjiang and Quanzhou,

China. His current research interest is focused in industrial heritage, re-mapping of historic urban maps and planning and design in urban historic context.

Devising an Adaptable Urban Shelter and Evacuation System in Disaster Situations

Su Jing-yu
Liu Chao-feng
Wang Wei

Su Jingyu, Professor of College of Architecture and Urban Planning, deputy director of Safety and Disaster Reduction Center of City & Engineering at Beijing University of Technology, is an expert of China National Committee for Disaster Reduction, the secretary-general of Academic Committee of Urban Safety and Disaster Prevention Planning, Urban Planning Society of China. He graduated from Tsinghua University in 1979. He has wide ranging research fields and is mainly engaged in research in the fields of safety and disaster reduction of city & engineering, structural seismic (vibration) isolation and seismic (vibration) reduction, synthetic disaster prevention & reduction of region and city, and disaster prevention & reduction of cultural heritage.

Liu Chao-feng, Ph.D candidate of College of Architecture and Civil Engineering at Beijing University of Technology, is mainly engaged in the study of synthetic disaster prevention & reduction of region.

Wang Wei, Dr, assistant research fellow of Safety and Disaster Reduction Center of City & Engineering at Beijing University of

Technology, major in the risk evaluation of disaster.

A Study of Target Groups for Affordable Housing

Zhang Jie
Jiao Yang

Zhang Jie, Professor of Urban Planning at Tsinghua University since 1999, is Director of Centre for Historic Conservation in Tsinghua Institute of Urban Planning and Deputy Director of National Centre for Heritage Conservation in Tsinghua University. He has wide ranging research interests in the fields of urban planning, urban design, heritage conservation and housing studies, which are mainly supported by Ministry housing, urban rural construction of China. He has rich practical experience in protecting and revitalizing traditional villages and towns across China. His current research on key technologies for protection and revitalization of traditional villages and towns is supported by Ministry of science and technology of China while his major projects focus on the conservation for historic and cultural villages in Kunming and Yunnan China in 2011.

Jiao Yang is a Doctoral candidate of the School of Architecture at Tsinghua University, where he completes his Bachelor of Engineering in Construction Management of School of Civil Engineering. He also has Master of Science in Real Estate of Faculty of Architecture at The University of Hong Kong. He has previously worked as an intern at General Contractor of National Stadium Project in Beijing. His current interests focus on urban housing development and public housing in China.